]

AND THE ENGLISH NOVEL
SINCE 1945

Manchester University Press

End of empire and the English novel since 1945

Edited by Rachael Gilmour and Bill Schwarz

Manchester University Press

Published by Manchester University Press
Altrincham Street, Manchester M1 7JA, UK
www.manchesteruniversitypress.co.uk

British Library Cataloguing-in-Publication Data is available

Library of Congress Cataloging-in-Publication Data is available

ISBN 978 0 7190 9745 4 paperback

First published by Manchester University Press in hardback 2011

This paperback edition first published 2015

The publisher has no responsibility for the persistence or accuracy of URLs for any external or third-party internet websites referred to in this book, and does not guarantee that any content on such websites is, or will remain, accurate or appropriate.

Printed by Lightning Source

Contents

Acknowledgements

We are grateful to the Department of English at Queen Mary, University of London, in particular to Tim Bell; and to Matthew Frost and his colleagues at Manchester University Press.

Contributors

David Alderson is Senior Lecturer in English and American Studies at the University of Manchester and Visiting Professor at Shanghai Jiao Tong University. His publications include the co-edited collection *Territories of Desire in Queer Culture* (Manchester University Press, 2000), and most recently, *Terry Eagleton* (Palgrave, 2004). He has written about Alan Hollinghurst, Will Self and Mark Ravenhill as part of a larger project on post-gay culture currently being completed.

Elleke Boehmer has published four widely praised novels, *Screens against the Sky* (Bloomsbury, 1990; short-listed David Higham Prize), *An Immaculate Figure* (Bloomsbury, 1993), *Bloodlines* (David Philip, 2000; short-listed Sanlam Prize) and *Nile Baby* (Ayebia Clarke, 2008). Internationally known for her research in international and postcolonial writing, she is the author of the world best-seller *Colonial and Postcolonial Literature: Migrant Metaphors* (Oxford University Press, 1995 and 2005), the monographs *Empire, the National and the Postcolonial, 1890–1920* (Oxford University Press, 2002) and *Stories of Women* (Manchester University Press, 2005) and of *Nelson Mandela* (Oxford University Press, 2008). She has also produced the acclaimed edition of Robert Baden-Powell's *Scouting for Boys* (Oxford University Press, 2004). In 2009 she co-edited essay collections on J.M. Coetzee and on 'postcolonial terror'. She is the General Editor of the Oxford Studies in Postcolonial Literatures Series. *Sharmilla and Other Portraits* (Jacana, 2010) is her first collection of short stories. Elleke Boehmer is the Professor of World Literature in English at the University of Oxford.

Sarah Brophy is Associate Professor in the Department of English and Cultural Studies at McMaster University, Hamilton, Canada. She is the author of *Witnessing AIDS: Writing, Testimony, and the Work of Mourning* (University of Toronto Press, 2004); writers discussed in this study include Derek Jarman, Amy Hoffman, Eric Michaels and Jamaica Kincaid. She has published articles in *Contemporary Women's Writing* (on Andrea Levy), *Literature and Medicine*, *scrutiny2* and *PMLA*; and chapters in *Teaching Life Writing* and *Critical Essays on Pat Barker*. With the support of a Social Sciences and Humanities Research Council of Canada grant she is currently writing a book on sexualities in British fiction, film and autobiography since 1945. She is also editing a collection of essays on embodied politics in visual autobiography in collaboration with Janice Hladki.

Rachael Gilmour is Lecturer in Postcolonial Studies at the School of English and Drama at Queen Mary, University of London, where she teaches postcolonial and Black British literature. Her research focuses primarily upon issues of language, translation, and linguistic encounter in colonial and postcolonial contexts – from eighteenth- and nineteenth-century South Africa, to contemporary multilingual Britain. She is the author of *Grammars of Colonialism: Representing Languages in Colonial South Africa* (Palgrave 2006). Her current research addresses the work of translingual writers in twentieth- and twenty-first-century Britain. She is on the editorial board of *Literature and History*, and is a contributing editor of *Wasafiri*.

Suzanne Hobson is Lecturer in Twentieth-Century Literature in the School of English and Drama, Queen Mary, University of London. Her research focuses on British and American modernism and literary theory and she has published articles on D.H. Lawrence, Mina Loy and H.D. She is co-editor of the *Salt Companion to Mina Loy* (Salt, 2010) and author of *Angels of Modernism: Religion, Culture, Aesthetics, 1910–1960* (Palgrave Macmillan, 2011). She has been co-organiser of the London Modernism Seminar since 2007.

Cora Kaplan is Honorary Professor of English at Queen Mary, University of London and has held chairs in English at Southampton University and Rutgers University. A feminist cultural critic with a particular interest in women's writing, popular culture and questions of race, gender, class and empire from the late eighteenth century to the present, her work includes *Sea Changes: Essays in Culture and Feminism* (Verso, 1986) and, with David

Glover, *Genders* (Routledge, 2000). Her most recent book is *Victoriana: Histories, Fiction, Criticism* (Edinburgh University Press, 2007). She is the General Editor, with Jennie Batchelor, of a forthcoming ten-volume series *The History of British Women's Writing* (Palgrave, 2010–).

Huw Marsh gained his Ph.D. ('"What has defeated historical enquiry": the representation of the past in the novels of Beryl Bainbridge') in the School of English and Drama, Queen Mary, University of London, where he is currently a Teaching Associate. His research interests lie mainly in the field of contemporary anglophone fiction, and he has previously published articles on Beryl Bainbridge and Nicola Barker. His Ph.D. research was funded by the AHRC.

Patrick Parrinder is the author of *Science Fiction: Its Criticism and Teaching* (Methuen, 1980), *James Joyce* (Cambridge University Press, 1984), *Shadows of the Future: H.G. Wells, Science Fiction and Prophecy* (Liverpool University Press, 1995), *Nation and Novel: The English Novel from its Origins to the Present Day* (Oxford University Press, 2006) and other works. He is General Editor of the forthcoming multi-volume *Oxford History of the Novel in English* and Editor, with Andrzej Gasiorek, of volume 4 in the *Oxford History, The Reinvention of the British and Irish Novel, 1880–1940*. He is a Vice-President of the H.G. Wells Society and has edited ten of Wells's science fiction titles for Penguin Classics, including *The Country of the Blind and Other Selected Stories* (2007). He is an Emeritus Professor of English at the University of Reading.

Deborah Philips is Professor of Literature and Cultural History at the University of Brighton. Her publications include *Writing Romance, Women's Fiction 1945–2005* (Continuum, 2006); with Ian Haywood, *Brave New Causes* (Cassell, 1998); and with Debra Penman and Liz Linington, *Writing Well: Creative Writing and Mental Health* (Jessica Kingsley, 1998). She has just published *Fairground Attractions* (Bloomsbury, 2011) on the function of narrative in the carnival site and is currently working on a study of the use of literary figures in tourism.

James Procter teaches postwar British and postcolonial literatures at Newcastle University. He is the editor of *Writing Black Britain, 1948–1998: An Interdisciplinary Anthology* (Manchester University Press, 2000), and with Michelle Keown and David Murphy, *Comparing Postcolonial Diasporas* (Palgrave, 2008); and the author of *Dwelling Places* (Manchester University

Press, 2003) and *Stuart Hall* (Routledge, 2004). Between 2006 and 2010 he was principal investigator on a collaborative AHRC project exploring the relationship between reading, location and migration (www.devolvingdiasporas.com/).

Michael L. Ross is an Emeritus Professor of English and Cultural Studies at McMaster University. He is the author of *Storied Cities: Literary Imaginings of Florence, Venice, and Rome*, and *Race Riots: Comedy and Ethnicity in Modern British Fiction*. He has also published articles on various aspects of nineteenth- and twentieth-century literature.

Bill Schwarz teaches in the School of English and Drama, Queen Mary, University of London. Most recently he has co-edited, with Susannah Radstone, *Memory. Histories, Theories, Debates* (Fordham University Press, 2010) and with Cora Kaplan, *James Baldwin. America and Beyond* (University of Michigan Press, 2011). He is an editor of *History Workshop Journal* and *New Formations*.

Richard Steadman-Jones is a Senior Lecturer in the School of English at the University of Sheffield and his research is mostly concerned with the way in which language and communication are figured in texts that deal with cross-cultural encounters, especially in the context of colonialism. He is the author of *Colonialism and Grammatical Representation* (Blackwell, 2007), and he has recently written articles on questions of language as they relate to the experience of exile. He first became interested in John Masters because his heroes frequently count multilingualism among their many accomplishments.

Introduction: End of empire and the English novel

Bill Schwarz

Some impression of the event must have been left inside me. Where is it now? (Freud to Fleiss, 1897)

At the bar a florid man in a black suit was predicting the imminent collapse of the nation. He gave us three months, he said, then curtains. … 'Trouble is,' [he] was saying, over the top of his drink, 'we won't even know it's happened.' (John Le Carré, *Tinker, Tailor, Soldier, Spy*, 1974)

The England that bore the classical English novel has gone forever, and we can't expect a country of high-rise flat-dwellers, office workers and factory robots and unassimilated multi-racial minorities, with a suburbanized countryside, factory farming, sexual emancipation without responsibility, rising crime and violence, and the Trade Union mentality, to give rise to a literature comparable with its novel tradition of a so different past. (Q.D. Leavis, 'The Englishness of the English novel', 1980)

In August 1957 the novelist Anthony Burgess returned to England having spent three years working as a teacher in Malaya. He was a self-consciously anti-establishment figure, to use a term of the times, who had little regard for the pieties of empire. At the start of his posting he had learned Malay quickly and well, although his headmaster at Malay College found his easy terms with the native Malays inappropriate. His *A Malayan Trilogy*, published between 1956 and 1959, was careful to depict and give voice to the Malays, and was at the same time sensitive to the ethnic complexities of the non-European

1

populations.[1] In comic manner the novels reveal the absurdities of formal political, national and imperial ideologies, and dwell on the ambiguous status of the various white characters who were obliged to contend with 'an Empire now crashing about their ears'. Indeed in the novels Englishness itself appears to be on the point of extinction, kept alive – in the figure of Mr Lim, for example, whom the hapless protagonist identifies as 'the last Englishman' – only in the mimicry of distant colonials.[2] Yet the irreverence toward empire harboured by Burgess did nothing to still his hostility toward the Chinese Communists, who were fighting for independence, and he remained convinced that decolonisation, when it occurred, was premature. Looking back on the trilogy in the 1980s he recalled that its purpose was 'to record one white man's Malayan experience before it was too late, before the white man was thrown out of this final corner of the British Empire, as he was being thrown out of everywhere else'.[3]

The England Burgess returned to he saw through the eyes, as he put it, of an 'exile'. *Right to an Answer*, published in 1960, was designed, he explained, 'to bridge the gap between the novels about the East and the novels about England I intend to write, because it has as its main character a man who'd lived in the East, and who sees what's happening in postwar England through the eyes of a man who's really an exile'.[4] The two 'English' novels which followed – *The Doctor is Sick* (1960) and *One Hand Clapping* (1961) – provided decidedly unheroic, sub-Joycean romps through the degraded urban landscapes of contemporary England. When he came back home on leave during his posting, and when he finally returned in the summer of 1957, he had been distressed by the violence of the emergent youth subcultures of the time, evident to him particularly in the teddy boys, whom he perceived to be a throwback to an earlier chauvinistic, imperial age.[5] By April 1961 he had embarked on what he called his 'novel about juvenile delinquents'.[6] This was *A Clockwork Orange*, which appeared at the end of 1962 and which, as readers will know, comprises an extraordinary exploration of dystopian violence.[7] Although not definitively set in England, there can be no doubt that it was a visionary future England which the author was determined to evoke.

Yet the passage from *A Malayan Trilogy* to *A Clockwork Orange* is significant in revealing the connections between the end of the British empire and the dispositions of the English novel. Burgess's time in Malaya coincided almost exactly with the final years of British rule. The struggle for independence was marked by prolonged, systematic violence.[8] Burgess himself was clearly more concerned about the violence perpetrated by those fighting for independence than by the violence of the British; he was, for example, fiercely critical of Alan Sillitoe's novel, *Key to the Door*, for the sympathy it displayed toward the Chinese militants. 'For those of us,' he wrote in a review, 'who, living in terrorist territory, saw the garrotted bodies of our friends, the political naiveté of a book like this is nauseating.'[9] However his recent biographer suggests that no mention of 'garrotted friends' or the like appears in Burgess's surviving letters of the time, and that he himself was living in a region relatively free from violence. He does concede, however, that there were plenty of stories circulating about such outrages.[10] Burgess certainly imagined himself to have been witness to a violent colonial war, 'in terrorist territory', and in many respects this was so.[11] Yet when he came to write about his time in Malaya the violence disappears from the page and the comic vein predominates, a comedy proximate to that employed by Kingsley Amis, in the same period, to recount the travails of English campus life in *Lucky Jim*.[12] On the other hand, however, on being confronted with the violence of youth subcultures on English streets, or with the threat of such violence, he felt impelled to draft *A Clockwork Orange*, which offered an unsparing engagement with its subject-matter.

Why, we might ask, was the colonial violence deleted from Burgess's fiction, while the male bravado of the teddy boys was amplified out of all proportion? What does this tell us about the manner in which late colonialism was comprehended by the English eye, and what – also – about the purview of the English novel?

It is these larger questions which the following chapters address. The weight of recent criticism, over the past two or three decades, has – properly, fruitfully – turned our attention to the margins: that is, more particularly in this context, to the novels by colonials and migrants, and to those by their sons and daughters, and to rethinking the racial, sexual and gendered organisation of inherited narrative forms. There is now an established canon of such writing, which we know as postcolonial. That this new writing has changed forever the literary landscape is irrefutable. But this focus on the margins has perhaps concealed what occurred historically at the centre, and this is our concern here: that is, the English novel, at the time of decolonisation, *at its most centred*. This is what I understand as the Anglo-English or – to avoid the paradox – the Anglo-British novel, a designation which turns on matters of ethnicity, and on the commensurate ethnic sexual codes.[13] I shall say more about centre and margins, and how the centre might be demarcated, later.

It has now become commonplace to describe a certain sector of the postwar English novel, often resolutely English and upper- or middle-class in its preoccupations, as parochial. Historically, this represents a profound shift in consciousness. In the 1890s Thomas Hardy was commonly regarded as a provincial, and in many respects as a parochial, writer; sixty years later, novels located in Mayfair or St James's, or in Bloomsbury or Kensington, signalled the new parochialism.

This transformation was principally due to the dramatic recomposition of class relations in mid-twentieth-century Britain. But in part it was also a consequence of the influence of new anglophone writing from overseas.[14] When, for example, the Barbadian George Lamming, the future author of *In The Castle of My Skin*, arrived in England from the West Indies in 1950 he was conscious that he was arriving in the metropole at a critical historical moment: the time of decolonisation. As he later recalled, he barely read 'English writers' – he specifically mentions Evelyn Waugh and Graham Greene – for, with decolonisation his urgent concern, they 'didn't interest me very much'. He was drawn instead to the French: to Jean-Paul Sartre, Simone de Beauvoir and Albert Camus. It was they, he argues, who enabled him to bring together politics and letters and who, more particularly, understood the historical significance of the ending of the epoch of the European colonial powers.[15] This sense of the parochialism of England is about all that Lamming has ever shared with V.S. Naipaul, who came to believe that his arrival at Oxford University in 1950, due to ill-fated historical timing, coincided with the collapse of English civilisation and the onset of mass vulgarity. 'With the destruction of a century-old order in England, nothing is settled, and the pace of disturbance increases.'[16] For all Naipaul's overblown jeremiads, a consistent theme in his reflections on England has been his sense that a deep insularity has prevented the English from grasping their own history. Early on in his career, with the empire uppermost in his mind, he indicted the indigenous novelists, observing, for example, that 'No novelist has chronicled the astonishing changes in England in the fifty imperial years after the Indian Mutiny'.[17] Much later in life, in an important essay, 'An English way of looking', he considered the works of his close friend, Anthony Powell. In a devastating assault Naipaul concluded that Powell 'leaves English social life just where the writer found it', which, he implied, was a function of – precisely – Powell's 'English way of looking'.[18]

From a radically different perspective from within the metropole, the cadres of the emergent New Left (composed by as many migrants from the colonies as by the English themselves) also came to agitate for a renewal of the national culture, insistent that the culture which was most highly acclaimed, and which carried the most authority, was little more than half dead on its feet, inert and insular, and incapable of recognising the new world which was unfolding at such speed.[19] From this point on, the identification of English literary culture as provincial became something of a truism. Patricia Waugh's identification of 'the complacency of a suburban realism and platitudinous Englishness', or Ken Worpole's claim, in his discussion of the widespread popular enthusiasm for American fiction in the 1960s, that 'it was reasonable to wonder whether any English novels were being written other than those set in North West London', could have been repeated a hundred times.[20] Views like this have currency in the contemporary critical literature as well. They form the central argument of two commentaries from North America – Hugh Kenner's *A Sinking Island* and Jed Esty's *A Shrinking Island* – as well as Patrick Swinden's *The English Novel of History and Society*, while Marina Mackay and Lyndsey Stonebridge open their exploration of the mid-century novel, *British Fiction after Modernism*, with the emphatic statement that: 'By the time that England had shrunk to the size of a campus novel, the novel (much like Britain itself) was in dire need of rescue from its own parochialism.'[21]

Yet we need to ask, if an insularity did indeed organise the 'Anglo' English novel in the period of decolonisation, how did it function, and why should we be concerned?

English parochialism and insularity have, historically, functioned as screens which have obscured an entire stratum of colonial realities. However things may have appeared, or been experienced, for long English civilisation has been constituted by its colonial others, even when this has remained invisible or opaque. The idea of 'England alone' has largely been a fabrication, forcing out from the national field of vision awkward truths, and working to disconnect metropole from colony, white from non-white. Parochialism, in this context, signals a psychic incapacity to register the social realities which made metropolitan lives possible or, to use a more usual formulation, a forgetfulness about the historical work of empire. But inside such forgetfulness *The* there may occur signs or clues – memory traces – which partially reveal what *solution* has been repressed or occluded. For this reason, to read the English novel *and* at its most centred, insular or not, may illuminate the historical question *preas* of the impact of end of empire on the culture of the metropole. Indeed, *for* given the degree to which novels can be read as distillations of historical *recovery* consciousness, interventions in their own right in the field of historicity, to *a* follow Georg Lukács, the English novel may provide a privileged site from *historical* which to approach this question.

But parochialism, in this sense, was not simply the preserve of the English novel. It inhabited the political culture, and underwrote the class and gender customs prevailing in private life. Indeed, we are faced with the startling paradox that the end of the British empire – a properly global historical event of some consequence – was paraded for home consumption as the latest vindication of the peculiar English genius, as if Westminster,

Whitehall and Oxford University really did constitute the presiding centre of the planet. In the public culture of the 1950s and 1960s the prevailing story of the end of the British empire was, notwithstanding much evidence to the contrary, one of beneficent far-sightedness, in which wise and able rulers in London, realising that the empire had had a good innings, conferred with a new generation of colonial leaders at Lancaster House and passed on to them the ancient mysteries of Westminster constitutionalism. From this perspective, the end of empire was barely a historical event at all: it was, more properly, an act of providence – in the manner of G.M. Trevelyan's Glorious Revolution of 1688, but bigger.[22] Long ago E.P. Thompson alerted us to the imperatives of a national culture in which profound historical ruptures can enter collective memory as exemplifications of English tranquillity and continuity. The brunt of Thompson's argument was to suggest that too insistent a conviction that nothing transformative ever really happened in England was to confuse ideological representations for historical realities.[23] It's difficult to know whether anyone ever believed the official rendering of the end-of-empire story, but this is not to say that it was bereft of purchase. It did, after all, create the founding narrative for the Commonwealth. Yet this mythologising served to take decolonisation out of history, and to insulate the home population from the historical realities of what had occurred. The parochialism of the English novel, in this sense, reflected the sensibilities of an entire, late colonial social order. The empire may have been 'crashing' through the pages of Burgess's *A Malayan Trilogy*, but it functioned as no more than a weak *mise-en-scène*: it possessed no historical palpability and had no means to enter the lives of its characters. In this it was symptomatic of a larger mentality.

'End of empire' and 'the English novel' are both large abstractions, and greater specification is required. Thompson, in reflecting on the making of English civilisation, adopted an approach which foregrounded questions of displacement, emphasising the unpredictabilities of historical change, and the belief that 'history' often operates where we least expect it. My own sense is that it would be very curious if, at the very moment of empire's end, all consciousness of the imperial past suddenly vanished. With Freud I'm inclined to suppose that 'some impression' must still be left 'inside' the collective self. But also with Freud we are compelled to ask where those traces, or symptoms, are to be located, and how might we identify them when we see them. Much depends, I argue, on the displacements.

End of empire

There exists an enormous literature which analyses the end of the British empire. However there is still relatively little discussion about the impact of the end of empire on the metropole, and even less on the cultural and political, as opposed to the economic, connections.[24] Given the shifts in imperial history over the past couple of decades, with a greater emphasis now falling on the mutual interconnections between metropole and colonies, this question is gaining new prominence. If it is the case that Britain's overseas empire systematically shaped the internal properties of the home society, as I believe it did, then, as I have suggested, there is every reason to explore what occurred when formal imperial relations came to an end.[25] But in this respect, the articulation of competing historical times is critical.

We have chosen in this volume, pragmatically in part, to focus on the period since the second world war, although there can be no doubt that decolonisation was structured in a much longer duration than this allows.[26]

The war itself did much to destabilise Britain's global authority, generating a huge deficit in the home economy and undermining the capacity of sterling to function as an international currency. The Labour administrations of 1945–51 were beset by a series of financial crises, and in the immediate postwar years privation was evident in every aspect of daily life. But at the same time, the fact that national defeat had been averted and the German empire destroyed profoundly organised the collective perception the English had of themselves. The mythic properties of the war – England alone in 1940, on the brink of annihilation; the pluck of those on the home front enduring the Blitz; 'Monty's' decisive campaigns in North Africa; D Day – remained highly charged well into the 1950s, and arguably long beyond.[27] To what degree these popular memories worked to screen other historical realities, not least the end of empire, is a difficult question, and little researched, but at the very least it remains a plausible proposition.[28] And as I suggest in a moment, there occurred a complex interplay between the memories of the salvation of England in 1940 and the perceptions that, in the 1960s and 1970s, with the empire gone, the nation was being destroyed by malign internal forces. For an entire generation the war provided the touchstone by which to comprehend the predicament of England.

The main external historical trajectory, after 1945, is relatively clear and uncontested. Amongst the British political class at the end of the war there was perhaps not a single figure who anticipated the speed and thoroughness of the collapse of Britain's world-system. As much as the two leading Conservative politicians in 1945, Winston Churchill and R.A. Butler, were wrong about the fate of private education (they believed it doomed), so they, and others, were wrong about the empire, though for contrary reasons.[29] The independence of India, and with it the catastrophe of Partition, were the consequence of the severe weakening of the power of the British state in the new global system which had emerged in the mid-1940s, of the presence of an effective, organised anti-colonial movement within the sub-continent itself, and of a concatenation of short-term panic and confusion on the part of the ruling bloc in London.[30] Well before Independence in 1947, effective British authority in India had ebbed away. But it was not simply India which broke from the formal, or informal, empire in these years. Between 1947 and 1948 Ceylon, Burma, Palestine and Greece were abandoned, all of which a little while earlier had been deemed paramount to British interests. Despite the shock this induced amongst those charged with managing the British state, it led few of them to conclude that the continuation of the empire without India was an impossibility. Indeed, from this point on there took place a reinvigorated imperial endeavour, notwithstanding the continuing currency difficulties, which saw a concerted shift of British imperial activity from southern Asia to the Middle East and to central and eastern Africa.[31] The nationalisation of the Suez Canal Company by Egypt in 1956, and the subsequent failures of the Anglo-French-Israeli invasion, did much to undermine the formal and informal areas of British interest in the Middle East. The tide of black nationalism in Africa – combined with the collapse of the Central African Federation in 1963 after only ten years, which put paid to the grandiose plan of creating a vast new white-settler dominion in the heart of the African continent – marked the high point of decolonisation, etched in the public mind by the image of the Union Jack, in one colonial capital after another, being lowered in order to be replaced by the newly minted emblems of the emergent postcolonial nations. By the end of the 1960s, with the onset of another financial crisis, Britain's commitments east of Suez were finally abandoned and – with the exception of Ian Smith's white redoubt of Rhodesia and a handful of tiny entrepôt or island territories – empire existed as little more than a memory.

These external events, though, moved at a different tempo from the internal events of the metropole: there was never an immediate correspondence between the two. There was no emergency in British politics – as there was in France in this same period – in which the repercussions of the struggle between colony and metropolis threatened to destroy the constitutional system, although the situation in Northern Ireland complicates the story. In France there existed a direct, visible connection between the colonial disasters in Vietnam and in Algeria and the run of

profound political crises which threatened the state in the metropole.
In 1958 the *pied noir* insurrection in Algeria broke the Fourth Republic.
Continued uprisings and mutinies in the colony throughout 1961 and 1962
impacted directly on the politics of the centre. In Britain there was no
comparable experience of attempted coups, bombings and assassinations.
Londoners were never obliged to scan the skies, on the lookout for mutinous
troops parachuting into the city, as the French were in their capital on
Sunday 23 April 1961.

In Britain the invasion of Egypt in November 1956, heavy with symbolism,
represented a moment of great drama when those who opposed the war
sensed that a terrible mendacity prevailed. The famous demonstration in
Trafalgar Square on 4 November, when Nye Bevan's soaring oratory scattered
the pigeons far and wide, the angry chants of the massed crowd echoing
within Number Ten Downing Street, indicated the degree to which the
nation was polarised. And indeed, the consequent censure by the Eisenhower
administration, which forcefully reasserted Britain's subaltern role on the
world stage, combined with the destruction of Sir Anthony Eden, did mark
a critical caesura in Britain's imperial hegemony. Yet popular agitation
against the Suez adventure was relatively short-lived, and never sufficiently
powerful to mobilise a sustained anti-colonial opposition. From the moment
in 1957 when Harold Macmillan succeeded Eden until the mid-1960s the
impact of decolonisation within the metropole was relatively *underdetermined*,
the transfer of colonial power managed – in terms of the domestic state –
within the formal constitutional institutions, without generating any great
mobilisation of populist politics. So far as the metropole was concerned,
decolonisation was largely a passive revolution, in Gramsci's terms. It was
a historical process which – if not exactly invisible to the metropolitan
population – was at the very least heavily mediated. The chaos and violence
generated by decolonisation barely touched metropolitan lives. One need
only think of the dreamy newsreels, complete with epic commentaries and
stirring musical scores, to get a sense of the deep affective power of the
mediations. Knowledge gleaned from the popular press, from the radio and
from the newsreels, let alone from the more sensational medium of the
cinema, did not encourage the making of an informed home population.
The memories which came to be condensed in the rituals of end of empire
– the symbolics of the lowering of one flag, the raising of another – served
to obliterate other decisive histories.[32]

But informed or not it is in fact possible to locate the slow emergence
of a metropolitan politics generated by decolonisation. In *The Wretched of the
Earth*, first published in 1961, Frantz Fanon declared – 'obviously', as he put

it – that decolonisation equalled 'a programme of complete disorder'.[33] This interpretation arose from Fanon's experience of the Algerian situation, and he had in mind events in the colony rather than in the metropole. Even so, to understand decolonisation as a process of *disorder* is helpful, particularly in overcoming the residues of the mythic screen of British decolonisation as a history which was, providentially, conducted in good order. The concept of disorder, furthermore, is one which privileges race. In Biblical mode, Fanon observed that 'the last shall be first', referring precisely to the wretched of the earth who had given him his title.[34] For the emancipation of the racially subjugated to occur, he insisted, the old colonial social order, in both colony and metropole, would need to be destroyed. Inevitably, 'disorder' would follow.

If the impact of decolonisation on the metropole was, from the end of the 1950s through to the middle of the 1960s, relatively underdetermined, it is nonetheless the case that during this period apprehensions of disorder assumed a new valency in English public life. A new public mood appeared in which the state of the nation was persistently perceived to be in jeopardy, arising from the threat embodied in a variety of seemingly disconnected internal disorders. Perceptions of disorder became ever more strident, slowly reshaping the currents of the domestic nation-state. Few of the overarching social dysfunctions which preoccupied the public media, with the exception of 'coloured' immigration, arose directly from empire: the putative affluence of the new working class, the prominence of 'youth', the emergence of new sexual and gender aspirations, and so on.[35] One might say, however, that they were all interconnected in that each was understood to be undermining the social values of the old colonial nation.[36] Indeed, the term which we now use to describe the imaginings of such disorder – moral panics – was coined to describe precisely this period. Stanley Cohen's book, *Folk Devils and Moral Panics*, first published in 1972, explored the responses to the clashes between mods and rockers during the Easter weekend of 1964. The moral guardians of the old order repeated time and again the old refrain: these disturbances, arising from an internal enemy, were, they proclaimed, bringing about 'the disintegration of a nation's character'.[37] Going back and re-reading the statements of those who were orchestrating the panic, from the perspective of our own postcolonial present, it becomes clear that a common, if perhaps a subordinate and inchoate, motif was supplied by memories of the imperial past.[38] Many determinations underwrote these emergent moral panics. Yet the recurrence of the idea that the nation itself was in peril was not, I think, a mere rhetorical flourish, for the identity of England had been actively constituted by the historical realities of race and empire. Mods and rockers brawling on Brighton beach may seem a long way from the imperatives of decolonisation. But why the inflated response? Why the fear that this brought the nation itself to the lip of destruction?

Or we could look to the decisive sequence of state and legal responses to the perceived sexual crises and scandals which took hold of the nation in these years. The *Wolfenden Report* of 1957, concerned with the place of male homosexuality and of female prostitution in the public life of the nation's great cities; the proceedings of the 1960 trial against Penguin Books for publishing an unexpurgated edition of Lawrence's *Lady Chatterley's Lover*; and the *Denning Report* of 1963, which attempted to repair the damage inflicted on the state and nation by the Profumo scandal: all dramatised the break between two conflicting Englands. In each we can see the fear that a disorderly femininity and an unmanly, wayward masculinity were undermining the moral authority of the respectable, reasonable male citizen whose right it was to travel on the Clapham omnibus without unwanted anxieties impeding his otherwise virtuous journey.[39] Low life, within this reigning if beleaguered mentality, often turned out to be associated with libidinous black men – in the Profumo case with 'rich men in high places and coloured men in low', or in the *Lady Chatterley* trial with 'the backstreets of Port Said'.[40] Forces of corruption which, it might once have seemed, had previously been *over there* now appeared to be rampant *over here*.[41]

There was a longer, if barely visible, history at work here.[42] The great proconsular conceptions of empire which emerged in the late Victorian and Edwardian years, adumbrated most effectively by Lords Milner, Curzon and Cromer, were founded on the conviction that the overriding purpose of imperial expansion overseas was to maintain the domestic nation. Without the empire, the argument went, and without the manly, martial values which derived from the experience of colonial life, the English nation would disintegrate. Milner, Curzon and Cromer were not figures who could claim great currency in the public life of England in the 1950s and 1960s, or not consciously at any rate: in fact it was effectively their conception of empire which came to be the butt of the new strain of satire which accompanied, as a countervailing force, the outbreak of moral panics. But the idea that England without its empire was no England at all – an enfeebled third-rate nation, squandering the virtues of its unique past – was a common one in the 1960s, and could be heard right across the social formation. The idea that the popular heroism of 1940 had been undone by the degeneracy of a new rock and roll generation encapsulated, with perfect economy, an entire history. The laments for England carried within them, sometimes spoken, sometimes not, laments for empire.

More particularly, the idea of a lost England was most keenly felt by a particular class stratum who had been trained as an imperial elite, only to discover that there was no empire to administer. In 1959, one insider, Peregrine Worsthorne, put it like this:

> What is the point of maintaining a Queen Empress without an empire to rule over? Or a public school system designed to produce a race of colonial administrators without any colonies to administer? Or an Eton on whose playing fields battles are won, if Britain can no longer win battles without relying on the Americans? Everything about the British class system begins to look foolish and tacky when related to a second-class power on the decline, like the ceremonial robe cut for a young Apollo hanging loosely around his shrunken limbs in old age.[43]

Worsthorne's image of a confidently imperial Britain as a young Apollo is appropriately homoerotic, if inappropriate in every other sense. But these same questions were posed in many different registers during the years of decolonisation.[44]

The transformations in the moral and civil sphere had their counterparts in party politics, notably in the reinvention of a radical right-wing politics within the Conservative Party itself, signalled organisationally by the foundation of the Monday Club in 1961. The Monday Club in large part became the institutional medium by which a white-settler conception of the world, from the British territories in central Africa, was carried into the mainstream of political life in the metropole.[45] The virtues personified by sturdy, independent white Rhodesians seemed, to the tyros of the new radical right, exactly what was required in order to reverse the decline of the English nation. This radicalism on social issues was fused within the Monday Club with an assertive commitment to the principles of the market, anticipating in the field of ideas the Powell–Thatcher transformations within Conservatism of the later 1960s and 1970s.

Organisationally in the early 1960s the Monday Club was never much more than an outrider of the Conservative Party, and its significance should not be overrated. Once Harold Macmillan had appeased the White House in the aftermath of the Suez debacle, and managed to curb his rebellious pro-empire diehards in the immediate years which followed, any profound crisis in the domestic state was averted. Yet it is difficult to get the measure of the ideological shifts which punctuated the period from the later 1950s and into the middle 1960s, both in terms of the succession of moral panics over civic matters, and in terms of the strategic recasting of the Conservative right. What can be concluded, I think, is that while there was no prolonged crisis of the state, there did take place a critical transformation within the field of ideology, which imposed an increasing strain on the social-democratic consensus, and the moral agenda which underpinned it.[46] And this reaction to the 'middle way' of postwar party politics was, in part, informed by the experience of the end of empire and driven by the conviction that the nation was going to the dogs.

Much of what was taken to be disorderly was racially encoded, where whiteness signified order and blackness disorder. What allowed this to work were memories of an imagined colonial past in which the appropriate racial hierarchies were in place. It was memories such as these which underwrote the Powellite moment of 1968–70 – a moment, in contrast to the decade after Suez, which domestically was *overdetermined* – in which the displaced lineaments of decolonisation can be discerned.[47] The moment of Powellism undermined not simply the Labour administration, but the postwar political regime – although Enoch Powell himself was destroyed politically in the process. This did mark an authentic crisis of the state which inaugurated the long road to Thatcherism. And the degree of popular support for the Powellite programme, from below, suggests that this was a political transformation which was far from passive.

On 13 June 1970, a few days before the general election, Enoch Powell spoke at Northfield, a few hundred yards away from where he had grown up. In the anthologies the speech goes under the title of 'The enemy within'.[48] He opened by observing that 'When the *Prince of Wales* and the *Repulse* disappeared beneath the waters of the Gulf of Siam, at least we knew that Britain had suffered a defeat.' Here, in the old Labour heartlands of Northfield, Powell revived the memory of the disasters which presaged the collapse of Singapore. He himself drew the connection between Singapore in 1942 and England in 1970:

Britain at this moment is under attack. It is not surprising if many people still find that difficult to realise. A nation like our own, which has twice in this century had to defend itself by desperate sacrifice against an external enemy, instinctively continues to expect that danger will take the same form in the future. When we think of an enemy, we still visualize him in the shape of armoured divisions, or squadrons of aircraft, or packs of submarines. But a nation's existence is not always threatened in the same way. The future of Britain is as much at risk now as in the years when Imperial Germany was building dreadnoughts, or Nazism rearming. Indeed the danger is greater today, just because the enemy is invisible or disguised, so that his preparations and advances go hardly observed.

There was, he proclaimed, an enemy inside the nation, invisible to the people and, wilfully or not, ignored by those whose job it was to govern the state. The tale told at Northfield was lurid, extravagant and wild in its appeal to a homely reasonableness. The enemy, plague-like, was all around, winning victories without anyone comprehending their enormity, and breaking the moral foundations of the nation. The speech rehearsed the convictions which Powell had long been advocating: that madness was reason and reason madness, that truths were lies and lies truth. 'The public,' he declared, 'are literally made to say that black is white.'

As one might have presumed, this terminology – black and white – was not fortuitous. It lay at the heart of the matter. Powell was outraged that there were those who could bring themselves to deny that 'the English are a white nation'. This he regarded as 'heresy', the product of 'a sinister and deadly weapon' which entailed 'brainwashing by repetition of manifest absurdities'. In his overarching scenario of decline and anarchy, black immigration constituted a significant factor.

> 'Race' is billed to play a major, perhaps a decisive, part in the battle of Britain, whose enemies must have been unable to believe their good fortune as they watched the numbers of West Indians, Africans and Asians concentrated in her major cities mount toward the two million mark, and no diminution of the increase yet in sight.

But race signified more than immigration. It was, in Powell's imagination, the issue which bound together all the arenas of disorder, the single principle with the capacity to articulate all that threatened 'the peaceable citizen'. 'The exploitation of what is called "race",' he said, 'is a common factor which links the operations of the enemy on several different fronts.' Race, in this larger sense, became a means for signifying ethics itself, for 'the battle of Britain' was to be 'fought and won in the moral sphere'.[49]

Memories of imperial loss, combined with the arrival of non-white citizens, increasingly represented for Powell the end of a world whose homeliness could be measured by the natural assuredness of white authority. England was not politely contracting but breaking up in the midst of the traumas of defeat. As much as in Singapore in 1942 the ruling classes were busily abnegating their historic responsibilities. In 1970, with continuing black immigration, treachery was abroad again. The stakes could not have been higher. What had been averted in the summer skies of England in 1940 had finally come to fruition – in Birmingham, in Wolverhampton – a generation later. The Battle of Britain was being fought again in earnest. 'There are at this moment parts of this town,' he announced in Wolverhampton, 'which have ceased to be part of England, except in the sense that they are situated within it geographically.'[50] England was now as strange a land to its native inhabitants as the colonies had once been to their settler forebears, while the Englishman was becoming a stranger to himself. England had been defeated by race: by blackness itself.

Race, in this idiom, had been given life by the imperial experience. When supporters of Powell declared themselves to be white men and women; when they wrote to him complaining that black people had secreted themselves under the eaves of their own homes, invading a space which did not belong to them; when they urged that blacks should be 'sent back'; when they professed to know the ways of the migrant, and derided his or her insolence; when they dreamed of sunlit lands overseas where white rule prevailed; when they imagined their nation to have been defeated, or no longer what it once was, or even that it no longer existed – all drew upon memories of the imperial past. Inside the nation's forgetfulness about empire, the memory-traces remained.

To read the domestic repercussions of end of empire in this way, with Powellism as a constituent feature of the metropolitan experience, is to offer an expansive interpretation, and one which is alert to the displacements which operated. What could not be spoken in one sphere of the society appeared elsewhere in the social landscape, transformed, elliptical, perhaps not even fully conscious, but nonetheless meaningful. As Powell himself recognised, by the late 1960s race did indeed function as the articulating principle which held in place a myriad, disparate set of otherwise inchoate fears of disorder: and where race was operative, memories of empire were proximate.[51] To suppose that, with the empire gone, England was on the point of imminent collapse ('curtains', as John Le Carré's character has it in the epigraph above) was to rehearse, in new conditions, much older conceptions of proconsular imperialism.

English novels

In the high imperial era England often signified not only the nation at the political centre of the British metropole, but the entire civilisation of Anglo-Britain and its empire – a conflation which for many of the great imperial thinkers transmuted into an act of faith.[52] That it is no longer possible, or desirable, to think in these terms leaves the question of England, as a postcolonial nation, precisely that: a question. By extension, the idea of the English novel seems as irresolvable as ever. At the very beginning of our period, in 1948, in inimitable mode F.R. Leavis opened *The Great Tradition* with the striking observation that 'The great English novelists are Jane Austen, George Eliot, Henry James and Joseph Conrad.'[53] For Leavis the English novel was a matter of shared sensibility, and could effortlessly incorporate a displaced Pole and a New Englander. It is not that Leavis ignored the respective ethnic backgrounds of Conrad and James; it was rather that these were entirely secondary, and seemed not to touch the essentials of their literary imaginations. Moving on a generation, Randall Stevenson's penultimate volume in *The Oxford English Literary History* takes for its title *The Last of England?*, the question mark indicating that some distance exists between Stevenson's own interpretation and the more apocalyptic notions of the end of England which haunted the Powellite years.[54] It is significant that, for the reasons I have suggested above, his investigation opens in the 1960s rather than in the initial phase of formal decolonisation. And as he shows, the period he analyses – from 1960 to 2000 – was dominated by the convergence of the English novel, narrowly conceived, on the one hand, with its multiple postcolonial, anglophone manifestations, on the other, such that the very categorisations – English literary history, the English novel – came to conceal more than they were able to explain.

Yet the relationship between these two sets of writing has been porous from the start, even while the distinctions between them are becoming ever more blurred. The fiction of Hanif Kureishi, Zadie Smith and Andrea Levy, for example, represents a decisive recasting of the characteristic, inherited practices of the postwar novel in that these are authors who determined to draw out the connections between Britain's imperial past and the post-imperial present (if that is what it is), seeking to undermine a parochial forgetfulness and in so doing they, with others, have crafted a new aesthetic. At the same time, however, their novels are self-evidently written in an English idiom; they are demonstrably conscious of English precursors; and they address the predicament of the English nation. The memorable opening of Kureishi's *The Buddha of Suburbia*, first published in 1990, is notable in this respect:

> My name is Karim Amir, and I am an Englishman born and bred, almost. I am often considered to be a funny kind of Englishman, a new breed as it were, having emerged from two old histories. But I don't care – Englishman I am (though not proud of it), from the South

London suburbs and going somewhere. Perhaps it is the odd mixture of continents and blood, of here and there, of belonging and not, that makes me restless and easily bored. Or perhaps it was being brought up in the suburbs that did it.[55]

The strategic 'almost' of the first sentence makes it clear that Kureishi, here as elsewhere, has a complicated relationship not only to England, but to the Englishness of the English novel, for he knows full well that his postcolonial inclinations have to operate within the force-field of Englishness itself, just as Karim's lack of pride in his status as an Englishman, or almost-Englishman, has to as well.[56] It is much the same for the critics. Strictly speaking, there may be many sound theoretical and practical reasons to dispense with the national prefix. But its presence highlights a set of problems which remain pressing, and which do not easily go away. England, after all, has not vanished.

For these reasons we make no attempt in this collection to codify the internal co-ordinates of the English novel, in general.[57] As I've indicated, our starting point was to explore the fiction which appeared to be most centred in terms of ethnicity. By this, I mean those novels in which England and its ethnic forms were most naturalised or in which 'the culture and traditions which were called England' (to borrow George Lamming's formulation from 1961) were most taken for granted.[58] In part, this is simply to recognise what for long has been appreciated in postcolonial readings: that ethnicity – pace Leavis – works as a significant determinant in the imaginative organisation of an author's fiction. But this can never be total. Alongside the ethnic formation of an author, many other determinations shape which novels come to occupy the centre of the national literature, and how they do so.

To say this goes against the grain of much contemporary postcolonial scholarship, which has sought to displace the centre and privilege the margins, offering an expansive reading of the history of the novel rather than the restricted one we follow here. All of our contributors are, to varying degrees, postcolonial scholars. Our purpose is emphatically not to question the findings of postcolonial critique: it is rather to extend its remit to those works which at first glance do not seem to fall within the postcolonial field of vision.[59] Nor do we have any desire to rehabilitate what we take here to be the centre, either in terms of aesthetics or of politics, though there are surprises. Our discussion is a heuristic one, no more. Its purpose is as much historical as it is textual or literary: we are keen to examine a significant constituent of English culture in order to reflect on the responses to the end of empire which arose in the metropole, and to discover what was happening inside the 'parochial' literary imagination of the mainstream English.

In order to proceed we established some broad protocols which have served us as guidelines, although not as absolutes. We were less interested in those authors for whom England was second, rather than first, nature. This meant that we excluded the vast array of colonial writers who, originating in the overseas possessions of the British empire, contributed to the evolution of the anglophone novel. Thus we chose not to consider the non-white writers from south Asia, from Africa and from the Caribbean. On the same grounds we have largely excluded from our attention white writers who were in one way or another formed in the colonies, and then came to settle in Britain. (This – and the fact that for long they have been the object of sustained postcolonial investigation – explains the absence of, for example, Jean Rhys, born in Dominica from Welsh ancestry; of Colin MacInnes, born in England to one branch of the English intellectual aristocracy, who spent his childhood and schooldays in Australia; and of Doris Lessing, born in Persia to an English family and who grew up in Southern Rhodesia: all of whom have been identified, sometimes powerfully so, with the English novel.)[60] We have, though, allowed Penelope Lively to slip in, who made the journey from Cairo to England when she was twelve. For rather different reasons we concluded that we would not include the children of non-white migrants who grew up in Britain (Hanif Kureishi, Zadie Smith or Andrea Levy to continue the example), nor – for rather different reasons again – writers who strongly identified themselves as Scots, Welsh or Irish.[61]

These are writers who are either well known in the postcolonial canon or who in some way regard or regarded themselves as postcolonial (the Scottish writer, James Kelman, for example).[62] But we need to be clear why we are thinking in these terms. The decisive issue is not the – assumed – racial or ethnic identity of any single individual, as such, but rather their determinate *historical experience* of England. None of these writers can be said to have inhabited England or Englishness immediately, as if it were the most natural thing in the world. In part, the power of their writing derives from their tangential connection to the England they confronted: it was not necessary for them to work at defamiliarising England, for to them – frequently – it was already a curious, often menacing, phenomenon but one which they nonetheless knew from the inside. England, after all, had defamiliarised them. The story of the encounter between those coming from an outpost of England overseas and thence confronting actually existing England has been recounted many times.[63] It forms a critical element in the fiction of many of the writers mentioned.[64] This, though, was a general experience which included those who were born into the traditions of the colonisers, as the career of Doris Lessing, amongst others attests, as well as those who were designated the colonised, or natives.

Long ago Raymond Williams wrote a short account of George Orwell which highlighted the colonial determinations in his life. Eric Blair, the future Orwell, had been born in Bengal in 1903 to a long-serving colonial family. As an infant he was sent to England where he later attended prep schools, and then went on to Eton. When he completed his schooling he travelled to Burma to join the police force. In 1927, while on leave in England, he resigned from the imperial police in order to become a writer, adopting the name of George Orwell. As Williams suggested, when Orwell first began to travel through his native land, documenting the home civilisation of the English, he discovered the disjuncture between actually existing England, previously unknown to him, and 'the culture and traditions which were called England', which – from the redoubts of the empire and Eton – were virtually the only England he had ever known. Williams contends that Blair/Orwell himself was a split subject, and that the colonial – and class – experience lay at the heart of this internal divide.[65] This reminds us of the degree to which the empire was never simply an extension or confirmation of the home nation; it could unsettle English men and women, and fracture Englishness itself.

In turn, it also demonstrates the fact that it was perfectly possible for a 'lower-upper-middle-class' white Englishman, as Orwell liked to describe himself, to divest himself of his imperial instincts (in some senses at any rate), and thereby to see England anew. 'Parochialism' was never a static condition, immune to transformation. Indeed, although we might immediately alight on particular novelists of the early 1950s as parochial – Anthony Powell, perhaps, or Angus Wilson or Kingsley Amis – the deep transformations which England underwent in the postwar period, including the end of empire, made it increasingly less plausible to take English ethnicity on trust, as a self-evident marker of civilisation.[66] Even with those novelists we might identify as most deeply English, their collective mental world was far from uniform. If in the early years after the war English ethnicity gave the novel a certain coherence, by the 1960s and 1970s any shared ethnic investment in the novel was unravelling.

But nor was England, even at its most insular, ever quarantined from the imperatives of empire. 'England alone' is as much a myth in the field of literature as in any other. Empire persistently impinges. For this reason, in choosing the authors we wished to discuss, it would have proved self-defeating (if not impossible) to have stuck uncompromisingly to a hermetic, empirically verifiable English identity.

There's an engaging moment in Raymond Williams's *The English Novel* when he discusses the 'very specific Englishness' of the nineteenth-century novel. After considering the Brontës and George Eliot he comes to Disraeli. 'Disraeli, yes,' he writes: 'that's a case on its own but I'd settle for Beaconsfield, as he did; that's how the consciousness went.'[67] 'That's how the consciousness went.' This is a characteristic phrase of Williams, but we can see what he means. As has often been remarked, if one were to take away from the English novel the colonials and the migrants, their sons and daughters, the Welsh, the Scots and the Irish, the resulting canon would appear singularly lopsided, eccentric even. In fact, England itself is left looking something of a chimera. But this is no surprise, for Englishness itself is always deferred. It is always somewhere else, or some time else. England is its own fiction.

That this is so has important ramifications for our own project. One author after another, seemingly impeccably English, turns out to be little of the sort. We have stayed as close as we believe is practicable to our original prospectus. But we might note here that Orwell (discussed by Patrick Parrinder in the opening chapter, and as noted above) was a son of the Raj; Josephine Tey was born in Scotland; John Masters came from a long line of colonial administrators and soldiers, but was not himself posted to India until he had completed his Sandhurst training in the 1930s; William Boyd, of Scottish descent, was born in the Gold Coast and spent much of his childhood in Nigeria; as we have seen, Penelope Lively's natal city was Cairo, where she spent her early life; and Ian McEwan, although born in Aldershot into a military-Scottish family, followed his father through his childhood to his postings in Asia, Germany and North Africa. Englishness remains as elusive as ever. But that is 'how the consciousness goes'.

The novel at the end of empire

There are a number of ways one might think through the connections between fiction and the end of empire. There is a relatively small grouping of authors who have endeavoured to tell the story of decolonisation.[68] There are many more who, from the standpoint of the postcolonial epoch and for various ends, choose to return to the empire in order to tell their stories of the present.[69] Others, of whom William Golding was perhaps the most prominent, as Rachael Gilmour shows later, work by allegory. There are the occasions when an author returns to a colonial text, or (in the case of Tim

Parks's relationship to D.H. Lawrence, discussed by Suzanne Hobson) to the entire work of an author, in order to recast it for the contemporary period. Some of the most interesting fiction is that which does not appear to concern itself in any way with empire or its demise, but which nonetheless carries the memory-traces of these former histories; or those which document the fate of England (including, for example, the piquant subgenre of the decline of the country house), or the onset of disorder or the question of race, and which can be situated in the larger public debates about the end of empire.[70] There are those which, while set in colonial situations, display little interest in the workings of empire but which employ the overseas 'background' as a means to drive forward a generic narrative – as in the female romances reviewed by Deborah Philips – but which nonetheless are revealing.[71] There exist interesting generic continuities between older colonial forms and contemporary writing, particularly in the fields of adventure stories, thrillers and spy novels; in the growing domain of travel reportage; and, the vehicle for ironic self-detachment, perhaps even in the form of the comic novel itself. There is at least one novel – Philip Hensher's *The Mulberry Empire* – which, in a putatively post-Saidian flourish, works entirely by pastiche and sleight of hand.[72] We should note too the fiction which, knowingly or not, continues to echo the mentalities, in our own neo-liberal globalised world, of a previous imperial epoch.[73] And any final settling of accounts would need to attend to those novelists who believe that the demise of the colonial empires requires the historical imagination itself to work in new ways.

Some of these questions are taken up in the pages which follow, while others suggest the need for future work. The dialectic between colonial order and postcolonial disorder, for all its phantasmagoric properties, turns out to be one theme which is prominent, although in many variants – from the 'invasion' literature of the postwar fiction discussed by Patrick Parrinder in the opening chapter to the novels of Pat Barker and David Peace which James Procter surveys – while the desire for a remembered colonial order, palpable in the work of John Masters, or in the postwar popular romances, also haunts the writings of more contemporary figures, such as William Boyd and Ian McEwan. And as I suggest in a moment, disorder, or a disorderly sense of history, has also impinged on the novel form itself.

I principally came to these issues as a historian, intrigued by the political and emotional landscape of England after empire. As I see it, a number of key works of fiction of the postwar period provide the analytical means *for historians* to comprehend the domestic and racial configurations of decolonisation, and to grasp the elusive conjunctions of the memory and forgetting of empire in the lives of the inhabitants of the metropole. Much turns, I think, on the systematic silences which have accrued, and which continue to accrue, around the issue of race. The crucial novels in this regard I found to be Doris Lessing's *The Grass is Singing*, published in 1950, and Paul Scott's *The Raj Quartet*, published between 1966 and 1975, both of which explore the dynamics of racial whiteness.

For our purposes here, Scott is perhaps the more interesting, for it was his encounter with India in 1943, as a serving soldier early on in his adult life, which enabled him to see in his native English culture the racial mentalities which had previously been invisible to him. Indeed Scott's reading of the end of the Raj came to be motivated by his understanding of the racial politics of Britain in the 1960s, and by Powellism in particular. Above all, though, the significance of his *Quartet* lies in its temporal structure: Scott's narrative articulates distinct historical times, bringing together the end of empire in India in the 1940s, with the time of his own present in the metropole in the 1960s and early 1970s, and links both to the long durational memories of the 'Mutiny' (1857) and of the Amritsar massacre (1919). This allows him to explore how *those* pasts work in *this* present, connecting at the same time both colony and metropole. In Scott's hands, I suggest, the fiction can explain competing temporalities with a depth and complexity which the histories rarely possess.

The core of the narrative of the *Raj* novels turns on the fate of a young white Englishwoman, Daphne Manners, who arrived in India from England in February 1942. In the months which followed she falls in love with an Indian, Hari Kumar and subsequently, in the midst of the turmoil of the Quit India insurrection which occurred in the following August, she is raped by unknown Indian men in the ominously named Bibighar Gardens. The varied reconstructions of these initiating events dominate the succeeding architecture of the *Quartet*, in which conflicting personal and official memories begin cumulatively to undercut the certainties of the white colonial vision. The unfolding of the story, though, is contradictory. On the one hand, the novels are obsessively, claustrophobically repetitious, returning time and again to the initiating trauma of the rape. In form, the narrative *acts out* this history, as if incapable of either leaving it or resolving it, and in so doing embodies a pathological or neurotic time. On the other hand, there are occasions when the narrative opens the possibilities for the subversion of racial whiteness as a given way of seeing, allowing us to imagine a process of *working through* the travails of the past. A handful of the characters tentatively seek to look outside the field of whiteness which presses in on them, and to re-imagine their lives on new terms. Others who do not, or who are not able to, or for whom the dispositions of whiteness accumulate, are destroyed. In this rendering, history as nightmare – as continuing trauma – is attributed to the imperatives of racial whiteness.

In his preliminary notes for the second volume Scott referred to the 'ghost of transference to the days of the Mutiny'.[74] The scene of Daphne Manners's rape – the Bibighar Gardens – redramatises the Bibighar massacre of white women and children at Kanpur (Cawnpore) in 1857. The 'transference' of 1857 echoes from the first sentence of the first volume, and it punctuates the narrative. Memories of Amritsar are more consequent but also more mediated, though the idea of transference recurs. In the earliest moments of drafting the *Quartet* Scott commented on what he identified as a 'dangerous racial memory' released by the defeat of colonial powers; by the time the novels were completed, in 1975, he was citing racism as the dominating force in the contemporary world.[75] Yet for Scott the great difficulty was that there existed for him no available language in which these apprehensions – these repressed *memories* of colonial violence – could be spoken, for what he himself termed the 'liberal humanism', to which he was instinctively drawn had, he'd decided, come to be complicit with racial violence.[76] Like many of the characters in his *Quartet*, he too discovered himself to be trapped in history – the history, indeed, bequeathed by the 'dangerous racial memories' created by the unfinished historical trajectory of decolonisation.

Scott's writing of the novels coincided with the rise and consolidation of Powellism, in which the old dreams of the 'master-race', as he saw it, took on a new, domestic syntax.[77] Through these years Scott was a keen observer of Powell. India, for the two of them, had proved decisive. They had both served the Raj in the critical years of the mid-1940s, though they had taken with them from this shared experience contrary positions on race and empire. The character of Merrick in the novels is a composite of historical time, functioning both as a police officer of his period, in realist mode, and as a premonition of what Powellism in the metropole was to be, retrospectively imagined. Part of the difficulty in reading *The Raj Quartet*, however, is that Scott's later experiences of India, in 1964 in particular, created in his own mind – as he explained – a measure of identification between his own racial instincts and those of Powell. He recounted the details of his experience on a number of occasions; once, significantly, in a talk on Powell, which he entitled 'Enoch *sahib*: a slight case of cultural shock', delivered to the Commonwealth Countries League in London in November 1969. Interwoven with a persuasive denunciation of Powell, he nonetheless felt obliged to confess, with unnerving candour, that 'India always did, still does and probably always will bring out the Enoch in me'.[78]

This leaves us with a difficult, contradictory figure. Opinion on *The Raj Quarter* is polarised. Its critics point to the relative absence of non-white voices and to the fact that the founding traumatic event of the sequence involves the rape, not of an Indian, but of a white English woman. Those who defend it do so on the grounds that it portrays a luminously textured account of white lives lived on the edge of an impending historical disaster. Opinion on Scott himself is, legitimately, equally divided. On the one hand we have the fierce opponent of Powell; on the other he advocated a certain sympathetic understanding of Powell's motivation. Scott, in his own life, was unable to reconcile these contraries, or to discover a means by which he could articulate the enormity of the 'dangerous racial memories' which he saw all about him. The more he wrote, the more a deep isolation took hold of him and the self-destruction which followed caused intolerable pain both to him and to those close to him. As the pages of his fiction multiplied so his own life disintegrated. And yet I take him to be England's first serious novelist of decolonisation. The fiction he produced carries many ambiguities, and the costs were high. He understood the weight of the historical past with which he was contending but could find no public voice in which his fearful sense of England, after empire, could be spoken. Like the doomed characters who populate his novels he could discover no way, personally or politically, of working through the past.

Memories of racial violence structure Scott's *Raj Quartet*, and in this respect – as in many others – the contrast to Anthony Burgess's *Malayan Trilogy* is significant. Indeed the more general question of violence in the postwar novel, viewed from the perspective of end of empire, deserves fuller attention. Here, particularly, the displacements may be most pronounced. If the comic novel eschews acknowledging violence there may be much to be learned from its counterpart: the detective genre, where violent deeds appear to come clean out of the sky, often in otherwise genteel circumstances.[79] In the chapters which follow we can catch something of the subterranean locations of racial violence, from William Golding's apprehension in *Close Quarters* of a dark corruption clinging to the hull of the ship – a 'black and streaming' 'thing' originating in the Caribbean – to the disinterred corpse, in the heart of England, of the young black woman in Ruth Rendell's *Simisola*. How the operations of violence have been imagined in the English novel, and mapped onto the metropolitan landscape, may prove to be symptomatic, illuminating one aspect of the inchoate complex of ideas and emotions which underwrote England after empire.

This returns us, finally, to the question of postcolonial history and to the historicity of the novel form. In simple empirical terms, the degree to which historians figure as characters in postwar fiction is striking. There are the absurd history dons in *Lucky Jim*, and the more steely medievalists of Angus Wilson's *Anglo-Saxon Attitudes* who have to contend with the possibility that their historical knowledge is nothing more than a fabrication. Guy Perron in *The Raj Quartet*, Tom Crick in Graham Swift's *Waterland*, Claudia Hampton in Penelope Lively's *Moon Tiger*, Esther Breuer in *The Radiant Way* by Margaret Drabble, and Edward in Ian McEwan's novella *On Chesil Beach* are also all historians of one sort or another. Their presence is not fortuitous. A.S. Byatt, like many others, has commented on 'the sudden flowering of the historical novel' in postwar Britain, coinciding with the highpoint of decolonisation.[80] What this explicit turn to the discussion of history represents is a matter of contention, even if the connection to the end of empire barely figures in most accounts.

Margaret Scanlan usefully distinguishes between the historical novel represented by Walter Scott and Tolstoy, and those which are more sceptical, ironic and discontinuous, on the model of *Vanity Fair*, and which are more expressly about the means by which we come to know history.[81] It is this latter metafictive form, she argues, which has come to dominate the postwar novel, and which emphasises the degree to which memory, history and tradition function as artifice. The engagement with history, in other words, is paradoxical, for it is in part driven by a distrust of history, or at least by a distrust of the formal protocols of the discipline of history, narrowly conceived.[82] In this, the fiction parallels many of the developments associated with the emergent academic histories of the past generation, in which recognition of the multiple ways in which historical agency is constituted requires us to rethink how to reach the past – whether through the means of formal history or through the novel form.

There are many examples we could turn to, but we can take one influential instance: Graham Swift's *Waterland*, first published in 1983. Tom Crick, a history master, faces the end of his career due to the fact that the history department in his school is due to be abolished. In his final lessons he abandons the conventional history curriculum and, reflecting on the contingencies of multiple temporalities, begins to relate to his class the story of his native region, the fenlands of East Anglia, in which he weaves together aspects of his own autobiography. In a riveting, fictive account of eighteenth-century primitive accumulation – based on the interconnection of the cultivation of cash crops, brewing and water-transport – he sets out a story of capitalist progress, in which his various protagonists come to believe that history is theirs, and in which the products of the Armstrong Brewery find their way throughout the empire, each bottle of ale a sign of modernity and confirmation of the civilisation of the English entrepreneur. But as the success of Armstrong's foundered in the Great Depression of the late nineteenth century, the 'nation-time' beloved of the fenland capitalists collapses, and a more uncanny, mysterious and menacing – a more Gothic – sense of time interposes itself, in which Tom, and others of his generation, have to learn to accommodate themselves.

In important respects, this shifting, fissile conception of time in the novel is explicitly post-imperial. So too is the discussion of temporality in Penelope Lively's *Moon Tiger* (published in 1987), a novel replete with fractured tenses, multiple narrative voices and a range of competing times, in which the reminiscences of the dying Claudia Hampton are reproduced in the narrative structure of the story. At one point she exclaims that 'History is disorder'.[83] A 'disorderly' conception of history, however, belongs to no-one: in that lies its disorderliness. To employ such a term is not to suppose that the past cannot be reached, or that it is un-narratable, or that it needs to be jettisoned. On the contrary, it may be exactly from such an idea of historical time that we can best understand England after empire.

Notes

1 From early on he was persuaded that the future of the English novel depended upon the fiction emerging from the old colonies: Anthony Burgess Wilson, *English Literature. A survey for students* (London: Longmans, Green, 1958), p. 12; and Anthony Burgess, *The Novel To-Day* (London: British Council and Longmans, Green, 1963), p. 9. I am very grateful to my co-authors for their responses to an earlier draft of this introduction.

2 Anthony Burgess, *The Long Day Wanes. A Malayan trilogy* (London: Penguin, 1981: comprising *Time for a Tiger*, 1956; *The Enemy in the Blanket*, 1958; and *Beds in the East*, 1959), pp. 210 and 450.

3 The recollection is from July 1980, cited in Andrew Biswell, *The Real Life of Anthony Burgess* (London: Picador, 2006), p. 169.

4 In a radio talk of 23 April 1959, cited in Biswell, *Anthony Burgess*, p. 200.

5 The teddy boys, he suggested, 'wore a kind of costume which evoked a period of chauvinism and imperial expansion', representing 'a nostalgia for an old Britain. ... The collective aggression of the imperial epoch had transformed itself into a debased violence of which youth had the monopoly', Anthony Burgess, *Little Wilson and Big God. Being the first part of the confessions of Anthony Burgess* (London: Heinemann, 1987), p. 41.

6 Letter, April 1961, cited in Biswell, *Anthony Burgess*, p. 256.

7 Though in many ways *A Clockwork Orange* is considerably less disturbing than a novel which followed it by a few months: Colin Wilson, *The World of Violence* (London: Pan, 1965; first published 1963). Dave Wallis, *Only Lovers Left Alive*

(London: Pan, 1966; first published 1964), of the same genre, is altogether more engaging.

8   Much can be gleaned from subsequent accounts which analyse how the British sought to shift from frontal assault to 'low intensity' warfare: Richard Stubbs, *Hearts and Minds. Guerrilla warfare in the Malayan Emergency, 1948–1960* (Singapore: Oxford University Press, 2004), and John Cloake's biography, *Templer: Tiger of Malaya. The life of Field-Marshall Sir Gerald Templer* (London: Harrap, 1985). Frank Kitson, an important theorist of counter-insurgency who served in Malaya, Kenya and Northern Ireland, and who retired as Commander in Chief, UK Land Forces in 1985, produced a classic account: *Low Intensity Operations. Subversion, insurgency, peace-keeping* (London: Faber and Faber, 1971), in which his Malayan experience proves central.

9   *Yorkshire Post*, 28 December 1961, cited in Biswell, *Anthony Burgess*, p. 153; and Burgess, *The Novel To-Day*, p. 39.

10 Biswell, *Anthony Burgess*, pp. 153–4.

11 Burgess, *Little Wilson and Big God*, pp. 378–9.

12 The significance of the campus novel has been discussed by Ian Carter, *Ancient Cultures of Deceit: British university fiction in the post-war years* (London: Routledge, 1990). See too Michael L. Ross, *Race Riots. Comedy and ethnicity in modern British fiction* (Montreal: McGill-Queen's University Press, 2006), which is very close to the concerns of this volume – as is his 'Passage to Krishnapur: J.G. Farrell's comic vision of India' *Journal of Commonwealth Literature* 40: 3 (2005) – and Andy Medhurst, *National Joke: Popular comedy and English national identities* (London: Routledge, 2007).

13 J.G. Ballard thought in these terms to describe the prominent English novels of the 1950s, citing in particular C.P. Snow, Kingsley Amis and Anthony Powell: *Archive Hour*, BBC Radio 4, 26 September 2009.

14 Bruce King, *The Oxford English Literary History. Vol. 13, 1948–2000. The internationalization of English literature* (Oxford: Oxford University Press, 2004). A significant moment in what may be taken as the modernisation of the English novel occurred at the first Writers' Conference at the Edinburgh Festival in 1962, organised by John Calder and Sonia Orwell, where there appeared, amongst others, Henry Miller, Norman Mailer, Lawrence Durrell, Kingsley Amis, Mary McCarthy, Muriel Spark, Rebecca West, Stephen Spender, Alexander Trocchi and Angus Wilson.

15 David Scott, 'The sovereignty of the imagination. An interview with George Lamming', *Small Axe* 12 (2002), p. 112; and for Lamming's contemporaneous response to English politics and letters, first published in 1960, see his classic *The Pleasures of Exile* (London: Pluto Press, 2005).

16 See V.S. Naipaul, *Letters Between a Father and a Son* (London: Little Brown, 1999).

17 V.S. Naipaul in the *Illustrated Weekly of India*, 14 April 1963, cited in Patrick French, *The World Is What It Is. The authorised biography of V.S. Naipaul* (London: Picador, 2008), p. 238; he noted in particular that playwrights and novelists

revelled in 'jokes about the Foreign Office and Eton and Harrow ... and London, so far as literature goes, remains Dickens's city ... on the modern mechanised city, its pressures and frustration and sterility, English writers have remained silent.'

18 V.S. Naipaul, 'An English way of looking' in his *A Writer's People. Ways of looking and feeling* (London: Picador, 2007), p. 40.

19 This emergent sensibility is well represented in the pages of the *Universities and Left Review*, published between 1957 and 1959, one of the two precursors of the *New Left Review*, which through the 1960s and 1970s unleashed its own war of manoeuvre against assorted practitioners of English insularity.

20 Patricia Waugh, *Harvest of the Sixties. English literature and its background, 1960–1990* (Oxford: Oxford University Press, 1995), p. 77; Ken Worpole, *Dockers and Detectives. Popular reading: Popular writing* (London: Verso, 1983), p. 25; see too p. 36. In his diary for 16 August 1962 John Fowles observed 'The provincial: one who fears others and otherness', John Fowles, *The Journals. Volume I*, ed. Charles Drazin (London: Vintage, 2004), p. 522. Fowles imagined himself at this time, and for much of his life, to be anti-Tory and anti-colonial. But with his unsettling sense of human life *as* biology, his disregard for the other grew deep, as becomes increasingly evident in *The Journals. Volume II*, ed. Charles Drazin (London: Vintage, 2007), which encompass the period from 1965 to 1990. See too John Fowles, 'On being English but not British' (1964) in his *Wormholes. Essays and occasional writings*, ed. Jan Relf (London: Vintage, 1999).

21 Hugh Kenner, *A Sinking Island. The modern English writers* (London: Barrie and Jenkins, 1988; first published 1987); Jed Esty, *A Shrinking Island. Modernism and national culture in England* (Princeton: Princeton University Press, 2003); Patrick Swinden, *The English Novel of History and Society, 1940–1980* (London: Macmillan, 1984), and Marina Mackay and Lyndsey Stonebridge (eds), 'Introduction' to their *British Fiction After Modernism. The novel at the mid century* (Houndmills: Palgrave, 2007), p. 1. In fact, this collection aims to dispel the received views of the mid-century English novel as uniformly dull. 'Too often characterized as a conservative literature of retreat, this book argues instead that mid-century fiction has a complex and under-thought relation to its own history – both in its historical and literary legacies and to the history of which it was such an uneasy part', p. 2. Yet while modernism appears to provide the authors with their organising category, the historical dimensions of end of empire appear only gesturally.

22 The purest expression of these sentiments can be found in Earl Attlee, *From Empire to Commonwealth. The Chichele Lectures* (Oxford: Oxford University Press, 1961).

23 E.P. Thompson, 'The peculiarities of the English' in his *The Poverty of Theory and Other Essays* (London: Merlin Press, 1978).

24 For the growing critical literature on the cultural consequences see, alongside Stuart Ward's pioneering collection, *End of Empire and British*

Culture (Manchester: Manchester University Press, 2002): Wendy Webs *Englishness and Empire, 1939–1965* (Oxford: Oxford University Press, 2007), and her *Imagining Home: Gender, 'race' and national identity, 1945–1964* (London: University College Press, 1998); Priya Jaikumar, *Cinema at the End of Empire: A politics of transition in Britain and India* (Durham: Duke University Press, 2006) and Christine Geraghty, *British Cinema in the Fifties: Gender, genre and the 'New Look'* (London: Routledge, 2000); Simon Faulkner and Anandi Ramamurthy (eds), *Visual Culture and Decolonisation in Britain* (Aldershot: Ashgate, 2006); and Mark Crinson (ed.), *Modern Architecture and the End of Empire* (Aldershot: Ashgate, 2003).

25 For a significant review of the recent debates, see Catherine Hall and Sonya Rose, 'Introduction' to their edited collection, *At Home in the Empire: Metropolitan culture and the imperial world* (Cambridge: Cambridge University Press, 2006).

26 The most insightful general introductions can be found in John Darwin's two accounts: *Britain and Decolonisation: The retreat from empire in the post-war world* (Basingstoke: Macmillan, 1988) and *The Empire Project. The rise and fall of the British world-system, 1830–1970* (Cambridge: Cambridge University Press, 2009). This should be supplemented with his 'The fear of falling: British politics and imperial decline since 1900', *Transactions of the Royal Historical Society*, 36 (1986), and with A.G. Hopkins, 'Rethinking decolonization', *Past and Present*, 200 (2008). I have offered my own interpretation, drawing from Darwin, in Bill Schwarz, 'End of empire' in Paul Addison and Harriet Jones (eds), *The Blackwell Companion to Contemporary Britain, 1939–2000* (Oxford: Blackwell, 2005). And in the literary field, for the earlier period, see John Marx's significant *The Modernist Novel and the Decline of Empire* (Cambridge: Cambridge University Press, 2005). Reed Way Dasenbrock's 'The novel and the end of empire', although appearing in Brian W. Shaffer (ed.), *A Companion to the British and Irish Novel, 1945–2000* (Oxford: Blackwell, 2005), curiously ends with Partition in India in 1947.

27 Angus Calder, *The Myth of the Blitz* (London: Jonathan Cape, 1991).

28 Or as J.G. Ballard put it, 'In fact we had suffered enormous losses, exhausted and impoverished ourselves, and had little more to look forward to than our nostalgia', *Miracles of Life. Shanghai to Shepperton. An autobiography* (London: Fourth Estate, 2008), p. 126.

29 Bill Schwarz, 'The tide of history. The reconstruction of Conservatism, 1945–51' in Nick Tiratsoo (ed.), *The Attlee Years* (London: Pinter, 1991).

30 The most moving accounts of recent scholarship include Yasmin Khan, *The Great Partition: The making of India and Pakistan* (New Haven: Yale University Press, 2007), and the collaborative volumes by Christopher Bayly and Tim Harper: *Forgotten Armies: Britain's Asian empire and war with Japan* (London: Penguin, 2005); *Forgotten Wars: The end of Britain's Asian empire* (London: Penguin, 2008). Aamir R. Mufti, *Enlightenment in the Colony: The Jewish question and the crisis of postcolonial culture* (Princeton: Princeton University

Press, 2007) provides a provocative reflection on this strategic moment of postcolonial history.

31 Wm. Roger Louis, *Imperialism at Bay, 1941–1945. The United States and the decolonization of the British empire* (Oxford: Clarendon Press, 1977); and his *The British Empire in the Middle East, 1945–1951. Arab nationalism, the United States, and postwar imperialism* (Oxford: Clarendon Press, 1984).

32 How this has entered collective memory is of great interest: for example, in Paul Scott, *Staying On* (London: Pan, 1977), pp. 170–1, where the ambivalence of the protagonists seeing the flag lowered finds a close echo in the final part of Jan Morris's history of the empire which came out the following year: *Farewell the Trumpets. An imperial retreat* (London: Penguin, 1979; first published 1978). And see Philip Murphy, 'African Queen? Republicanism and defensive decolonization in British tropical Africa, 1958–64', *Twentieth Century British History* 14: 3 (2003).

33 Frantz Fanon, *The Wretched of the Earth* (Harmondsworth: Penguin, 1971), p. 27.

34 Fanon, *Wretched of the Earth*, p. 28.

35 Ian McEwan's *On Chesil Beach* (London: Vintage, 2008; first published 2007) explores the lived forms of this shifting sexual history, which he explicitly locates against the backdrop of the end of empire. The narrator knows, as the protagonists cannot, that sexual adventure is just around the corner – or at least, that is what he or she believes: 'In just a few years' time, that would be the kind of thing quite ordinary people would do. But for now, the times held them', p. 18.

36 I have made an initial exploration of these developments (focusing, in part, on John Arden's play *Serjeant Musgrave's Dance*, first staged in 1960) in 'Disorderly politics' in Brian Meeks (ed.), *Stuart Hall. Culture, politics, race and diaspora* (Kingston, Jamaica and London: Ian Randle, and Lawrence and Wishart, 2007).

37 Cited from the *Birmingham Post*, 19 May 1964, in Stanley Cohen, *Folk Devils and Moral Panics. The creation of the mods and rockers* (St Albans: Paladin, 1972), p. 52.

38 This reading would conform to the interpretation of British youth cultures provided by Dick Hebdige, *Subculture. The meaning of style* (London: Methuen, 1979). So far as I'm aware no-one has commented on Stanley Cohen's South African provenance: the apartheid world may have attuned him to hear a politics of national and racial fear whose significance others might not have so readily grasped.

39 With the possible exception of Colin MacInnes, the only author who properly registers this in the fiction is Sam Selvon in *The Lonely Londoners* (Harlow: Longmans, 1986; first published 1956), pp. 101–9. This passage is conventionally read as a lyrical evocation of summertime eroticism, when the English can at last dispense with convention, and get on with all manner of polymorphous pleasures. What this misses is the violence, disaffection and

despair which these racial-sexual energies release, and which Selvon was careful to calibrate.

40 The Committee on Homosexual Offences and Prostitution, *Report of the Committee on Homosexual Offences and Prostitution* (London: HMSO, 1957); C.H. Rolph (ed.), *The Trial of 'Lady Chatterley'. Regina v. Penguin Books Limited* (Harmondsworth: Penguin, 1961), p. 1; and *The Denning Report* (London: Pimlico, 1992), p. 22. On the eruption of wayward sexualities in the heart of the state, Gillian Swanson, *Drunk with the Glitter: Space, consumption and sexual instability in modern urban culture* (London: Routledge, 2007); on male homosexuality, Matt Houlbrook, *Queer London. Perils and pleasures in the sexual metropolis, 1918–1957* (Chicago: University of Chicago Press, 2005), and Richard Hornsey, *The Spiv and the Architect: Unruly life in postwar London* (Minneapolis: University of Minnesota Press, 2010); on the legislative dimensions, Stuart Hall, 'Reformism and the legislation of consent' in National Deviancy Conference (ed.), *Permissiveness and Control. The fate of the sixties legislation* (London: Macmillan, 1980). And for the larger view: Frank Mort, *Capital Affairs: The making of the permissive society* (New Haven: Yale University Press, 2010). Paul Johnson's novel, *Merrie England* (London: Pan, 1966; first published 1964), presents a comic reworking of the Profumo crisis, with the imperial determinations pronounced.

41 It would be important to tell the story of how a specifically working-class feminine voice entered the prose of the period. There is much that is revealing in the short stories of Shelagh Delaney, *Sweetly Sings the Donkey* (London: Methuen, 1964), and of Nell Dunn, *Up the Junction* (London: Pan, 1966; first published 1963), and in her novel, *Poor Cow* (London: Virago, 1988; first published 1967). In 1959 Dunn moved from her upper-class locale of Chelsea to the then 'unknown' region of Battersea, where she documented the lives of her young female friends and acquaintances, attempting to remain true to their voice – providing one of my favourite lines in postwar British fiction: '"He drove me out to London Airport for a snoggin' session"', *Up The Junction*, p. 74. D.A.N. Jones responded to *Up the Junction* by commenting: 'Nell Dunn has been accused of slumming. This is not fair. She has been reworking a national literary tradition, the love-affair between the classes, and if her stories sometimes sound like a Liberal White living it up in Sophiatown, perhaps that's not surprising', *New Statesman*, 22 November 1963.

42 The connections, in the field of sexuality, can be tracked through the evidence compiled by Philippa Levine, *Prostitution, Race and Politics: Policing venereal disease in the British empire* (New York: Routledge, 2003).

43 Peregrine Worsthorne, 'Class and conflict in British foreign policy', *Foreign Affairs* 37: 3 (1959), p. 431.

44 Another insider who posed these same questions was John Le Carré, whose novels are essentially framed by the end of empire, progressively charting the destructiveness of post-imperial nostalgia. In Le Carré's fiction we see

reconstructed a political class in ideological, moral and personal disarray, whose representatives are, at every point, conscious of what they have lost. It is little surprise that the Kim Philby figure, Bill Haydon, believes himself to have been betrayed *by England*, nor indeed that his successors feel obliged to make common cause with assorted neo-cons. Le Carré says of himself that he had entered the secret service 'in the spirit of John Buchan and left it in the spirit of Kafka', quoted by Christopher Tayler, 'Belgravia cockney' *London Review of Books*, 25 January 2007. When I say that these questions could be asked in different registers, I have in mind the contemporaneous fiction of Alan Sillitoe, John Braine, Stan Barstow, Barry Hines and David Storey.

45 Philip Murphy, *Party Politics and Decolonization: The Conservative Party and British colonial policy in tropical Africa, 1951–1964* (Oxford: Clarendon Press, 1995).

46 For a demonstration of the influence of the moral movements 'from below' in these years, see Michael Tracey and David Morrison, *Whitehouse* (London: Macmillan, 1979).

47 Bill Schwarz, 'Actually existing postcolonialism', *Radical Philosophy* 104 (2000); Kobena Mercer, 'Powellism. Race, politics and discourse' (Goldsmiths College, University of London, Ph.D., 1990); and Camilla Schofield, 'Enoch Powell and the making of postcolonial Britain' (Yale University, Ph.D., 2009).

48 Some of these local determinations of Powellism – Selly Oak, Northfield, Longbridge – work as the backdrop to Jonathan Coe, *The Rotters' Club* (London: Penguin, 2002; first published 2001).

49 Enoch Powell, 'The enemy within' in John Wood (ed.), *Powell and the 1970 Election* (Kingswood, Surrey: Elliot Right Way Books, 1970), pp. 104–12.

50 Enoch Powell, 'Immigration' in Wood, *Powell and the 1970 Election*, p. 98.

51 This famously is the argument of Stuart Hall, Chas Critcher, Tony Jefferson, John Clarke and Brian Roberts, *Policing the Crisis. Mugging, the state and law and order* (London: Macmillan, 1978).

52 Exemplary in this regard is Sir John Seeley, *The Expansion of England* (London: Macmillan, 1883).

53 F.R. Leavis, *The Great Tradition* (Harmondsworth: Penguin, 1974), p. 9. An acute discussion of this text, and of the Leavises more generally from the point of view of end of empire, occurs in Francis Mulhern, 'English reading' in Homi K. Bhabha (ed.), *Nation and Narration* (Abingdon: Routledge, 1990).

54 Randall Stevenson, *The Oxford English Literary History. Vol. 13, 1960–2000. The last of England?* (Oxford: Oxford University Press, 2004).

55 Hanif Kureishi, *The Buddha of Suburbia* (London: Faber and Faber, 1990), p. 3. Stephen Connor says of this passage: 'Within its short compass, this opening paragraph seems to play out the characteristic swings of the novel as a whole, slightly caught-out, but also somewhat arch deflection of serious enquiry into pose, performance and the disorderly pulsations of the body', *The English Novel in History, 1950–1995* (London: Routledge, 1996), p. 95.

56 'I think English literature has changed enormously in the last ten years,

because of writers from my background – myself, Salman Rushdie, Ben Okri, Timothy Mo. You know, there are many, many of us, all with these strange names and some kind of colonial background. But we are part of English literature ... writing about England and all that implies. Whatever I've written about, it's about England, in some way, even if the characters are Asian or they're from Pakistan or whatever. I've always written about England, usually London. And that's very English. Also the comic tradition, I think, is probably English, the mixture of seriousness and humour ... and the interest in popular music is a very English thing. Everything I write is soaked in Englishness, I suppose.' Hanif Kureishi in Kenneth C. Kaleta, *Hanif Kureishi. Postcolonial storyteller* (Austin: University of Texas Press, 1998), p. 3. I am grateful to Mark Williams for this reference.

57   Patrick Parrinder's intervention is indispensable: *Novel and Nation. The English novel from its origins to the present day* (Oxford: Oxford University Press, 2006), as is Simon Gikandi, *Maps of Englishness. Writing identity in a culture of colonialism* (New York: Columbia University Press, 1996). See too David Rogers and John McLeod (eds), *The Revision of Englishness* (Manchester: Manchester University Press, 2004).

58   *West Indian Gazette*, December 1961.

59   There can be no doubt, now, that there exists an entire postcolonial method of interpretation, in which texts are read for what they conceal, marginalise or repress concerning the place of colonialism in the metropolitan imagination. In the British case, certainly, we are suggesting that in the period of the end of empire, when for those in the metropole the histories of decolonisation were so heavily mediated, we need to elaborate an appropriate hermeneutics: in other words, reading for empire in Austen or Dickens represents a different procedure from reading for empire in William Golding or A.S. Byatt.

60   Or one might think of J.G. Ballard, born in Shanghai in 1930 and educated at the cathedral school (where, as punishment, he had to copy out lines from G.A. Henty, but found he could write more quickly if he made it up himself). Arriving in England in 1946 he encountered an unreal, alien world, 'a dream of English life which had gone forever', and found Cambridge to be 'a Gothic pageant, a theme park before its time', *Archive Hour*. 'The more I learned about English life, the stranger it seemed ... most English novelists were far too "English"', Ballard, *Miracles of Life*, p. 132.

61   We might note here as well the comment by Emmanuel Litvinoff, born in 1905 in Bethnal Green to a Russian Jewish family, that he never wished to become an 'English writer': cited by Patrick Wright in his 'Introduction' to Litvinoff's *Journey Through a Small Planet* (London: Penguin, 2008), p. xxviii.

62   For Kelman, and much else of great historical interest, see Roxy Harris, Sarah White and Sharmilla Beezmohun (eds), *A Meeting of the Continents. The International Book Fair of Radical, Black and Third World Books revisited: History, memories, organisation and programmes, 1982–1995* (London: New Beacon Books, 2005). I am conscious there is much more to say about the literary

politics of Celtic Britain. And more generally, Ian Bell (ed.), *Peripheral Visions. Images of nationhood in contemporary British fiction* (Cardiff: University of Wales Press, 1995).

63 The Caribbean version of this story, for example, is discussed in Bill Schwarz (ed.), *West Indian Intellectuals in Britain* (Manchester: Manchester University Press, 2004).

64 And see as well: Doris Lessing, *In Pursuit of the English: A documentary* (London: MacGibbon and Kee, 1960), and Colin MacInnes, *England, Half-English* (London: Hogarth Press, 1986; first published 1961). Of the latter, V.S. Naipaul wrote that 'He wants people to *see*', *Listener*, 7 September 1961; while Bernard Levin, with all the charmless bewilderment one might associate with him, commented: 'Until quite recently I believed (consequent upon reading *City of Spades*) that Mr Colin MacInnes was a black man. Indeed I not only believed it; I told other people as much. ... The trouble is that having read *England, Half-English* I am rather more inclined to believe that I was right all the time. At least, if Mr MacInnes is not black, then he must be green. Or he has two heads, or three legs, or a cyclops eye, or telepathic powers. ... At any rate, he is different from us', *Spectator*, 1 September 1961. Indeed.

65 Raymond Williams, *Orwell* (London: Fontana, 1971).

66 Readers may think that Anthony Powell is too easy a target, and not an appropriate one. Yet the group around the *New Left Review*, for example, hostile to Little Englandism, are unusually indulgent to Powell: see Tariq Ali, who delivered the first Anthony Powell lecture, and who contends that Powell was 'the most European' of twentieth-century British novelists, comparing him not only to Proust but to Robert Musil, 'Come dancing' *Guardian*, 26 January 2008. There is a moment in Powell's *O, How the Wheel Becomes It* (Harmondsworth: Penguin, 1986; first published 1983) when a TV pundit tries to get Shadbold, the main protagonist, to reflect on 'the sunset of imperialism', p. 98. No answer is forthcoming.

67 Raymond Williams, *The English Novel. From Dickens to Lawrence* (St Albans: Paladin, 1974), p. 99.

68 I am doubtful of the degree to which Burgess's *A Malayan Trilogy* does rehearse the story of the end of empire, though Burgess himself clearly thought it did. From the standpoint adopted in this collection, in addition to those works addressed in the substantive chapters, we could also cite: H.E. Bates. Mainly remembered for his English novels, he wrote also on Burma and Kashmir at the time of the end of empire: *The Purple Plain* (London: Michael Joseph, 1947), *The Jacaranda Tree* (London: Michael Joseph, 1949) and *The Scarlet Sword* (London: Michael Joseph, 1950). According to Andrew Whitehead, *A Mission to Kashmir* (New Delhi: Penguin Viking, 2007), Bates had never visited Kashmir, and *The Scarlet Sword* was exclusively based on reports from the *Daily Express*, 222–5. The *Observer*'s Alan Moorehead also wrote a novel about the fate of Kashmir at the same time: *The Rage of the Vulture* (London: Hamish Hamilton, 1948).

Gerald Hanley, *The Consul at Sunset* (Glasgow: Fontana, 1962; first published 1951), whose earlier *Drinkers of Darkness* (Harmondsworth: Penguin, 1958; first published 1955) is revealing on the relations between sex and race. David Caute, *At Fever Pitch* (London: André Deutsch, 1959) is compelling and surprising. John Masters, *To the Coral Strand* (London: New English Library, 1968; first published 1962). Iris Murdoch, *The Red and the Green* (London: Chatto and Windus, 1965). Paul Scott, *The Birds of Paradise* (Harmondsworth: Penguin, 1964, first published 1962), and his *The Jewel in the Crown* (London: Panther, 1983; first published 1966); *The Day of the Scorpion* (London: Granada, 1982; first published 1968); *The Towers of Silence* (London: Panther, 1983; first published 1971); *A Division of the Spoils* (London: Panther, 1983; first published 1975) – known collectively as *The Raj Quartet*. J.G. Farrell, *Troubles* (London: Jonathan Cape, 1970); *The Siege of Krishnapur* (Harmondsworth: Penguin, 1982; first published 1973); *The Singapore Grip* (London: Weidenfeld and Nicolson, 1978). Olivia Manning, *The Levant Trilogy: The Danger Tree, The Battle Lost and Won*, and *The Sum of Things* (Harmondsworth: Penguin, 1982; first published 1977–80), which should be read alongside Artemis Cooper, *Cairo in the War, 1939–1945* (London: Hamilton, 1989). Allan Massie, *Shadows of Empire* (London: Sinclair-Stevenson, 1997). Linda Grant, *When I Lived in Modern Times* (London: Granta, 2000). Gillian Slovo, *Black Orchids* (London: Virago, 2009; first published 2008). Alan Sillitoe, *Key to the Door* (London: Star Books, 1978; first published 1961) and Leslie Thomas, *The Virgin Soldiers* (London: Constable, 1966) are two novels which recount the experience of national service overseas in the last days of empire. The Suez crisis provides the material for P.H. Newby, *Something to Answer For* (1969) and for Stevie Davies, *Into Suez* (Aberteifi: Parthian, 2010) – the latter juxtaposing Suez in 1956 and the invasion of Iraq in 2003. Maggie Gee's *The White Family* (London: Telegram, 2008; first published 2002) has its white protagonist a veteran of the war in Palestine, and – with recourse to James Baldwin – sets out to link the end of empire to contemporary racism. A work which takes for its subject the Mau Mau rebellion is Beverley Naidoo's children's novel, *Burn My Heart* (London: Puffin, 2007). Paul Scott, *Staying On*; Kazuo Ishiguro, *The Remains of the Day* (London: Faber and Faber, 1989); and Jane Gardam, *Old Filth* (London: Abacus, 2005; first published 2004) and her *The Man in the Wooden Hat* (London: Chatto, 2009) reflect on end of empire and the subjective, inner world. Adam Thorpe, *Pieces of Light* (London: Jonathan Cape, 1998) explores how the mysteries of a colonial childhood reverberate in a late twentieth-century life, while Marina Warner's *Indigo* (London: Vintage, 1993; first published 1993) creates a startling interplay between colonial and postcolonial. Luke Strongman reviews the Booker prize winners from the point of view of empire in *The Booker Prize and the Legacy of Empire* (Amsterdam: Rodopi, 2002). The more well-known novels about the end of empire have been written by men. Deborah Philip's thoughtful *Women's Fiction, 1945–2000. Writing romance* (London: Continuum, 2007) does not refer to the histories of decolonisation: it seems that the impressive feminist re-readings of empire in the historiography do not operate to the same degree in the fiction.

69 Note should also be made of the popular male romances of empire which continue to secure high sales: George MacDonald Fraser's Flashman series; C.S. Forester's Hornblower novels; Bernard Cornwell's stories of rifleman Richard Sharpe; and the novels of Wilbur Smith and Patrick O'Brian, the latter respected critically, the former not.

70 Constantine Fitzgibbon, *When the Kissing Had to Stop* (London: Panther, 1978; first published 1960), and Douglas Hurd and Andrew Osmond, *Send Him Victorious* (London: Fontana, 1969; first published 1968) both portray, in a popular idiom, political-racial crises in the metropole, the former as a result of Soviet machinations (but with many echoes of the end of empire), the latter consequent upon events in Rhodesia. Hurd was subsequently foreign secretary. Both novels speak to the desires for a 'strong' England after empire, in reaction to the disorders besetting civil society.

71 In this respect Emma Smith's *The Far Cry* (Harmondsworth: Penguin, 1952; first published 1949), set in an unspecified time in pre-Independence India, is of great interest. Consciously following in the wake of Forster's *A Passage to India*, the novel is undoubtedly ashamed by English racism. But India itself, and anti-colonial feeling, appear as little more than abstractions – as when, for example, Mr Littleton, a tea-planter, declares: "'The country's in a very peculiar state at the moment. Riots going on all the time in one place or another. They were throwing acid about in the market the other day. Nasty stuff, acid'"; to which Teresa, the English schoolgirl, replies, "'They weren't throwing it about in my market. … Everyone was awfully nice'", p. 91.

72 Philip Hensher has taken a benign view of the history of the empire in his *Independent* columns over the years; his conviction that Said has become *passé* can be found in his 'Is it safe to revisit the harems?', *Independent*, 20 June 2008.

73 There are wonderful insights in Nicky Marsh, *Money, Speculation and Finance in Contemporary British Fiction* (London: Continuum, 2007).

74 Cited in Robin Moore, *Paul Scott's Raj* (London: Heinemann, 1990), p. 75. Over the years Scott has been an important figure for me. My arguments were first developed in 'An Englishman abroad … and at home. The case of Paul Scott', *New Formations* 17 (1992), and refined in 'Memories of empire' in Angelika Bammer (ed.), *Displacements: Cultural identities in question* (Bloomington: Indiana University Press, 1994), where I also discuss the various controversies about the *Raj Quartet*.

75 Paul Scott, *My Appointment with the Muse: Essays, 1961–1975* (London: Heinemann, 1986), pp. 31 and 145.

76 Scott, *Appointment*, p. 48.

77 Cited in Moore, *Scott's Raj*, p. 72.

78 Scott, *Appointment*, p. 95.

79 Until the moment, perhaps, of David Peace's occult *Red Riding Quartet*,

where daily life in West Yorkshire in the 1970s and 1980s is defined by its violence: *Nineteen Seventy Four* (1999), *Nineteen Seventy Seven* (2000), *Nineteen Eighty* (2001) and *Nineteen Eighty Three* (2002) – all republished in London by Serpent's Tail in 2008 – although the English *noir* of Derek Raymond, and maybe Ballard too, served as precursors.

80 A. S. Byatt, *On Histories and Stories: Selected essays* (London: Chatto and Windus, 2000), p. 9; Marriadele Boccardi, *The Contemporary British Historical Novel. Representation, nation, empire* (Houndmills: Palgrave, 2009); David Leon Higdon, *Shadows of the Past in Contemporary British Fiction* (London: Macmillan, 1984); Peter Middleton and Tom Woods, *Literatures of Memory. History, time and space in postwar writing* (Manchester: Manchester University Press, 2000); and Dominic Head, *The Cambridge Introduction to Modern British Fiction, 1950–2000* (Cambridge: Cambridge University Press, 2002).

81 Margaret Scanlan, *Traces of Another Time. History and politics in postwar British fiction* (Princeton: Princeton University Press, 1990). Scanlan is very good on Paul Scott, and on spy fiction and the end of empire.

82 As we can see when Margaret Drabble ponders the figure of 'the historian who denies the existence of history', *The Radiant Way* (London: Penguin, 1988; first published 1987), p. 36. Her essay of the same period, '*Mimesis*. The representation of reality in the post-war novel', *Mosaic* 20: 1 (1987), provides a good account of her own practice.

83 Penelope Lively, *Moon Tiger* (London: Penguin, 1988), p. 152.

1

The road to Airstrip One: Anglo-American attitudes in the English fiction of mid-century

Patrick Parrinder

Far from being a time of dramatic change in the novel, as 1750 and 1850 had been, the year 1950 in Britain shows all the signs of cultural exhaustion. The journals *Horizon*, *Penguin New Writing* and *World Review* all ceased publication, with the editor of *Horizon*, Cyril Connolly, firing a memorable parting shot in the final double number (December 1949–January 1950): 'It is closing time in the gardens of the West.' The June 1950 issue of *World Review* was a tribute to George Orwell, who had died five months earlier at the age of forty-seven. Much of this special number was given over to Orwell's unpublished notebooks from 1940–41, in which he commented on the progress of the second world war from Dunkirk to the German occupation of the Ukraine. In 1950 the aftermath of war was everywhere, both in literature – novels set in wartime London included Elizabeth Bowen's *The Heat of the Day* (1949) and Graham Greene's *The End of the Affair* (1951) – and in everyday life. Postwar austerity under the Attlee government included military conscription, food rationing, import restrictions, and a state petrol monopoly. Children who had never seen a fresh banana were brought up on cod liver oil and National Health Service orange juice.

Orwell's *Nineteen Eighty-Four* (1949) portrays a terrifying future which is, nevertheless, full of echoes of postwar London. As he enters Victory Mansions on the novel's opening page, Winston Smith immediately notices the smell of 'boiled cabbage and old rag mats' in the communal hallway.[1] He drinks Victory Gin (evidently a state brand), smokes government cigarettes and struggles to shave with a blunt razor-blade. Everything except political propaganda is in short supply. Orwell's satirical exaggerations have a real basis, as do the geopolitics of *Nineteen Eighty-Four*. The bomber squadrons of the US Strategic Air Command had returned to Europe in 1947, and the North Atlantic Treaty was signed in Washington in the spring of 1949.[2] This no doubt is why Orwell makes Britain the forward base of Oceania, suitably renamed as Airstrip One. War between the three great power blocs of Oceania, Eurasia and Eastasia is incessant in Orwell's novel, though for the most part remote from the metropolitan centres. The Korean war of 1950–53 was very much the kind of conflict he had envisaged.

Nineteen Eighty-Four is a story not just of ideological tyranny but of national humiliation and defeat. Historical memory has been crushed, and the familiar English language is being systematically eradicated. The currency of Airstrip One is no longer the pound sterling but the dollar. Nevertheless London, so far as we can tell, is still the centre of government (dominated by its three huge ministry buildings), and America and Americans are entirely absent. The ruling doctrine is Ingsoc ('English Socialism'), while Big Brother is far more reminiscent of 'Uncle Joe' Stalin than of Uncle Sam. It is hard to say whether this absence of anything directly connected with the United States (apart from the dollar) from Orwell's satirical targets is deliberate, or whether it results from an unconscious refusal to grasp the full implications of Britain's diminishing place in the world. At all events, Nineteen Eighty-Four is remarkably Anglocentric, even though the novel's worldwide fame might suggest otherwise. Its combination of local setting with universal relevance aligns Orwell's vision of a totalitarian future both with earlier British disaster fiction – most notably H.G. Wells's The War of the Worlds (1898) – and with such contemporary works as John Wyndham's The Day of the Triffids (1951).

The 'shrinking island' thesis

Not all English novelists of the mid-century restricted themselves to the local. In Graham Greene's oeuvre, for example, The End of the Affair was preceded by The Heart of the Matter (1948) set in West Africa and by the screenplay for The Third Man (1949) located in divided Vienna. Greene's pursuit of international perspectives would be continued in his Vietnamese novel The Quiet American (1955), to be discussed below. Similarly, C.P. Snow's The Masters (1951) seems at first sight to reduce the whole of political life to the narrow confines of a Cambridge college; but Snow's portrait of an academic microcosm forms part of a long novel-sequence tackling major historical themes including the development of atomic weapons and the co-option of scientific research into the defence and security establishment during the cold war.[3] Perhaps more representative of the time, however, is the insularity of William Cooper's Scenes from Provincial Life (1950), the story of a young physics teacher in an unnamed Midlands town which would influence writers as diverse as Kingsley Amis, John Braine, Alan Sillitoe, David Storey and John Wain. What appealed to Cooper's contemporaries was his quietly comic first-person narrative with its rejection of modernist experiment in favour of a more traditional, plain style of storytelling; nothing could be further removed from the complicated time-schemes and intricate theological ironies of Greene's best fiction.

In 1961, in a *Sunday Times* review of the Penguin edition of Cooper's novel, John Braine – by now the bestselling author of the equally insular *Room at the Top* (1957) – contrasted the impact of Greene and Cooper in the preceding decade:

> We hear a great deal about Greeneland now, and I don't deny its importance, I don't deny the appalling grandeur of its spiritual vistas. I lived there once myself; but since 1950, when I discovered *Scenes from Provincial Life*, I prefer the Cooper country.[4]

What Braine was discovering in 1950 could be expressed in the terms put forward by Jed Esty in 2004 in his *A Shrinking Island: Modernism and National Culture in England* as a 'resurgent concept of national culture', whose 'insular integrity' more than made up for its plain, even humdrum, mode of expression.[5] Esty, whose title alludes to Hugh Kenner's 1988 *A Sinking Island: The Modern English Writers*, sees the Anglocentricity of modern English writing as at once a reflection and a denial of the long decline in British power which began with the first world war. He is especially concerned with the work of writers from the Bloomsbury Group to the 1960s New Left who portrayed an England that was 'self-consciously historical, even antiquarian' – an England that, thanks to a reversal of the traditional ethnographic preoccupation with the exotic, could function as a 'symbolic replacement for its colonies'.[6] Both cultural analysis and the sense of the picturesque were turned inwards, so that 'England', having lost its status as the all-conquering heart of empire, became potentially (if not actually) a centre of resistance against the forces of metropolitan modernity. The same broad process, according to Esty, links the pageant plays of E.M. Forster and the visionary fiction of John Cowper Powys in the 1930s to the rise of academic cultural studies two decades later. The emotional and spiritual force of this new Anglocentricity is captured in T.S. Eliot's *Little Gidding* (1942) with its conception of history as 'a pattern / Of timeless moments', yielding the revelation that 'On a winter's afternoon, in a secluded chapel / History is now and England'.[7]

Nineteen Eighty-Four offers a crushing reply to such aspirations for national cultural resurgence, yet Orwell's novel has its own kind of Anglocentricity, as we have seen. When towards the end of *A Shrinking Island* Esty divides twentieth-century British writers and intellectuals into two camps – those who 'take *imperial* decline to imply some sort of *national* revival', and those, 'typically associated with the ebb of British power', who 'take imperial decline to imply national decline' – with Greene, Orwell and Evelyn Waugh in the second category – the oversimplification is manifest.[8] Representations of national decline at mid-century are as intricate, and often as ambiguous, as are the visions of national and provincial self-sufficiency. Sometimes the two are combined.

For example, Cooper's *Scenes from Provincial Life* looks back to the spring and summer of 1939 when the narrator, Joe Lunn, and his best friend Tom were convinced that British democracy was on the verge of collapse. They have no confidence in the Chamberlain government and spend much of their time making ineffectual plans to emigrate to the United States. These plans are quickly abandoned when Britain at last declares war on Germany. In a final chapter significantly called 'Provincial life-histories', Joe reveals that Tom did eventually get to America on a wartime diplomatic mission, and decided to stay on after the war. This leads to the following tight-lipped comment: 'In America Tom found a limitless field for his bustling bombinations, spiritual, emotional and geographical.'[9] Joe's disenchantment with both Tom and the United States corresponds to his belated discovery of the value of the provincial life he found so irksome in 1939. Once instinctively pro-American, he is now instinctively anti-American. Maturity has turned him into the first of the typically English heroes of the 1950s, chippy, resentful and small-minded.

Seen from the 'Cooper country', America is the new metropolis, a land of failed promise and a suitable destination for the big-headed and over-ambitious. But William Cooper was not Joe Lunn; nor, for that matter, was he 'William Cooper', since he had earlier published several novels under his real name, H.S. Hoff. While Hoff's own background is a little uncertain – he was born in Crewe and baptised as an Anglican – it is notable that Tom, an active bisexual who is first introduced to the reader as 'red-haired and Jewish – it fairly knocked you down', is always an outsider in the provincial milieu where Joe Lunn will eventually settle down.[10] Since Joe plays the straight man (more or less) to the outrageous Tom, it seems reasonable to speculate that Tom too is a self-projection, a version of 'Harry Hoff' where Joe is a version of 'William Cooper'. What is clear, at least, is that a novel which at first sight seems a perfect expression of Esty's 'shrinking island' thesis is less straightforward than it looks. One aspect firmly linking it to other novels of its time is its exploration of English provincial identity in relation to the cultural pressure of the United States, now acknowledged as Britain's imperial successor.

'The U.S.A. Threat to British Culture'

In 1951, the year of the dying Labour government's Festival of Britain, the Communist Party, not to be outdone, staged its own one-day national festival: a conference at Holborn Hall on 29 April devoted to 'The U.S.A. Threat to British Culture'. The proceedings, together with essays by the American radicals W.E.B. DuBois and Howard Fast, were immediately printed in the Party journal *Arena*. The contributions range from Diana Sinnot on 'Our historical tradition' and E.P. Thompson on 'William Morris and the moral issues to-day' to pieces on newspapers, film, and 'Children's reading' – a diatribe against American comics. A prefatory note (presumably by *Arena*'s editor Jack Lindsay) clarifies that 'the threat comes from the reactionary elements now dominant in U.S.A. society, and there is no question of an attack on American culture as such'. The enemy is not 'the U.S.A. common man', but 'the synthetic imperialist culture of the State, coldly and cynically devised for the debasement of man'.[11] Moreover, as E.P. Thompson (who would leave the Communist Party in 1956) tells his readers, US imperialist culture has its 'British apologists', such as T.S. Eliot and George Orwell.[12]

This was the height of the McCarthy period as well as the cold war, so that British Communists had particular reasons for detesting the 'American threat'. Their arguments were framed in the populist terms of a defence of national autonomy, not primarily as a commitment to the socialist societies of China and the Soviet Union. The Party's election manifesto at this time was *The British Road to Socialism*. As Sam Aaronovitch put it in his opening address at Holborn Hall, 'The American trusts aim to destroy ... the national independence of *all* peoples, British as well as Soviet'.[13] Speaking on behalf of 'Literature', Montagu Slater added that 'The threat to our culture is as definite as a physical occupation of our country'.[14] The spectre of physical occupation doubtless struck a chord at a time when a favourite street slogan in Britain, largely aimed at the unmarried male conscripts of the US Air Force, was 'Yanks go home!'

Slater's brief essay in *Arena* is the first of a group of contributions devoted to literature, publishing and the media, including films. The authors' warnings of a growing American monopoly in cultural expression might have been intensified had they looked at other areas of popular entertainment, including the genre which, ever since Wells, had specialised in fantasy scenarios of alien occupation – science fiction. British science fiction at the mid-century would not have existed had it not been for its authors' ability to sell to the US market. For example, 1951 saw the publication of *The Day of the Triffids* by John Wyndham, which became one of the best-known British fantasy novels of the century. From 1954 onwards, Penguin paperback editions of *The Day of the Triffids* included the following biographical information about the author: 'From 1930–9 he wrote stories of various kinds under different names almost exclusively for American publications. He has also written detective novels. During the war he was in the Civil Service and afterwards in the Army. In 1946 he went back to writing stories for publication in the U.S.A. and decided to try a modified form of what is unhappily known as "science fiction".'

Waiting for the Americans: mid-century British science fiction

Wyndham, whose real name was John Beynon Harris, mainly wrote for the 'slicks' such as *Collier's Magazine*, but his younger colleague Arthur C. Clarke sent his first work in 1946 to the American 'pulp' magazine *Astounding Science-Fiction*. (The term 'science fiction' itself was, of course, a recent American invention.) Clarke's first novel *Against the Fall of Night*, begun in 1936 when he was still a teenager, was rejected by *Astounding* but published in 1948 in another US pulp, *Startling Stories*. Much revised and expanded, it took its 'classic' form as *The City and the Stars* (1956). Clarke in the meantime had published several other novels including *Prelude to Space* (1951) – which he claimed to have written in twenty days in 1947 – and *Childhood's End* (1953). Thanks to his non-fiction work, *The Exploration of Space* (1951), he had become Britain's best-known champion of space flight.

In a 1961 preface to *Prelude to Space*, Clarke acknowledged that 'The chief respect in which reality has departed from my fiction is, of course, in the Russian dominance of manned space exploration'.[15] It is true that there are no Russian characters in this documentary novel (set in 1978) of events leading up to the first lunar voyage, but an even more striking aspect of Clarke's 1947 view of the world is the supposed British dominance of experimental space flight. The Americans are mere junior partners, a status that Clarke's narrator Dirk Alexson, a historian on secondment from the University of Chicago, takes in his stride. The novel offers a rather feeble rational justification for Britain's leading role, since Alexson maintains that a huge, unpopulated land area is needed for a space launch, with the only suitable location being 'the West Australian desert, where the British Government started building its great rocket range in 1947'.[16] At another level, *Prelude to Space* asserts that the British are at the forefront of lunar exploration because it is a continuation of empire. At the space mission's head offices overlooking the Thames, Alexson senses a 'historical continuity' stretching from Captain Scott and the *Discovery* back to Drake and Raleigh: 'only the scale of things had changed'.[17] The novel closes with the departure of the astronauts from Luna City in Australia and with Clarke's most explicit reminder of empire. The director-general, Sir Robert Derwent, ensures that the chimes of Big Ben are broadcast over the public address system at the moment of launching; Dirk realizes that 'for half a century Englishmen all over the world had waited beside their radios for that sound from the land which they might never see again. He had a sudden vision of other exiles, in the near or far future, listening upon strange planets to those same bells ringing out across the deeps of space.'[18] *Prelude to Space* is as proudly British as Dan Dare's adventures in the *Eagle* comic, which first hit the news-stands on 14 April 1950.

Prelude to Space, however, is one of Clarke's weakest and least characteristic novels, barely recognisable as being by the same author as *The City and the Stars*, *Childhood's End* (to which we shall return), or the filmscript for *2001: A Space Odyssey* (1968). These are works strikingly at variance with Clarke's public optimism and his championship of the space programme. In *Against the Fall of Night* and *The City and the Stars* the space pioneers explore an empty and seemingly dead universe, in which little is left of the former galactic empire except for its archaeological remains. As for *Childhood's End*, it teasingly states on the reverse-title page that 'The opinions expressed in this book are not those of the author', and, as a novel, it is all the better for this element of unendorsed fantasy.[19]

In contrast to Clarke, nearly all Wyndham's best-known novels are scenarios of hostile invasion. Britain comes under attack from 'natural' forces – plants in *The Day of the Triffids*, marine animals in *The Kraken Wakes* (1953) and, in *The Midwich Cuckoos* (1957), a new generation of unusually gifted children. *The Chrysalids* (1955) openly confronts the period's most pressing anxieties – being a post-nuclear catastrophe story set in Labrador – but all these titles, and particularly *The Day of the Triffids*, contain suppressed but disquieting echoes of the cold war. The triffids themselves are products of genetic modification, secretly developed in the Soviet Union and highly prized for their oil. Once the seeds have been stolen from a laboratory in Kamchatka, they rapidly colonise the whole world and are a familiar sight in English suburban gardens. Bill Masen, Wyndham's narrator, is a triffid farmer and one of the few people to recognise their dangers. His expertise proves crucial to survival once they unleash their stings and declare war on the human beings who exploit them.

Masen looks back from the 'day of the triffids' to the onset of the catastrophe and, before that, to what he now sees as the complacency and decadence of the years after the second world war. At critical moments he recalls two historical events which should have served as warnings: first the period of the Blitz when Britain stood alone against Nazi invasion, and then the bombing of Hiroshima in August 1945. The bombing of London is the precedent for the destruction unleashed at the beginning of *The Day of the Triffids*, when humanity succumbs to near-universal blindness after a spectacular astronomical display apparently caused by a cloud of comet dust. Masen, one of the tiny minority who retains his sight, recalls that:

> My father once told me that before Hitler's war he used to go around London with his eyes more widely open than ever before, seeing the beauties of buildings that he had never noticed before – and saying goodbye to them. And now I had a similar feeling. But this was something worse. Much more than anyone had hoped for had survived that war – but this was an enemy they would not survive. ... Unless there should be some miracle I was looking on the beginning of the end of London – and very likely, it seemed, there were other men, not unlike me, who were looking on the beginning of the end of New York, Paris, San Francisco, Buenos Aires, Bombay, and all the rest of the cities that were destined to go the way of those others under the jungles.[20]

Eventually Masen devises a theory (which is never confirmed) that the cause of the blindness was not comet dust but the triggering of satellite weapons orbiting the Earth and emitting radiations aimed at the optic nerve; in other words, it was a direct result of the cold war and the 'mutually assured destruction' that began with Hiroshima. The destruction is global and the small group of survivors realise that, if they are to fight back, it must be by their own efforts. They cannot wait for the 'arrival of the Americans who were bound to find a way', and Masen makes fun of the pathetic belief that '"The Americans will be here before Christmas"'.[21] However tough life may be under the triffids, at least Britain will not suffer the humiliation of the second world war and the cold war when it became a base for the American armed forces.

As Masen moralises in the opening chapter, 'It is not easy to think oneself back to the outlook of those days. We have to be more self-reliant now.'[22] Self-reliance involves escaping from the clutches of a fascist warlord, bringing up a family, fighting off the triffids and ensuring that scientific research gets started again. Finally our hero joins a group of resisters who have withdrawn from the mainland to the triffid-free Isle of Wight, a kind of Britain-in-miniature. The continent of Europe is still cut off, and nothing is heard from the rest of the world, but the survivors looking out across the Solent are effectively reliving the years between 1940 and 1945, seen as a specifically British odyssey from Dunkirk to D-Day and Berlin. The novel's final words articulate this vision in which a lost empire will be restored:

> So we must regard the task ahead as ours alone. We think now that we can see the way, but there is still a lot of work and research to be done before the day when we, or our children, will cross the narrow straits on the great crusade to drive the triffids back and back with ceaseless destruction until we have wiped the last one of them from the face of the land that they have usurped.[23]

Its tone of political reassurance, even self-congratulation, is one factor accounting for the popularity of *The Day of the Triffids*.

If *Childhood's End* never achieved anything like the same popularity it is doubtless because it is a fable of benign, not hostile, invasion. Clarke's novel in its original version opened with the United States and the Soviet Union competing to win a decisive advantage in the space race.[24] Humanity's ideological division is suddenly overcome as both sides are forced to recognise that they have 'lost [the race], not by the few weeks or months that [they] had feared, but by millennia'. The aliens' unexpected arrival means that 'The human race was no longer alone'.[25] The Overlords, as the invaders are called, set up a benevolent despotism that Clarke twice compares to the British Raj in India. Nevertheless, after fifty years the narrative takes a sudden twist when the hitherto unseen rulers reveal themselves to humanity for the first time. As Clarke puts it, 'The leathery wings, the little horns, the barbed tail – all were there. The most terrible of all legends had come to life, out of the unknown past.'[26] On the face of it, the satanic legend has been tamed, since it does not affect the Overlords' pretensions to liberal imperialism. Although there is an underground resistance against them, for Clarke this is a transient, barely significant movement. In the long run the extraterrestrials inspire not fear or hatred but simply disappointment. They can impose beauty but not sublimity, turning the Earth into a utopia without satisfying human aspirations for some kind of ultimate transcendence. In the novel's conclusion humanity has outgrown them, and outgrown its status as *homo sapiens*: an advance guard of transformed children ascends from a dying Earth to go to the stars. Clarke, like Wyndham, invokes the figure of a historian left behind among the ruins: 'Perhaps, lost in one of the still-intact cities, was the manuscript of some latter-day Gibbon, recording the last days of the human race.'[27] In their fantasies of invasion both *The Day of the Triffids* and *Childhood's End* function as a theatre of the repressed, of world-destruction and miraculous salvation. Is it merely coincidental, we may wonder, that Clarke's benign aliens take their name from the official military title of the D-Day landings, Operation Overlord? Are the horned extraterrestrials, at some level, simply the US infantry?

Seeing off the Overlords: Evelyn Waugh and Graham Greene

Both Waugh's *The Loved One* (1948) and Greene's *The Quiet American* end with the death of an American, and hinge on American attitudes to the death of others; and that seems to be all they have in common. In *The Loved One*, as in Waugh's rather feeble satire of a near-future scientific socialist England, *Love Among the Ruins* (1953), most people are '"half in love with easeful death"'.[28] Waugh's Californian crematorium, the Whispering Glades, is portrayed as the ultimate expression of American culture, even if, due to a piece of Anglo-American skulduggery, the remains of his heroine Aimée Thanatogenos are disposed of at the Happier Hunting Ground (the pet cemetery) instead. On his first visit to the Whispering Glades, the British protagonist Dennis Barlow feels '[a]s a missionary priest making his pilgrimage to the Vatican, as a paramount chief of equatorial Africa mounting the Eiffel Tower'.[29] Barlow, however, is a renegade from the established British community in Hollywood, whose members Waugh portrays as being lost in a time-warp and unable to grasp that the British empire has, so to speak, been superseded by the American.

At the start of *The Loved One*, by not specifying the location of his narrative Waugh completely deceives his readers:

All day the heat had been barely supportable but at evening a breeze arose in the west, blowing from the heat of the setting sun and from the ocean, which lay unseen, unheard behind the scrubby foothills. It shook the rusty fingers of palm-leaf and swelled the dry sounds of summer, the frog-voices, the grating cicadas, and the ever present pulse of music from the neighbouring native huts.

In that kindly light the stained and blistered paint of the bungalow and the plot of weeds between the veranda and the dry water-hole lost their extreme shabbiness, and the two Englishmen, each in his rocking-chair, each with his whisky and soda and his outdated magazine, the counterparts of numberless fellow-countrymen exiled in the barbarous regions of the world, shared in the brief illusory rehabilitation.[30]

It is only later that we realise that the 'barely supportable' heat is not that of tropical Africa, that the 'native huts' are the chalets of the Hollywood Hills and the 'dry water-hole' is a drained swimming-pool. The life of the British expatriates is one long pretence that they are still the lords of the Earth; their dread is of someone like Barlow who ostentatiously 'goes native'. As Sir Francis Hinsley explains, the British 'have a peculiar position to keep up':

They may laugh at us a bit – the way we talk and the way we dress; our monocles – they may think us cliquey and stand-offish, but, by God, they respect us ... it's only the finest type of Englishman that you meet out here. I often feel like an ambassador, Barlow.[31]

Barlow is, in the end, just another would-be colonist; he thinks that all young American women look alike, and after Aimée's suicide, he promptly decides to go back home, taking his (spiritual rather than material) plunder with him. Earlier we were told that 'He did not covet the spoils of this rich continent', but now: 'Others, better men than he, had foundered here and perished. The strand was littered with their bones. He was leaving it not only unravished but enriched.'[32] *The Loved One*, a relatively minor work in the Waugh canon, blatantly indulges in the national self-deceptions that it ostensibly satirises; however richly comic, it seems comparable to Clarke's *Prelude to Space* in its refusal to recognise that the days of British greatness are now over.

A similar judgement might be passed on Graham Greene's *The Heart of the Matter*, published in the same year as *The Loved One*; but by the time that he wrote *The Quiet American* five years later Greene's understanding of world politics had fundamentally changed. This novel stands out both for its political prescience – its outspoken critique of liberal imperialism remains hauntingly relevant in the twenty-first century – and for its reflection of the author's own shadowy involvement in the cold war. It differs, too, from both *The Heart of the Matter* and *The End of the Affair* in that Greene's Catholicism is only lightly insisted upon. Thomas Fowler, the narrator, is a British journalist separated from his Catholic wife; the theological dimension is, for once, understated and largely implicit. Instead, the novel's human relationships illustrate, and to some extend stand for, diplomatic entanglements between the British, the Americans, the Vietnamese and their French colonial rulers. Thus when Fowler loses his Vietnamese mistress Phuong to the CIA agent Alden Pyle, he comments that 'It was as though she were being taken away from me by a nation rather than by a man'.[33] Pyle is younger and more vigorous than Fowler, he has more to offer since he is ready to marry Phuong, and his love for her seems more genuine and less purely selfish – yet, as Fowler feelingly says, 'I never knew a man who had better motives for all the trouble he caused'.[34] Pyle preaches the cause of 'democracy', national self-determination and opposition to the European colonial powers, but he is in Saigon to fight the Communists and set up a client state pursuing America's objectives in the cold war.

Greene's strange mixture of cold war involvement and anti-Americanism has been traced by Adam Piette in his book *The Literary Cold War, 1945 to Vietnam*. During the second world war Greene worked for the British secret service in London, in office accommodation shared with his American counterparts; he later remarked that 'security was a game we played less against the enemy than against the allies on the upper floor'.[35] In 1950 he visited Malaya, where his brother Hugh was working for the colonial government's Emergency Information Services on secondment from the Information Research Department (IRD), set up by Clement Attlee in 1947 to promote anti-Communism.[36] Greene wrote articles for *Life* magazine reflecting the official British position but, moving on to Vietnam, he reacted strongly against what he had seen. In Piette's judgement, 'the animus against the kinds of procedures Hugh Greene and the IRD had been cooking up in Malaya is ferocious in *The Quiet American*', although it is directed not at the British or the French but at the American secret service official Pyle. For Piette, Pyle 'sounds like an American conjured up, or at least politically informed, by the IRD'.[37]

The Quiet American begins with Pyle's murder by Communist insurgents, and – following a complex time-scheme which, like other aspects of the novel, is strongly reminiscent of Joseph Conrad – it ends by revealing Fowler's complicity in his death. (A similarly cynical betrayal leading to murder is part of the denouement of *The Heart of the Matter*.) Fowler has been both Pyle's chosen confidant and his amorous rival; the murder works out very conveniently for the British journalist since he wins back Phuong. But Fowler also has high moral grounds for his action (so he thinks), since Pyle has been smuggling explosives into the country for the benefit of a local warlord, General Thé, whom he sees as a democratic 'Third Force' opposing both the Communists and the French colonial army. With Pyle's knowledge, Thé organises terrorist attacks (meant to be blamed on the Communists) against civilian targets in Saigon. Shortly before he is murdered, a bomb has gone off in a crowded market-place and Pyle has refused to show any remorse:

> 'They were only war casualties,' he said. 'It was a pity, but you can't always hit your target. Anyway they died in the right cause. ... In a way you could say they died for democracy,' he said.[38]

There is, then, a case for excusing Fowler along the lines set out (but later disowned) by W.H. Auden in his poem 'Spain 1937', that, if guilty at all, his is 'The conscious acceptance of guilt in the necessary murder'.[39]

Pyle, fresh from Harvard, is a devotee of the academic theorist York Harding, whose book *The Rôle of the West* sets out the doctrines of 'National Democracy' and the 'Third Force'. He believes that the US can credibly set up a Third Force because it comes to Asia with 'clean hands'.[40] Greene takes every opportunity to expose Pyle's doctrinaire callousness and to show Fowler patronising him in the name of the 'old colonial peoples', who have supposedly 'learnt a bit of reality' – in particular, 'not to play with matches'.[41] Fowler, who claims to be personally disengaged from the Vietnamese conflict, pours scorn on Pyle's liberalism: '"I've been in India, Pyle, and I know the harm liberals do".'[42] His critique of Pyle is ineffective, since Pyle never takes any notice of his arguments; but nor is it grounded in any real self-knowledge, a point which Greene insists upon in his own way by showing Fowler as a confirmed atheist. His claim to be uninvolved is manifestly false. Significantly, the French officer charged with investigating Pyle's murder is convinced of Fowler's implication in the crime even if he has no hard evidence for it.

A number of rhetorical touches in *The Quiet American* recall *Heart of Darkness*, Conrad's anti-imperialist masterpiece which some critics have accused of complicity with imperialism. Whatever the truth about *Heart of Darkness*, there is much less moral distance between Fowler and Pyle than there is between Conrad's narrator Marlow and the demonic imperialist Kurtz. The point is driven home by Fowler's indignation when, after the explosion in the market-place, Pyle looks down at his blood-soaked shoes and says, '"I must get them cleaned before I see the Minister"'.[43] Almost to the end of his narrative, Fowler claims to be a better man than Pyle without admitting that he too has blood – Pyle's blood – on his shoes. To the extent that Fowler represents the 'old colonial powers', Greene seems to be saying that, on the one hand, they lack the peculiar moral blindness of American neo-colonialism, and, on the other hand, they are more cunning. So Pyle has to die, and Fowler gets back Phuong. The facts that such claims rest on layers of self-deception and that Fowler is a deceitful, unreliable narrator seem designed to lie hidden from many readers.

In Greene's novel, if Fowler's amorous rivalry with Pyle stands for British–American diplomatic conflicts, then Fowler's vaunted disengagement from the Vietnamese struggle may also stand for England's growing disengagement from its erstwhile empire. Disengagement becomes a pretext for the denial of continuing moral responsibility. Pyle's slogans of 'National Democracy' and the 'Third Force' are, indeed, the modern equivalents of the European colonial crusade that aroused Marlow's disgust in *Heart of Darkness*. But American neo-colonialism simply replaces the French and, by implication, the British empires. Although Greene's novel reflects no credit on any of the colonial powers, past, present or future, like *Heart of Darkness* it is set in a foreign imperial domain, a dying colony in which (for once) the British are not involved. Was it a sign of weakness or a stroke of astonishing foresight that made Greene place this novel in Vietnam, where ten years later, after the defeat and withdrawal of the French, the United States would become mired in the bloodiest, the most devastating, and – for the Western powers – the most hopeless colonial war of the twentieth century?

Notes

1   George Orwell, *Nineteen Eighty-Four* (Harmondsworth: Penguin, 1954), p. 5.
2   By 1953 there would be a new monthly cultural journal, effectively replacing *Horizon* and paid for by the Congress for Cultural Freedom, an organisation set up in 1950 and much later revealed (to less than universal astonishment) to be a front for the CIA.
3   Other novelists beginning large-scale sequences at this time were Anthony Powell with *A Question of Upbringing* (1951) and Evelyn Waugh with *Men at Arms* (1952).
4   John Braine, 'The Cooper Country', *Sunday Times*, 22 January, 1961.
5   Jed Esty, *A Shrinking Island: Modernism and national culture in England* (Princeton and Oxford: Princeton University Press, 2004), p. 2.
6   Esty, *A Shrinking Island*, p. 42.
7   T.S. Eliot, *Collected Poems, 1909–1962* (London: Faber, 1963), p. 222.
8   Esty, *A Shrinking Island*, p. 215.
9   William Cooper, *Scenes from Provincial Life* (Harmondsworth: Penguin, 1961), p. 234.
10   Cooper, *Scenes from Provincial Life*, p. 12.

11 'Note', *Arena* 2: 8 (June/July 1951), p. 2.
12 E.P. Thompson, 'William Morris and the moral issues to-day', *Arena* 2: 8 (June/July 1951), p. 27.
13 Sam Aaronovitch, 'The American threat to British culture', *Arena* 2: 8 (June/July 1951), p. 3.
14 Montagu Slater, 'Literature', *Arena* 2: 8 (June/July 1951), p. 38.
15 Arthur C. Clarke, *Prelude to Space* (London: Four Square, 1962), p. 5.
16 Clarke, *Prelude to Space*, p. 23. The allusion is to the Woomera range in South Australia.
17 Clarke, *Prelude to Space*, p. 12.
18 Clarke, *Prelude to Space*, p. 154.
19 Arthur C. Clarke, *Childhood's End* (New York: Ballantine Books, 1953), p. iv.
20 John Wyndham, *The Day of the Triffids* (Harmondsworth: Penguin, 1954), pp. 86–7.
21 Wyndham, *Day of the Triffids*, pp. 201, 203.
22 Wyndham, *Day of the Triffids*, p. 16.
23 Wyndham, *Day of the Triffids*, p. 272.
24 Editions published since 1990 and the collapse of the Soviet empire contain a rewritten first chapter.
25 Clarke, *Childhood's End*, p. 5.
26 Clarke, *Childhood's End*, p. 65.
27 Clarke, *Childhood's End*, p. 204.
28 Evelyn Waugh, *The Loved One: An Anglo-American Tragedy* (Harmondsworth: Penguin, 1951), p. 111.
29 Waugh, *The Loved One*, p. 34.
30 Waugh, *The Loved One*, p. 7.
31 Waugh, *The Loved One*, pp. 12–13.
32 Waugh, *The Loved One*, pp. 46, 127.
33 Graham Greene, *The Quiet American* (London: Vintage, 2004), p. 132.
34 Greene, *Quiet American*, p. 52.
35 Quoted in Adam Piette, *The Literary Cold War, 1945 to Vietnam* (Edinburgh: Edinburgh University Press, 2009), p. 26.
36 Piette, *Literary Cold War*, pp. 154–8.
37 Piette, *Literary Cold War*, pp. 161–2.
38 Piette, *Literary Cold War*, p. 171.
39 W.H. Auden, *Selected Poems*, ed. Edward Mendelson (London: Faber, 1979), p. 54.
40 Auden, *Selected Poems*, p. 115.
41 Greene, *Quiet American*, p. 149.
42 Greene, *Quiet American*, p. 88.
43 Greene, *Quiet American*, p. 154.

2

Josephine Tey and her descendants: conservative modernity and the female crime novel

Cora Kaplan

Crime fiction has always thrived on the narrative possibilities of the social and political landscapes of modernity, building its plots on the real and imagined violence that change seems always to threaten. In Britain the male-authored thriller dominated the first two decades of the twentieth century, but from the 1920s onwards women writers led the genre, making a speciality of detective novels. Agatha Christie, Dorothy L. Sayers and Josephine Tey are now the best remembered representatives of the distaff side of Britain's Golden Age of crime fiction which extended well into the early postwar period. They were joined by a host of other women writers – Margery Allingham, Ngaio Marsh, Gladys Mitchell – whose work is still in print. Crime fiction's readership cut across both class and gender lines. Labour prime minister Clement Attlee enjoyed Agatha Christie's 'puzzles'.[1] In the same years Mass Observation made a survey of Tottenham's reading habits citing a 'young manual worker' who declared, 'There's nothing to beat a good detective story.' Edgar Wallace and Christie were among Tottenham's favoured writers.[2] Twentieth-century crime fiction's imaginative terrain, whether its setting is the village, the country house or the metropolis, is the violence – psychic and physical – which is the inevitable accompaniment of a ruthlessly modernising society. The stock view of crime fiction as a genre whose plots are always, or only, about the policing or restoration of social order is both a simplification and exaggeration of the nature of the genre's conservatism, and misses entirely the radical, if not always progressive, elements of its social and political agendas. Empire is rightly credited with playing a key role in the genesis of crime fiction, especially spy stories and the thriller, but the decline and fall of empire might equally be seen as a more powerful catalyst for the genre in the postwar period and beyond. Loved or hated, regretted or mourned, the loss of empire radically transformed British identity. Within the conventions of the crime genre the end of empire generates opportunities, most obviously the redeployment of imperial male subjectivity in the world of spies. Less obvious perhaps is the many ways in which crime novels set in Britain, whose concerns are largely domestic, reflect the longstanding culture of empire as well as its ideological preconditions – its hierarchies, prejudices, its violence and its administrative forms, now often seen as uncomfortable reminders of a world both outdated and well lost. The sins of imperial rule, as well as the bodies of its administrators and subjects, had definitively come home to roost. The sense that there was now no easy way to siphon off domestic discontent or injustice through emigration is immanent in the British crime genre from the late 1940s onwards, one of the constants that holds together its many mutations and reinventions.

This chapter traces the writing and rewriting of empire's effects in two connected novels by two British women crime writers of succeeding generations. The effects of empire are obliquely rendered in *The Franchise Affair* (1948), in which a teenage English girl accuses a mother and daughter of kidnapping and incarcerating her in their country house, forcing her to work as a captive servant. This is the work of Scottish-born Elizabeth Mackintosh (1896–1952) who wrote from the late 1920s under the pseudonym Josephine Tey. Tey's eight crime novels – six published in the immediate postwar period – were all adapted for radio, film and television in the 1950s or 1960s. *The Franchise Affair* was made into a feature film in 1950. In 1994 Ruth Rendell's *Simisola* reworked elements of Tey's plot for a police procedural whose initial case involved the disappearance of another young woman, twenty-two-year-old Melanie Akande, the daughter of a local GP and a hospital ward sister, long-time West African immigrants and British citizens. Born in 1930 of Scandinavian immigrants, and still writing today, Rendell published her first Inspector Wexford novel in 1964. Twenty-three of them – including *Simisola,* the first of what she calls her 'political Wexfords' – have been adapted for a television series which ran between 1987 and 2000. Unlike *The Franchise Affair* in which imperial traces are both present and disavowed, *Simisola* boldly confronts the effects of empire and neo-colonialism in modern multicultural Britain. Nevertheless this is a novel that comes from the centre, not the periphery, even if some of its more radical observations, when they re-appeared later in the decade in official reports and inquiries, might have been unpalatable to various governments. Rendell and her close friend P.D. James, the equally celebrated but more politically conservative crime writer, have both accepted honours. James received an OBE in 1983 and a life peerage in 1991 from Tory governments; Rendell, a loyal Labour supporter, and a leading financial contributor, a CBE in 1996 and a life peerage in 1997 from New Labour. Together they have inherited the mantle of the earlier generation of female crime writers. Like Agatha Christie in her vigorous old age they have become public figures and national treasures, paired 'Queens of Crime' of the last half century. The cultural and political imprimatur accorded nationally to this popular 'middlebrow' genre and its high profile women authors affords a particularly interesting window – one with both strong feminist and misogynist overtones – on the afterlife of empire.

The Franchise Affair

The Franchise Affair is itself a modern retelling of a well known eighteenth-century case, that of Elizabeth Canning, a London maidservant who claimed that she had been abducted and imprisoned by two elderly women (one of whom, Mary Squires, was identified as a 'gypsy') when she refused their request to become a prostitute.[3] Canning was initially believed and supported by the law – the writer and magistrate Henry Fielding became one of her champions – and a successful prosecution was brought against Squires's son John, and 'Mother' Susannah Wells, the former being sentenced to death. Popular feeling among the gentry and 'the mob' lay strongly on Canning's side, but the trial judge, Sir Crisp Gascoyne, uneasy with the decision, set up a private investigation which ended with the release of the defendants and the prosecution of Canning for lying. Nevertheless public opinion, shaped by the press, remained sharply divided, and although Canning was given a seven-year sentence of transportation to British America, her supporters saw that she was decently treated; she married well and died in the colonies in 1773. It was never conclusively proved how or where Canning spent the month of her disappearance. The original story is a rich one; the 'press frenzy' stirred up by Gascoyne's investigation reinforced stereotypical anti-Gypsy feeling united with sentiment on behalf of a poor girl defending her honour. Canning's transportation to the American colonies brings the empire into the story in a complicated way, as it proved, ironically, not so much a punishment as a means of her advancement.

The swell of public feeling around the Canning affair makes it a good instance of what Mary Poovey has defined as a 'border case' – an incident or issue which takes hold of the popular imagination and condenses and displaces social and political anxieties of particular historical conjunctures, especially where class boundaries and the policing of female sexuality are both at stake.[4] Tey's recasting of Elizabeth Canning's story to emphasise postwar class and gender antagonisms also fits Poovey's model, suggesting the durability of a story in which the probity of women becomes the occasion for violence and the symbol and symptom of simmering social discontent. In Tey's adaptation, an unmarried woman of forty, Marion Sharpe, and her eccentric mother, quintessential genteel Englishwomen of a declining class, inherit an ugly isolated late Regency house, The Franchise, outside the peaceful market town of Milford in the heart of the midlands, a town 'which could be duplicated a hundred times anywhere south of Trent.'[5] Milford is seemingly untouched by time but not the larger, more demotic, Larborough ('a million souls' crammed into 'dirty red brick' houses) only a short horizon away.[6] Out of the blue, a seemingly 'innocent' and all too plausible fifteen-year-old schoolgirl, Elizabeth Kane, named after her historical predecessor, accuses the Sharpes of kidnapping and beating her to make her work as an unpaid servant. A working-class Londoner by birth, Kane had been evacuated as a toddler in the early years of the second world war to Aylesbury. When her parents die soon after in the Blitz, she is adopted by her hosts, a thoroughly respectable but very modest middle-class family. Milford solicitor, Robert Blair, comes to the Sharpes's defence, determined to free them of suspicion and unmask the girl. As the case escalates, Kane's cause is taken up both by the popular press and the liberal 'do-gooding' publications, triggering mob attacks on the house and its owners. The Sharpes are targeted by different groups, as the idle rich, fascists and suspect foreigners – Marion Sharpe's 'gypsy swarthiness' echoes the description of Mary Squires, one of the supposed abductors in the Canning case. With determination and a little luck Blair and his Irish barrister friend, Kevin MacDermott, succeed in disproving Betty Kane's story when the case comes to court at the Assizes. At the trial's end, the police 'converge' on the perjurers: on Kane herself, and on two local servant girls – one dismissed from the Sharpes's service for stealing – who have got embroiled in the affair. But in a radical twist to its eighteenth-century counterpart, in which Elizabeth Canning was deported to the New World, it is the Sharpes who emigrate to North America, to Canada – in spite of the fact that Kevin McDermott predicts that the press will give them 'the most public vindication since Dreyfus' (271). For them, England will never be the same again. *The Franchise Affair* is written as a tribute to, and defence of, conservatism with a small 'c' in the face of the enormous changes brought in by Attlee's government. Published in the year which saw the arrival of West Indian immigrants on the *Windrush* and a year after Indian independence, the novel's anxious discourse about cultural difference and the breakdown of social hierarchy and order in the metropole is grounded in a phantasmatic evocation of traditional British values, values under threat in a country transformed by historical forces which largely go unnamed.

But not quite. The empire enters on the opening page of *The Franchise Affair* in the form of a 'lacquered tray covered with a fair white cloth and bearing a cup of blue-patterned china, and, on a plate to match, two biscuits; petit-beurre Mondays, Wednesdays and Fridays, digestives, Tuesdays, Thursdays, Saturdays' (1). Both tray and china are reminders of the two-centuries-long English passion for chinoiserie, imported or domestic items for middle- and upper-class home-use decorated with 'Chinese' scenes. That this orientalist vogue is now passé is signalled by the demotion of the tray from home to office use. The bearer is Miss Tuff, the firm's only female employee, a 'wartime product' (of the Great War); the recipient is Robert Blair, in his forties, who represents, through his family firm, 'English continuity', as does Milford itself through its architecture, a reassuring mix of Restoration, 'Georgian brick, Elizabethan timber-and-plaster, Victorian stone, Regency stucco' and Edwardian villa (4). Hand-me-downs from Robert's family, the tea things reinforce the prestigious, conservative image of Blair, Hayward and Bennet – tea was 'no affair of a japanned tin tray', that mass market symbol of imperial commerce (1). Once a 'sensation' and a 'revolution', Miss Tuff has become the guardian of the firm's genteel reputation, imposing her own lower-middle-class and mildly xenophobic tastes by covering the tray, whose pattern she found 'distracting, unappetising, and "queer"', with a 'cloth from home; decent, plain and white' (2). This careful orchestration of smug, virtuous Englishness with its self-consciously fine-tuned class discriminations, and its gently self-mocking tone about the insular habits of the different rungs of the middle classes, is the backdrop against which the novel's drama will be played out. Milford represents benign provincial stasis; one in which bloody national history is captured and pacified in stone, brick and lathe. Cups, trays, Miss Tuff – worn relics of empire and past social 'revolutions' – are all as thoroughly domesticated as Robert Blair's home, a place of highly polished furniture and excellent dinners, run by his comfortably woolly minded cousin, 'Aunt' Lin. Yet Robert himself is feeling a twinge of mid-life restlessness, even before The Franchise and its odd mother and daughter owners enter, and change, his life. As Alison Light suggests, a '"condition of England"' crisis is posed in the book's opening pages, in the form of Robert Blair's 'doubts as to the pleasures and possibilities of being a middle-class citizen after the war'.[7]

As is true of so many things in *The Franchise Affair,* the apparent stability of place and time in the novel is a narrative trick. Set ostensibly in the postwar present, it is key to the plot that the girl, Betty Kane, was evacuated

as a toddler – 'just a baby' (78). Both Milford and its citizens seem at first
to inhabit a kind of parallel, tranquilised Britain, one which the war and
its legacy of trauma and privations – local deaths or ongoing rationing are
glaring instances – have touched only lightly. Of Robert Blair's 'war' nothing
at all is said. The continuity of Englishness, which he and Milford must
represent for the oppositions of the novel to be sustained, works to minimise
the effects of the conflict within its borders, covering them discreetly and
discursively, in the manner of Miss Tuff's 'decent', 'plain' 'white' cloth.
Even as the story unfolds, and the disruption which the case engenders hits
the national press and engages the popular imagination, provoking violence
within Milford's borders, there seems to be a gentleman's agreement forged
between text and reader that there will be only a 'light-touch' reference
to the war. The death of Betty Kane's parents in the Blitz, for example, is
a narrative necessity. As if to justify the ambivalent presence and absence
of the war we are, if we look closely at the book's chronology, in a near
future. For if the year of the book's publication is taken as the fictional
present, the chronology of the story does not quite compute: Betty Kane
is almost sixteen when she is supposedly kidnapped, but a very small child
when evacuated in the early 1940s. If, then, the setting is the 1950s, the
text assumes that the war itself is becoming a memory, even if its effects
are not. The 'natural' forces of conservatism and Englishness, as the novel
represents them, are being undermined by the ugly forces of mass culture
and class hostility on the one hand, and the dangerously naïve liberalism of
an ascendant left on the other. The political and social watershed of 1945;
the election of a Labour government; the introduction of the welfare state;
extensive postwar nationalisation of industries and services; the loss of
Britain's empire, beginning with India in 1947; and the struggles of the Tory
party to regroup: these are nowhere directly present in Tey's novel. But the
threatening effect of these changes are immanent in the insistent, anxious
defence of 'traditional' English values of fairness and kindness, which range
from the obsequious service provided by Robert Blair's Jermyn Street hotel,
which always gives him his 'old' room, to the incorruptibility and humanity
of Scotland Yard, and to the police in general. The challenge to deference
and to justice is exemplified in the way in which the daily popular press,
the *Ack-Emma* (*The Daily Mirror*), and the upmarket liberal left weekly, *The
Watchman* (*New Statesman*), pre-empt the judgement by joining forces in
support of Betty Kane and against her supposed abusers. It is dramatised
through the escalating attacks on The Franchise, first by local youth, then
by yobs from the nearby city of Larborough and finally by more sinister
cosmopolitan thugs who use durable best paint (not whitewash) to scrawl

'Fascists' on the walls that surround the house, which is eventually burnt to the ground by one or another of these contingents.

Josephine Tey was one of two pseudonyms which Elizabeth MacKintosh adopted in her writing career, and the English persona assumed by the narrative voice of her detective fiction creates another layer of performative authorship, as it was also for the New Zealander Ngaio Marsh, and perhaps for the half-American Christie as well. National character, ethnic traits and the common sense physiognomy practised by many of her characters are leitmotifs in *The Franchise Affair*, the last almost a running gag which loses its comic character as events seem to confirm the pseudo-scientific prejudice behind them. National xenophobia writ small is flagged up early in the novel, not only by Miss Tuff's fear of the patterned tray, but by Milford's more general, typical, refusal to naturalise incomers, such as 'old Mrs. Warren' from Swanage who had been there twenty-five years (12). Marion Sharpe is suspiciously lean and dark skinned, Mrs Sharpe 'an uncomfortable old person' resembling in profile 'Whistler's Mother', but 'full face' with her 'bright, cold, pale seagull's eye' – a 'sibyl' (6). This antipathy to strangers is joined with the approving evocation, through Robert's eyes, of the surrounding lonely countryside, farmland 'Quiet and confident and unchanged since the Wars of the Roses' (11). Even this mention of a distant and very English war introduces the idea of internecine conflict – one between two kinds of Englishness, one represented by the Sharpes who, even if their circumstances have changed, are genealogically members of the same intricate network of lesser gentry to which Robert Blair and his cousin Lin belong. On the other side of the equation is Betty Kane, a displaced person taken in and nurtured by English kindness, but also part of a newly ascendant social formation, created by the violence of the second world war, and 'rootless', at least compared to families like the Blairs. It is hard not to see Betty as standing in for other kinds of child refugees not mentioned in *The Franchise Affair*, the thousands of Jewish children who arrived in Britain via the *kindertransport* between 1938 and 1939. Although the Sharpes seem like suspect foreigners to the settled Milford middle classes they have, significantly, arrived there through a traceable kinship network, inheriting their ugly house from a distant relative. When the police call, Marion initially contacts Robert Blair whom she's never met, for help, because he 'looked my sort', and is horrified when he suggests that his colleague at the other end of the street, Benjamin Carley, an experienced criminal lawyer, would be a better bet (8). She is offended that Robert would 'palm her off' onto 'that awful little man with the striped suits' (8). Clever Ben Carley with his 'bright black eyes' is not Robert Blair's cup of tea either; we are made to feel he is vulgar as well as physically small – and Jewish (51). The one discreet reference which confirms this identification is Blair's thought, later in the novel, that Carley has 'the pliant philosophy of a race long used to lying low and letting the storm blow past', a thought that contains an unmistakable sneer at the supposed passivity, even femininity, of Jews (155). Marion's instant apology to Robert for her 'silly' remark, if not the aversion that triggers it, contributes to the reader's sense of Carley's ethnic as well as his class otherness. At a later point, when Carley is clearly seen to be on their side, Robert 'very nearly' feels he'd like to 'hug Ben Carley' – 'very nearly' but not quite (155). The casual but overt anti-Semitism of interwar British fiction – Christie and Sayers are frequent offenders – might be considered out of place in a text so close to the war, but its subliminal presence helps to give credence and social value to the Sharpes's own class pretensions, which makes other characters of 'their sort' reluctant to believe them guilty of the crime of which they are accused. Indeed the several references to their predicament as somehow parallel to that of Dreyfus identifies them with martyred Jews defended by good Christians in an earlier era. This is an identification which the novel cannot quite contain, however. For while it substitutes the individual case of the virtuous patriotic Jew from the nineteenth century for more recent mass victims of anti-Semitism, and implies that it is now the true-born English, not the acculturated diasporic subjects, who are the targets of mob prejudice, it deepens the association of the Sharpes with ethnic alterity and difference.

Nevertheless in their first encounter with the police the Sharpes's upper-class accents and manners make both Inspector Hallam of the local force, who 'plays such a steady game on the golf course' (12), and Detective Inspector Alan Grant from Scotland Yard in his 'well-tailored suit' (14), disposed to believe them rather than the suburban cuckoo, Betty Kane. The reader herself is brought round to Marion by a more genetic marker that makes her seem less foreign: the moment occurs when Robert, meeting her for the first time at the door of The Franchise, notices that her eyes were not, as he had thought, 'bright gypsy brown' but 'actually a grey hazel' (13–14). Marion herself has a theory about eye-colour and transgressive tendencies, which she passes on to Robert after she has met her accuser. She believes that Betty – a girl with non-descript 'mousey brown' hair who presents herself as young for her age and innocent, is 'over-sexed', because she has 'never known anyone – man or woman' with her 'opaque dark blue' eyes 'who wasn't' (36). Rejecting Robert's suggestion that this is 'feminine intuition', Marion asks him to test her belief through his own observation, and he thinks immediately of the local potman paying child support to half the women in Milford. Inspector Hallam also has a theory about plausible liars with 'baby-blue' eyes; but more important for him is symmetry: eyes which are differently set, 'as if they belonged to different faces', are a sure mark of a potential murderer (46). Evidence of and about eyes are vital in *The Franchise Affair*. Betty Kane's 'photographic memory' allows her to take in the details of the house and its owners from a passing double-decker bus and so gives her the basis for her tale: she gets some elements wrong because she must claim that she sees the house only from inside the attic room, but these details she later glossed in her evidence during the trial (76). The novel's 'informal' case against her is partly built on the aggregate pseudo-scientific theories of eye-settings and colour, however conflicting this evidence proves; and yet since the reader is persuaded that the Sharpes are not guilty and that Betty is lying, they are all in some sense proved true.[8] These sedimented physiognomic myths are made to seem more reliable than the instinctive paternal and avuncular response of men and the maternal judgement of women. The latter includes Betty's adoptive mother, her teachers and her aunt – who are all taken in by her persuasive performance as a vulnerable, innocent, simply dressed English schoolgirl, whom only a dirty-minded observer would think of as a sexual object, or subject. But Betty, as the novel points out, is 'at an unstable age': and the age itself is suffering from an unstable view of adolescence, still looking at it with outmoded pre-war eyes (180). Hair up, with a bit of make-up, Betty is transformed into a teenage seductress, looking old enough to pass for a wife, and anticipating by only a few years the period's famous fictional prototype, Nabokov's Lolita. In the novel, face value, especially in regard to women, is hard to get right.

Robert has the 'Saxon's' traditional views about the Celts: Irishmen, whether posh like his old school friend, the charming barrister, Kevin Macdermott or like the husband of Kevin's char, who both find it difficult to get up in the morning. These forms of local knowledge allow the inhabitants of England to distinguish differences among themselves. The 'rule of difference' which was so essential to the governing of the overseas colonies as well as of maintaining hierarchies at home, is the very thing which structures not just national identity but also an individual's atavistic response or common-sense belief, which in itself becomes the mark of national virtue.[9] Tey has gone to great pains to seed her references to racial, physiognomic thinking, and to ethnic and class prejudice, across the novel. What is represented as the empirical observation of particular persons turns out to be a palimpsest of older ideas reaching back to the late eighteenth century when theories of human difference come into their own: particularly the impermeable divide between Celts and Saxons which is so important to racial theories in Britain from Robert Knox through Matthew Arnold and beyond. Gustave Johann

Lavatar's physiognomic theory, and its late nineteenth-century appropriation by Cesare Lombroso for identifying criminal types, also figures heavily, if silently.[10]

Ben Carley, less sanguine than Robert Blair about the pacific nature of English character, but no less contemptuous of the mass of people, predicts correctly that the 'midland morons' of Milford and Larborough are as capable of mob action stirred by moral panic as any other group (51). Through its narrative voice the novel takes a very dim view of the institutions and individuals responsible for triggering the panic. A rant against the rise of the popular press, in its fictional form of the *Ack-Emma*, is a passage worth quoting:

> The *Ack-Emma* was the latest representative of the tabloid newspaper to enter British journalism from the West. It was run on the principle that two thousand pounds for damages is a cheap price to pay for sales worth half a million. It had blacker headlines, more sensational pictures, and more indiscreet letterpress than any paper printed so far by British presses. Fleet Street had its own name for it – monosyllabic and unprintable – but no protection against it. The press had always been its own censor, deciding what was and what was not permissible by the principles of its own good sense and good taste. If a 'rogue' publication decided not to conform to those principles then there was no power that could make it conform. In ten years the *Ack-Emma* had passed by half a million the daily net sales of the best selling newspaper in the country to date. In any suburban railway carriage seven out of ten people bound for work in the morning were reading the *Ack-Emma*. (59)[11]

Like so many developments in postwar Britain deplored by the novel's narrator and her good characters, the *Ack-Emma* is characterised as a foreign import, on this occasion from the United States, and one which takes advantage of the liberal laws and consensual self-regulation of Britain's national culture in order to violate 'good sense and good taste'. Its name – first world war phonetic slang for AM, evoking guns and conflict – symbolises the violence such a morning paper can do, especially, perhaps, one like the left-leaning *Mirror* which in this period outstripped the popular right dailies, some equally sensationalist, such as the *Daily Mail* and the *Daily Express*. *The Franchise Affair* is especially venomous about the liberal clergy and readers of *The Watchman*, readers who might number among Tey's own. 'The Bishop of Larborough had long ago extended the Christian philosophy to include the belief that the underdog is always right. He was wildly popular with Balkan revolutionaries, British strike committees, and all the old lags in the local penal establishment,' espousing undeserving causes from 'Creches to Kaffirs' (50). The naïvely crusading Bishop and his organ, *The Watchman*, articulate the connection between the imperial and national ideologies which the book defends. The world outside Britain is full of killers operating under the false cover of revolutionaries fighting for a national cause – defending 'Kaffirs' speaks of anti-colonial struggles, and promoting creches refers to a domestic revolution which allowed women the freedom to stay in the postwar workplace, especially telling in a novel whose main theme is women out of place. The Polish 'patriot' Kotovich, the Bishop's current cause, is pronounced by Robert to be a criminal wanted 'in his own country' by the police, 'for two murders' (49). Britain's refusal to give him sanctuary contrasts with the nation's inability to keep the alien gutter press under control. The Bishop later loses some of his liberal cachet when he goes too far and defends an Irish 'patriot', Mahoney, who 'put a bomb in a woman's bicycle basket in a busy English street and blew four people to pieces, including the woman, who was later identified by her wedding ring' (166). The wedding ring is a particularly nice touch. But to ram home the political point Robert expands on the credulity of the Bishop, who had argued, he says contemptuously, that poor Mahoney 'was acting on behalf of a repressed minority – the Irish believe it or not' (166).

No subject of Britain's former empire escapes whipping. When garage-man Stan sees a picture of Betty Kane in the *Ack-Emma* it reminds him 'of a bint' he 'had in Egypt. Same far-apart eyes. Nice kid she was. Told the most original lies' (61). Fighting abroad offers an opportunity for yet another gag about eyes – this time both sexist and racist. And where it is not actually criminal the politics of resistance, right or left, is a foreign contagion which the weakening of the *cordon sanitaire* surrounding the nation in the postwar years is unable to contain. As the violence against the Sharpes escalates and the ever-loyal Stan is co-opted to clean the walls of The Franchise of abusive graffiti, he tells Robert that while he was in the 'Signals' he 'was a given a free tour of Italy' where he 'escaped the malaria, and the Ities, and the Partisans and the Yank transport' but 'took a great dislike to slogans on walls' (130).

There is, also, an internal enemy. This includes not only Betty, who increasingly emerges as a sociopath with an hereditary taint; her mother, Robert discovers, was an habitually unfaithful wife and an uncaring parent. Betty represents the failure of nurture over nature, and a warning against postwar dreams of class mobility, however modest. Independent but wholly fabricated support for Betty's story of beatings and incarceration come from Rose Glyn, the dismissed servant-girl who stole from the Sharpes, and from her friend Gladys Rees, another rural domestic. Thieving and malicious, Rose represents a whole fraction of the working class who historically went into domestic service, but who in the postwar world could no longer be contained by deference, discipline or need. Betty Kane's accusation against the Sharpes is only made credible by the fact that domestic service was in decline, with servants no longer willing to live-in.[12] That the 'public' believes that the Sharpes's desperation for domestic help in their draughty, unmodernised pile would lead them to kidnap and abuse a teenage girl is symptomatic of a much more general fear arising from the simmering resentment and potential class violence which had been stoked by the war. Tey needs the caricatured and despised Rose and Gladys borrowed, as it were, from the Canning case, but updated to show the depth of submerged social unrest.

In her acute analysis of class and gender in *The Franchise Affair* Alison Light shows just how Betty Kane comes to be 'a kind of psychic "dumping ground" for all the fears originally inspired by Marion Sharpe'.[13] Light's essay focuses on 'the fear which runs through the text and which is never finally quelled – the fear precisely that female desire, the demands of feminine sexuality, can never be fully regulated through the definitions and limitations of class.'[14] As Light goes on to argue, the 'good' characters in the novel freely and with relish express the violence they would like to inflict on Betty Kane – a fantasy made more permissible 'once her low class position' and her 'tainted and inadequate femininity has been revealed'.[15] Marion feels 'intense satisfaction' that someone has beaten Betty Kane until she is 'black and blue' (37); Robert Blair's deepest desire is to 'undress her in public' before the court (180); his young nephew Nevil should like to make *'a very nasty mess'* of Betty's face (71). Their fantasies, taken collectively, endorse the 'sick' violence supposedly done to Betty in the first place. The final '"sick" twist to the tale', as Light suggests, is the discovery that Betty's beating has been administered by the wife of the travelling salesman who Betty ran off with, a cheerfully unrepentant and very modern lower-middle-class woman.[16] The true 'victim' of the story, Marion tells Robert, is Betty's adopted mother, betrayed by the child she has so rashly taken in.

Light is surely correct to see the novel's high point as the torching of The Franchise. Ugly and unfashionable as it is, she argues that it comes to represent 'all that was good and uncomplicated about the "old England" of the Empire's ruler and servants, of an upper middle class whose days, by 1948, are patently numbered.'[17] The house-burning is done by unidentified thugs, perhaps those who have daubed 'Fascists' – the 'worst insult' they know – on the walls, but its demolition references, deliberately I think, the burning of other fictional great houses created by women writers:

Thornfield in Charlotte Brontë's *Jane Eyre* (1847), Danielstown in Elizabeth Bowen's *The Last September* (1929), Daphne du Maurier's Manderley in *Rebecca* (1938), each incendiary act a symbolic form of revenge, aiming to bring down elements of an historic English ruling class. As in these earlier novels, the house burning is not only destructive but offers new freedoms to fictional protagonists. Emigration to the colonies is a favoured resolution in the nineteenth-century novel for potentially disruptive rebellious elements in the metropole. In Tey's novel emigration to the Commonwealth is figured as a way for Robert Blair and the Sharpes to escape a nation in which the class war, unaccountably turned violent again, is being won by the wrong side. The inevitable march of democracy and modernity are nevertheless acknowledged: Canada is surely a place of the future which retains certain positive forms of Englishness but which has escaped its brutal and brutalising class conflict. Focusing on the traces and legacies of empire in the novel highlights its compulsive racial as well as class distinctions and its fear of an underclass with hereditary flaws whose composition and mood have altered. In spite of the centrality of femininity and its discontents in *The Franchise Affair* – the 'pleasurable and contradictory fantasy' it conjures up, as Light suggests – there is another important sense in which gender difference is itself a pretext and a displacement in the novel, a kind of brilliant fabrication not so unlike Betty Kane's.[18] The condition of women can from this perspective be seen paradoxically at once as the novel's reason for being and as a convenient vehicle, the *collective* 'dumping ground' for the novel's much broader social anxieties. In the postwar conservative imaginary conjured up by Tey and others, women may be both the agent and the victims of such anxieties, but never the real authors of the period's enormous social changes. The legacies of empire in the novel, especially the pervasive racialising discourse that are both a deliberate narrative ploy and an almost uncontrolled obsession has something of the same function as the discourse of gender, a scapegoat for a perceived cultural trauma which cannot be fully named or brought to justice.

Simisola

The Franchise Affair has stayed in print, and the story itself has lingered in the imagination of later novelists. Indeed one of Britain's pre-eminent writers of historical fiction today, Sarah Waters, considered, but eventually abandoned, 'a rewrite of Tey's fascinating but deeply troubling novel' which reflected the 'deep anxiety' amounting to 'a kind of hysteria' embedded in 'conservative postwar paranoia' about 'a changing social system and a newly confident working class'.[19] However fragments of Tey's plot and themes do resurface, if only suggestively and obliquely, in Ruth Rendell's 1994 novel *Simisola*. Rendell acknowledges her debt to women writers of the Golden Age, if not particularly to Tey, and *Simisola* reaches further back in the genealogy of women's writing, referring several times to Jane Austen's great houses, Mansfield and Pemberly, and once, tellingly, to *Northanger Abbey*, whose heroine, overdosed on Gothic novels, believes that there has been a woman or women shut up or murdered in the house. *Jane Eyre* is also referenced when a character asks whether the police are looking for 'A madwoman in the attic'.[20] However *Simisola* is firmly set in the present day, in Rendell's fictional Sussex town of Kingsmarkham towards the end the recession of the early 1990s, its penultimate scene a protest march of the unemployed. In the economic downturn even Inspector Wexford's social-worker daughter, Sylvia, and architect son-in-law, Neil, are out of work, reduced to applying for benefits. Class hierarchy is still alive and well in *fin de siècle* Sussex, although its composition is no longer monochrome or insular. The novel's cast includes Wael Khoori, supermarket owner, and his wife Anouk, Saudi aristocrats escaping the Gulf War, now part of Kingsmarkham's *nouveau riche* who have just built themselves a faux Georgian country mansion on the grounds of an old estate. The reader gets to know members of both the 'indigenous' white and non-white middle class, as well as respectable working-class immigrants and local petty criminals. The anxieties of a nation whose culture and complexion have been changed and challenged, not only by a half century of non-white immigration from its former colonies but by a more comprehensive movement of populations and capital across the globe, have replaced Tey's narrower postwar issues.

Simisola is a novel in which the struggles of the white liberal conscience are central. The disappearance of two young women, both black, one murdered, are at the heart of *Simisola*'s narrative, which paints contemporary racism as an ugly, everyday reality. And where *The Franchise Affair* seems both to dramatise and unconsciously act out its social fears, *Simisola* is all too painfully aware of its every political move, its aim to make readers equally uncomfortable by alerting them to the myriad ways in which England's tarnished history of empire has impinged on its late twentieth-century present. Real-life melodrama does lurk behind *Simisola*. Rendell was inspired by a contemporary case of modern day 'slavery' in Sheffield, cited near the novel's end, transferring its setting to Inspector Reg Wexford's patch, 'Kingsmarkham', which 'lies in that part of Sussex that was once the land of Celtic tribe the Romans called the Regnenses' who the colonists 'regarded only as a source of slave labour' (195). This history is the other of

Tey's evocation of landscape as part of an organic, timeless nation. Rendell's reference to Roman slavery echoes another of the leading issues of the 1990s: the scandal of the British participation in the international traffic in women. Race and violence against women are woven through the story. Reg Wexford and his outspoken feminist daughter Sylvia attend a rape-awareness meeting, another related contemporary campaign central to the novel's plot. Key scenes are set in the grim job-seekers' and benefits office, a place where frustrated clients of all classes can suddenly become both hysterical and abusive. Published in the year after the shocking street murder of Stephen Lawrence by young white men in south London on 22 April 1993, and while the implications of the police mishandling of their investigation were slowly unfolding, the novel focuses on the errors which even a well-intentioned, liberal police officer can make in a case that centred on racial difference.

The opening of *Simisola* makes an interesting contrast to the beginning of *The Franchise Affair*. Free indirect discourse – Tey through Robert Blair, Rendell through Wexford – sets the scene in both. The empire enters *Simisola* in the form of Wexford's Nigerian-born GP, Dr Akande, who the Inspector is consulting. The NHS waiting room, itself a kind of microcosm of the community, includes an 'olive skinned blonde', who is patently not 'English', in a 'designer track suit' who has come, incredibly, to consult the doctor for 'one' of her 'servants' (1–2). Akande is new to the town, and Wexford 'liked to believe' that on a previous visit they had 'taken to each other', but he immediately 'castigates himself' for so thinking, reflecting 'that he knew damned well that he wouldn't have involved himself with likings or dislikings if Akande had been other than he was', that is if he had been white (3). Urbane, literate, Christian, Akande himself introduces the subject of his race, wryly confiding to Wexford that he had 'a feeling – without foundation, I must tell you, merely intuition' that the woman who had come on behalf of her cook would not 'be too overjoyed when she finds I'm what my father-in-law's boss used to call "a man of colour"'. 'These things are always just under the surface,' he tells his patient, 'and sometimes they bubble up' (5). Professionally and personally Akande has the upper-hand in this exchange – it is he, not Wexford, anxious patient and anxious liberal, who sets the terms through which ordinary everyday racism in Britain can be discussed. In their next encounter it is Akande who is anxious, about the disappearance of his daughter Melanie, and Wexford whose professional reassurance is required. And as the search for Melanie intensifies without result, the body of a naked young black woman turns up, found by a local 'plying his metal detector' for Roman coins or treasure buried on the historic Downs (196). Ironically what the treasure seeker finds is not an ancient imperial coin, but a 'Victorian halfpenny, bearing the head of the young queen', perhaps another 'clue' to the history of empire (197). Wexford and Burden wrongly jump to the conclusion that it is Melanie, although the woman is nothing like the photograph which the police had nor conforms to her physical details. As Akande's wife, Laurette, angrily says, they made the identification just 'because she was black' (208). Laurette's anguished attack on Wexford – 'the great white man, condescending to us, so magnanimous, so liberal' (208) – brings home to him his own considered view that 'We're all racist in this country'. 'Without exception. People over forty are worse and that's about all you can say. You were brought up and I was brought up to think ourselves superior to black people' (13–14).

Liberal self-consciousness, even Wexford's agonistic sensibility, offers a flimsy protection against the historically embedded, systemic racism of post-imperial Britain. Wexford himself has an instinctive physical loathing of the utterly manipulative Anouk Khoori, whose 'olive-skinned' blondness seems to emphasise her ethnic alterity. And as the search for the identity of the dead black woman – dubbed 'Sojourner' by Wexford after the American ex-slave and campaigner for women's rights, Sojourner Truth – is added to the search for Melanie, the novel expands on the effects of the end of empire. A stream of possible relatives with missing persons come to look at the dead girl, including Kashyapa Begh in his Jaguar, Festus Smith from Glasgow, Mary Sheerman from Nottingham: Rendell's point is that the multi-racial hybrid nation stretches the length and breadth of Britain, and that its infinite variety is at least a generation old. The British themselves do not escape Rendell's / Wexford's racialising gaze: a local election is near and the 'bull-necked, red faced representative of the British National Party (BNP), with his ... small piggy eyes' (a John Bull caricature), and the 'vulture-faced Lib Dem', compare badly with an airbrushed portrait of the 'Independent Conservative', Anouk Khoori (245–6). Tracking the unknown dead woman, 'Sojourner', the police interview Mhonum Ling, a Nigerian married to a Chinese take-away owner, Mark Ling. Mhonum's sister, Oni Johnson, a school-crossing worker, and her unemployed son Raffy also become involved in the case. It is Oni, who, attacked and left for dead by Sojourner's murderer, provides the first clue to Sojourner's identity.

Sojourner turns out to be a fugitive from an isolated house on Kingsmarkham's posh outskirts (like The Franchise) where she has been a captive servant, virtually a 'slave', in the household of the impeccably English Swithun Riding, a well-known and esteemed paediatrician. Her flight takes her past the school, and at the crossing she addresses Oni in Yoruba, asking the way to the job centre. This small detail is crucial; the desperate black woman is not simply seeking refuge but more acceptably, work; a fact that perhaps should not, but somehow does, add to the pathos of her death. Before Sojourner's murder is solved, however, Wexford has found the missing Melanie Akande, who has taken a job looking after three mixed-race kids, whose parents are on holiday abroad. No Betty Kane, Melanie has been in flight from the punitive pressures to succeed academically from her over-ambitious family, who are part of what she scornfully calls the 'Ebony Elite' (307). Black 'Africans', says Laurette Akande proudly to Wexford, 'are the most highly educated members of British society' (23). The Akandes, in turn, look down on Melanie's feckless ex-boyfriend, Euan Sinclair, of West-Indian extraction, with his two families of illegitimate children. Sojourner's murderers, however, are true sociopaths, although it is made clear that their pathological behaviour is culturally constructed – historically, not biologically, inherited. The villains who have systematically beaten and raped their Nigerian maid, whose first name we learn is Simisola, turn out to be the paediatrician Swithun Riding, a man with a reputation for being particularly gentle with newborn babies, and his son Christopher. Riding and his family have been long-term expatriates, only recently returned to England from Kuwait, in flight from the Gulf War. The Middle East serves as a post-imperial context which reinforces Swithun's long-held belief that 'some people are born to be slaves and wait on others' (369). The Ridings are part of a privileged class that include the Khooris and their friends who employ maids from the Phillipines, women negatively represented in the novel as a culturally offputting but undeferential work force. The Khoori's servants represent a new social grouping, recruited by a domestics agency under the terms of the Immigration Act of 1971, the 'solution' for a leisured class to the longstanding dearth of British subjects willing to 'live in'.

Simisola, the dead woman, has, on the other hand, been 'sold' by her indigent father in Nigeria to a Kuwaiti who 'meant to educate her and treat her like a daughter' but who dies suddenly, and it is then that she is passed on to the unscrupulous Ridings (368). Brought to Britain as a consequence of a loophole in the Immigration Act as a putative friend or relative of the Riding family, she has been kept as a virtual slave in the household. It is Wexford's daughter Sylvia who explains to him the psychology of such abuse, as it connects with racial prejudice, citing the eighteenth-century American and 'Founding Father' Dr Benjamin Rush, the author of a 'Theory of Negritude', which argued that blackness was a contagious disease, like leprosy (296). What the novel strangely fails to say is that Rush also held strongly abolitionist views. This is a missed opportunity, for the paradox that Rush represents, between the historic liberal universalism of

Western culture and its equally embedded racial thinking, is precisely the contradiction that Rendell's novel sets out to explore.[21]

I know of no other genre fiction by a white English author in the 1990s that aims with such ambition and courage to integrate the range of political, economic and social discontents of the period. Its premises anticipate by some years the conclusions of the *MacPherson Report* (1999), on the Lawrence case, and the *Parekh Report on the Future of Multi-Ethnic Britain* (2000), commissioned by the Runnymede Trust. Like *Parekh*, *Simisola* suggests that the residue of empire is evident in systemic racism, in a country now irrevocably multi-ethnic and multi-racial. The novel argues that endemic racism combines with other inequalities in a nation which has not eradicated class hierarchies or violence against women. In *Simisola* the BNP is a local presence, and the kind of opportunistic conservatism, with its own 'liberal' masque, peddled by the international rich as represented by Anouk Khoori, signals a new danger. Neo-imperial wars have chased home Englishmen like Swithun Riding and his family, whose lives in Kuwait fostered and preserved the prejudices of their British colonialist forefathers, attitudes which they bring back unamended to Britain. These prosperous class-conscious 'refugees', with their sense of innate privilege, are seen by Rendell as a major threat to social justice and to the establishment of a more truly egalitarian, multi-racial and multi-cultural society. Wexford and his colleagues may solve the murder of Simisola, but not the wider contradictions that the novel raises. In this sense, like *The Franchise Affair*, it resists closure. Yet its terms remain within the parameters of Wexford's/Rendell's own ethnocentric historic understanding, a basic liberal belief in humanitarian progress and the rule of law, tempered by a healthy scepticism about its application. Quoting a passage from William Cowper's *The Task* (1985), which refers to Lord Mansfield's groundbreaking 1823 decision that 'Slaves cannot breathe in England, if their lungs Receive our air, that moment they are free; They touch our country and their shackles fall', Wexford reflects that 'it may have been true once, it isn't any more' (348). Yet apart from Wexford's 'error' about the identity of Simisola, the police's behaviour is seen as exemplary, a sharp contrast to the emerging scandal of the Lawrence case. Wexford's 'fault' originates rather in his compensatory liberalism which gives the Akandes 'special consideration', not in a lack of concern over Melanie's disappearance or, later, over the murder of Simisola. The educated Melanie can voice her discontents, but Simisola (unlike many 'real-life' slaves who continue to run away from their employers) is an almost silent victim in the novel, reproducing, one might argue, the abjection she is made to suffer.[22] English racism may be culturally embedded in a legacy that extends from Roman times, a legacy which includes but does not romanticise its own anti-slavery movements, but the violence in the novel is laid, perhaps problematically, perhaps correctly, at the door of a global rather than a simply national history of oppression. Yet the novel has many strengths. *Simisola* asks the reader to accept the given of multi-ethnic Britain, an instance of the inexorable global movement of populations which, while it may have its emancipatory effects, is also responsible for hidden crimes, like that of modern 'slavery', whose female victims highlight the ongoing misogyny of contemporary societies. David Glover has argued that it is the imaginative function of novels about migrants to provoke 'a critical understanding of the worlds of others' and, at their best to offer readers a sense of their 'own otherness'; this surely is the admirable ambition, if not the absolute achievement, of Rendell's novel.[23] Yet Tey too, from her more reactionary and 'hysterical' conservative stance, believed, if pessimistically, in the inevitable fact that a modernising global culture would change England – and for England we should read Britain – out of all recognition. Perhaps in this sense the two novels, in spite of their very different takes on national history and the legacies of empire, are connected by a deeper, residual continuity of concerns.

Notes

1   See Peter Hennessy, *Never Again: Britain, 1945–51* (London: Penguin, 2006) p. 318; Hennessy sees this as indicative that the period was 'the era of the middle-brow'.

2   David Kynaston, *Austerity Britain, 1945–51* (London: Bloomsbury, 2008), pp. 210–11.

3   The account of the Canning Case is drawn from the very detailed Wikipedia entry, wikipedia.org/wiki/ElizabethCanning. Three recent studies – John Traherne, *The Canning Enigma* (London: Jonathan Cape, 1989), Judith Moore, *The Appearance of Truth: The story of Elizabeth Canning and eighteenth-century narrative* (Newark: University of Delaware Press, 1994) and Kristina Straub, *Domestic Affairs: Intimacy, eroticism and violence between servants and masters in eighteenth-century Britain* (Baltimore: Johns Hopkins University Press, 2009) – further analyse the significance of the case in its period.

4   Mary Poovey, *Uneven Developments: The ideological work of gender in mid-Victorian England* (Chicago: University of Chicago Press, 1988), pp. 12–13.

5   'Milford' is also the name which Noel Coward and David Lean took for their typical English town in the film *Brief Encounter*, in 1945. Thanks to Bill Schwarz for this interesting appropriation.

6   Josephine Tey, *The Franchise Affair* (London: Arrow, 2003), p. 11. All future references to this novel appear in parentheses in the text.

7   Alison Light, 'Writing fictions: femininity and the 1950s' in Jean Radford

(ed.), *The Progress of Romance: The politics of popular fiction* (London: Routledge and Kegan Paul, 1986) pp. 139–56, and 152. I am greatly indebted to Light's reading of the novel in this essay, which focuses on questions of class, gender and sexuality in the context of postwar anxieties.

8 A positive emphasis on the making of common-sense, everyday distinctions between ethnic types in Britain's heterogeneous population, including those between Celts and Saxons, goes back at least as far as the late 1840s and to the post-emancipation rise of racial thinking. See for example Robert Knox, *The Races of Men: A fragment* (London: Henry Renshaw, 1850). As with all scientific racism, moral, as well as biological, discriminations are embedded in these judgements which drew from and helped to sustain colonial and imperial hierarchies.

9 For the operation of the 'rule of difference', see Frederick Cooper and Ann Laura Stoler, 'Between metropole and colony: rethinking a research agenda' in Cooper and Stoler (eds), *Tensions of Empire: Colonial cultures in a bourgeois world* (Berkeley: University of California Press, 1997) pp. 1–56, and Catherine Hall, *Civilising Subjects. Metropole and colony in the English imagination, 1830–1867* (Cambridge: Polity, 2002).

10 On the popularisation of Lavater, see Lucy Hartley, *Physiognomy and the Meaning of Expression in Nineteenth-Century Culture* (Cambridge: Cambridge University Press, 2001).

11 The paper, the first to adopt the format and appearance of the New York tabloids, is easily identifiable to contemporary readers as the *Daily Mirror*, by the late 1940s selling 4.5 million copies a day, outstripping the *Express*; for some thirty years afterwards, it dominated the British daily newspaper market, selling over 5 million copies a day at its peak in the mid-1960s. For an analysis of the popular press see A.C.H. Smith with Elizabeth Immirzi and Trevor Blackwell, *Paper Voices: The popular press and social change, 1935–1965* (London: Chatto and Windus, 1975) especially the introduction by Stuart Hall. Tey would have had it in for the *Mirror*, which supported Labour and was vital in the orchestration of Labour's success in the 1945 general election and afterwards.

12 See Alison Light, *Mrs Woolf and the Servants: The hidden heart of domestic service* (London: Penguin, 2007), pp. 4–5.

13 Light, 'Writing fictions: femininity and the 1950s', p. 152.

14 Light, 'Writing fictions: femininity and the 1950s', p. 149.

15 Light, 'Writing fictions: femininity and the 1950s', p. 156.

16 Light, 'Writing fictions: femininity and the 1950s', p. 157.

17 Light, 'Writing fictions: femininity and the 1950s', p. 158.

18 Light, 'Writing fictions: femininity and the 1950s', p. 160.

19 Sarah Waters, 'On writing *The Little Stranger*', *Guardian 'Review'*, 7 August 2010, p. 6.

20 Ruth Rendell, *Simisola* (London: Arrow, 1995), p. 322. All further references to the novel are in parentheses in the text.

21 Rendell returns to some of the issues treated in *Simisola* in the final Wexford novel, *The Monster in the Box* (2009).

22 Two television programmes broadcast on Channel 4 on 30 August 2010 highlight the widespread, ongoing problem of the 'slave' trade in Britain. *Dispatches: Britain's Secret Slaves* interviewed women of various nationalities who had escaped from situations similar to Simisola's. It was followed by a compelling drama on the same subject, *I Am Slave*.

23 See David Glover, 'Preface' in Maria Isabel Romero Ruiz and Sylvia Castro Borrego (eds), *Cultural Migrations and Gendered Subjects: Colonial and postcolonial representations of the female body* (Newcastle: Cambridge Scholars Press, forthcoming).

3

Colonial fiction for liberal readers: John Masters and the Savage family saga

Richard Steadman-Jones

The American Liberal ... taught me much, above all to look afresh at institutions and ideas which I had held as fixed pillars of the universe. Without his abrasive presence and pressure around me, I could not have written anything better than potboiling thrillers. (John Masters, 1971)[1]

An issue of reception

Between 1951 and 1962, John Masters published a sequence of seven novels, each set at a different moment in the history of British India.[2] The heroes of the books are all members of the same family, their surname is 'Savage', and so the sequence is often known as the 'Savage family saga'. Until 1947, Masters had been an officer in the Indian army, but, when his regiment – the 4th Gurkhas – was incorporated into the forces of the newly independent state, he chose not to accept a commission in the British army and instead moved to the USA, where he thought that he would find more opportunities for adventure than in England.[3] His decision to become a writer was a solution to the problem of how he could support his family in this unfamiliar context and he pursued his new career with the kind of systematic determination that had been inculcated in him in the army. Between 1951 and 1955 he published a novel every year. The first, *Nightrunners of Bengal*, was adopted by the US book club, The Literary Guild, as its 'Book of the Month' for January 1951, a choice which guaranteed Masters royalties of over $16,000 and the kind of publicity that costs a small fortune to buy.[4] This and a series of generally favourable reviews meant that by the mid-1950s his work was very well known in both Britain and the USA and, although his star has faded in recent decades, the story of the Savages was widely read in its hey-day, particularly in the 1950s and 1960s.

The focus of this chapter is a particular issue in the reception of Masters's writing, and to appreciate what is at stake here we need to consider the way in which he handles his historical material. The events dramatised in the 'Savage family saga' are mostly ones which had a strongly emblematic status within British colonial discourse. For example, the first novel, *Nightrunners of Bengal*, deals with the Indian 'Mutiny', a moment of crisis that became crucial to British conceptions of imperialism in the second half of the nineteenth century and beyond.[5] The uprising of 1857 was variously figured as an act of treachery, an outbreak of barbarity and, as the term 'Mutiny' implies, an irrational eruption of lawlessness. Furthermore, it was often presented as the justification for a hardening of attitudes towards the governance of India in the later years of the nineteenth century. Thus, to write about the 'Mutiny' at the beginning of the 1950s was clearly to revisit one of the tropes of British imperial rhetoric. Of course, one might revisit such a trope in order to reinterpret it. One might develop a fictional account which in some way acknowledged the nationalist interpretation of the 'Mutiny' not as an isolated outbreak of disorder but as a moment in the long sequence of anti-colonial action which finally led to independence in 1947. But, while Masters's novel is a long way from those earlier texts that make explicit use of terms such as 'treachery' and 'barbarity' in their descriptions of the uprising, his narrative is so insistently focalised through its British hero that we experience the events almost entirely in the terms that he does and it is hardly strange that his response is one of shock, sadness and anger rather than of dispassionate analysis.

Yet, despite this, it is evident that, on both sides of the Atlantic, Masters's work was favourably received by a range of readers who were at the very least unsympathetic to Britain's status as an imperial power. The relatively uncritical nature of his engagement with Indian history does not seem to have deterred people whose own attitudes were, in fact, highly critical of that history. My aim here is to examine why that should have been. In doing so, I shall look first at the comments of the critic, Ronald Bryden, who was born in Trinidad and educated in Canada but who spent much of his adult life in Britain and was very much immersed in the country's political and cultural life during the period we are discussing. Bryden identifies Masters's approach to the creation of characters as a crucial element in the dynamics of his historical writing, an idea I shall develop by looking at the way in which his interactions with US editors shaped his work. In the final sections of the essay I shall examine how Masters's handling of characterisation relates both to the literary critical culture of the period and to the temporality of the 'Savage family saga' as a whole. Crucial is the idea that the moral qualities of the novel as a genre lie in the sphere of characterisation. Why this is important for a reading of Masters's work is something Bryden can show us.

'The bitter winter after Suez'

In 1961 Ronald Bryden published a short article on Masters's fiction in *The London Magazine*, which effectively constitutes a 'confession'. Avowedly anti-imperialist in their politics, he and his friends were not the obvious audience for Masters's writing and yet, in the late 1950s, having made his way through the first tranche of Fleming's Bond stories, Bryden found himself part of a circle of ambivalent readers who, despite their political qualms, were entirely captivated by the ongoing story of the Savages:

> We knew our shared guilt: what we were indulging was intellectual vice blacker in our code than any gratified by Bond's gloating torturers. We prided ourselves we were liberals, leftwing, 'literary'. It was the bitter winter after Suez, our sodden pamphlets strewed Trafalgar Square. Yet here we were revelling in walnut-stained exploits beyond the Khyber, in last-minute rescues by John Company's lancers, in the parrot-splendours, raw silks, jewels and regimentals, of a Calcutta Residency ball. We were allowing ourselves vanished, forbidden pleasures, nostalgia for the unrecoverable simplicity of a dead and deadly virtue. For us, the saga of the Savages, heroes and conquistadors of the Raj, was a political pornography in which we savoured the illicit sensualities of imperialism.[6]

Bryden goes on to argue that, while Masters frequently treads the paths taken by unashamedly imperialist writers, presenting India as a space of exotic spectacle and revisiting the usual tropes of colonial legitimation, his central characters are, in many ways, awkward figures who do not fit straightforwardly into the settings in which they find themselves:

> Each Savage, on the face of it, is a bundle of doubts: uneasy about power, the need to kill, about his own instincts. He is always a slight imperial anachronism, devoted to Indian India, hating the colour-bar, worried over Britain's right to this sprawling empire.[7]

For Bryden, it was this awkwardness, this sense of 'doubt', that gave 'liberal, leftwing' readers like himself and his friends a point of entry into the material. The fact that Masters's heroes spend so much time toiling through their internal ethical conflicts ensures that they are read not as mere imperial automata, blinkered and blimpish, but as moral actors capable of engaging in serious self-examination. The Savages always do their 'duty', but the fact that they struggle so deeply with their consciences along the way provides just enough purchase for a reader in search of some political escapism to climb into their world.

As we have seen, the phrase that Bryden uses in describing this escapism is 'nostalgia for the unrecoverable simplicity of a dead and deadly virtue'. The term 'colonial nostalgia' is now well established in the postcolonial lexicon but it is important to point out that the phenomenon it labels comes in a number of different varieties. Whereas the cultural production of the 1980s has often been seen as displaying an aggressive form of historical nostalgia, one which undoubtedly did lament the passing of Britain's imperial 'greatness', the nostalgia invoked by Bryden is that of people actively involved in anti-imperialist politics. The reference to the 'bitter winter after Suez' is important here. On 4 November 1956 some 30,000 people had gathered in central London to demonstrate against the invasion of Egypt by British, French and Israeli troops, and this is the event to which Bryden alludes when he talks about 'sodden pamphlets strew[ing] Trafalgar Square'. The criticism levelled at Sir Anthony Eden and the Conservative Government had both pragmatic and ethical dimensions. At the former level, the decision to invade Egypt seemed to betray a fundamental failure to understand Britain's position in the postwar world. As Aneurin Bevan put it in a speech to the demonstrators: 'We are stronger than Egypt but there are other countries stronger than us. Are we prepared to accept for ourselves the logic we are applying to Egypt?'[8] At the ethical level, the decision to embark on an adventure of this kind at a time when it could not even be justified on pragmatic grounds seemed to betray an absurd and depressing level of commitment to a discredited idea. A term which Bevan uses in this context is 'shame'. The government, he declared, has 'besmirched the name of Britain. They have made us ashamed of the things of which formerly we were proud'. This is revealing when one considers Bryden's account of his response to Masters. His is not the nostalgia of a reader for whom the loss of India was itself a source of regret but that of someone seeking respite from a kind of political shame, an opportunity to spend a little time in a world where the notion of virtue was altogether more straightforward.

Such reading, of course, entails a process of disavowal – an acceptance of the material masked by a simultaneous act of distancing. And, for Bryden, the act of rejecting narratives such as these involved a display of humour: 'You have to smile apologetically for owning them, laugh when challenged to defend them, protest their merits with mock-indignation.'[9] But the point of this laughter is not simply to ridicule a book which one finds absurd but to conceal an underlying sense of identification, and Masters produces this identification through his approach to characterisation. For Bryden's friends, the attraction of spending time in Masters's world was that, in that fictional space, they were relieved of the pressure to feel the kind of political shame associated with the Suez debacle. The fact that Masters's heroes have a strong moral dimension meant that liberal readers were able to bracket their own critical responses and, for a moment, accept the characters' decisions on the basis that they were, at least, taken in good faith. This sense of 'good faith' emerges in a number of ways. As Bryden implies, the books often stage a conflict between what (with an appropriate level of irony) one might call 'good imperialism' (paternalistic, compassionate, intellectually engaged) and 'bad imperialism' (exploitative, racist, ignorant). The fact that the hero always aligns himself with the former immediately gives the reader scope for sympathy. But more than this the conflict Masters sets up often has a strong personal dimension which does not relate to the ethics of imperialism at all, a fact that gives his novels a distinctly moral texture, while disguising a lack of engagement with the specific context of the narrative. This too opens up the possibility of identification by moving the political elements of the novel into the background and placing a different kind of ethical problem in the foreground.

Towards the end of his essay, Bryden describes the 'Savage family saga' as a 'huge myth-cycle of historical apology' and no doubt that is a reasonable description. But more interesting, perhaps, is this observation on his reaction to the work as a reader:

> What [Masters] has poured out ... is his faith, against all fact we know to the contrary, that British India was for the best. We should like desperately to believe it. If we could, he would give back an imperialism purified, made innocent, beneficent, and with it the continuity of virtue, whole and unquestioning, which Britain has lost.
>
> So we go with him, defensive, half-laughing, half-credulous, as he unstitches the story of British India and weaves it afresh in untarnished colours ...[10]

It is significant that in that final sentence Bryden pictures Masters as a kind of travelling companion, for as one moves through the landscape of the books it is actually the Savages with whom one makes the journey. And it is for this reason – the need to reassure the reader that all this is presented in good faith – that the characterisation of Masters's heroes assumes such significance.

The policeman and the 'terrorists'

Since he became a novelist only after moving to the USA in 1948, Masters's approach to fiction was shaped by the experience of working with American editors, a point well illustrated in a passage where he describes his early experiences of submitting stories to US magazines. Striking here is the extent to which his comments focus on problems of identification and sympathy, problems which have already emerged in Bryden's discussion and which arise from the political perspective of the work. To illustrate the point, Masters describes how editors responded to a story in which a British police officer 'ambushed and killed three Indian terrorists'. The term 'terrorist' is now so contested that it is difficult to see how a story which hinged on its use could possibly be read apolitically. But for Masters the editors' response seems to have come as a surprise:

> The theme of the story was the skill and bravery of the police officer. The editors wanted to know why he was shooting Indians. They could not, for themselves or on behalf of their readers, see my hero as a hero, or even as a good man.[11]

To anyone familiar with Bryden's essay, Masters's use of the phrase 'good man' is striking. US editors doubted that an imperial agent could be represented to their readers as a morally comprehensible character. However, as Bryden indicates, Masters did manage to square this circle. And in doing so he produced a type of fiction which was especially appealing to that other kind of reader – one committed to the idea of a British identity which was not imperial but in search of a momentary escape from the labour of living the anti-imperial idea. Interestingly, Masters and Bryden use the same term, 'liberal', to describe these two groups of readers – Americans instinctively critical of tales about the British empire and British readers with an anti-imperialist perspective – although Masters's use of the term seems less precise than Bryden's. He employs the term frequently throughout his autobiography, usually in a critical way. Indeed, he often uses it to characterise the views of the US literary establishment and perhaps implies that the problems of political identification had more to do with the opinions of the editors than with those of the mass readership on whose behalf they read his work.

In this vein, he describes the editors' response to the 'terrorist' story as his first meeting with the 'American Liberal Establishment', a phrase which he later reduced to 'A.L.E.'[12] He was scathing about their political commitments:

> [T]he A.L.E. had taken sides in many questions of the day, and believed that writers should do so too. I did not. I had come to believe that the writer's duty, as a writer, is to offer some effectively worded insight into the human condition. If anything else, a particular situation, for example, is at the centre of his work – that is, if the situation and not the humans are the essentials of it – it will not last, because all situations change.[13]

The trope of prioritising the 'human condition' over the 'political situation' has been the object of extensive discussion in postcolonial criticism and it seems unnecessary to labour the point. It's interesting, though, that Masters's views on the insufficiency of quotidian politics as a focus for fiction led him to participate in public debate about the work of an emerging postcolonial writer. When Edith Efron published a review of Sam Selvon's novel, *A Brighter Sun*, in the *New York Times*, Masters responded contesting Efron's critical comments.[14] She had remarked on Selvon's apparent 'anxiety to spare British colonialism' and the 'oddly timid' way in which he depicted his hero's 'response to colonial race-prejudice'. In his reply, Masters returned to the issue of the relationship between reader and character, arguing that in the case of certain people 'who would probably call themselves "liberals"', the quality of sympathy 'has become a compulsion for resentment', which he believed was not in fact sympathy, 'but bias'. In short, he claimed that Efron's sympathy for the oppressed had led her to make assumptions which she was not justified in making.[15] In her reply, Efron gave as good as she got and the row fizzled out until Masters revisited it in his autobiography.[16] Yet the exchange revealed Masters's sensitivity to the kind of political critique which he himself had received. It offers a good example of his sense of the so-called 'American Liberal' as an 'abrasive presence', placing a 'pressure' on him which he had never anticipated when he first began to write.

After his first encounters with American publishers Masters realised that, in order to make a living as an author, he would need to find a way of responding to the criticisms of 'liberal' editors and enable US readers to 'identify' with his heroes. He discussed this problem in his autobiography and described his dawning sense that if people were going to interpolate 'other values' into his fiction then the best way to respond was to complicate the dynamics of the stories himself. As an example, he re-imagined the narrative of the policeman and the 'terrorists' thus:

> Suppose ... that the chief terrorist had had an affair with the policeman's wife, and the policeman knew it. The policeman could be put into a situation where he would not be sure whether he was only doing his duty, or taking a private revenge. Every reader would see the problem without my having to shout it in his ear every few lines. Such a device, very simple, would add enormously to the story.[17]

The introduction of this complication is powerful because it means that the hero has constantly to question the nature of his commitment to 'duty'. But this questioning does not arise from any fundamental uncertainty about the nature of the 'terrorist' cause. It is really no more than a sleight of hand which gives the illusion of introducing critical reflection without leading to any engagement with the ethics of imperialism. This story of the policeman and the terrorists, in fact, provided the prototype for the more complex narratives of the 'Savage family saga', a point I will demonstrate by examining the first two books of the sequence.

As we saw earlier, Masters's first novel, *Nightrunners of Bengal*, deals with one of the most contested moments in British imperial history – the 'Mutiny' of 1857 – and focuses almost entirely on the hero, Rodney Savage, an officer in the Bengal Infantry. But rather than treating the actions of the British characters as obviously justified by the wrongs perpetrated against them, as a propagandist text might, Masters instead constructs his hero's reaction to the 'Mutiny' as itself a moral problem. In the early chapters Rodney displays all the virtues of 'good imperialism': a paternalistic interest in his troops and considerable intellectual curiosity about India and its cultures. But, after the uprising, he is virtually transformed into another person: cynical, mistrustful and consumed with anger, an incarnation, almost, of 'bad imperialism'. This is the ethical dilemma at the heart of the book – as Masters puts it 'hatred breeds hatred'[18] – and the problem is resolved when Rodney eventually manages to put aside his pathological anger and regain his original qualities of openness and respect, albeit he is a little sadder and less trusting. The moral complexity of Masters's protagonist emerges not because he experiences any doubt over the political significance of events but as a result of his struggle to master his own feelings. The personal crisis effectively eclipses any consideration of the politics of the 'Mutiny', which remains little more than a catalyst for Rodney's subjective descent into hell.

A different perspective might have been introduced through the character of the Rani of Kishanpur, the ruler of a nearby 'princely state'. Early in the book Rodney becomes romantically involved with her but the romance turns out to be built on deception when it emerges that she is one of the leading figures behind the rebellion. The character is modelled on a real historical figure, Rani Lakshmibai of Jhansi, who is often seen as a kind of nationalist heroine, an interpretation which informs Sohrab Modi's film, *Jhansi ki Rani*, released in 1953, just two years after the publication of *Nightrunners*.[19] But rather than using the Rani to render his account of the 'Mutiny' more politically complex, Masters figures her relationship with Rodney through the trope of the 'star crossed lovers' whose relationship is doomed because they are *necessarily* on different sides of a larger divide. The result is that their relationship simply becomes another facet of the protagonist's personal crisis rather than an encounter which challenges him in a more profound – or, indeed, political – way. Thus, in the end, the narrative works in a manner similar to the story of the policeman and the 'terrorists'. It focuses attention on the personal dimensions of Rodney's experience and figures his return to a more balanced state of mind as a moral triumph such that, when he finally assumes his 'imperial duty' and – saddened but not bitter – goes to fight the rebel troops, the reader is presented with a sense of ethical closure which masks the unresolved issue of the 'Mutiny' itself.

Masters's second novel, *The Deceivers*, deals with another trope of colonial discourse, the suppression of 'Thuggee', the cult of ritual murder which became the focus of British attention in the 1830s.[20] Whereas British writers often figured the 'Mutiny' as a means to discredit and delegitimise opposition to British rule, the campaign against the 'Thugs' was typically presented as one of the regime's achievements. Like 'Suttee' the immolation of widows on their husbands' funeral pyres, 'Thuggee' became an emblem of the presumed disorder and cruelty of Indian society, and hence the suppression of both practices emerged as signs of the supposedly beneficent nature of the British administration. Several key texts appeared which presented the phenomenon in this way, foremost among them Henry William Sleeman's *Ramaseeana* (1836), a particularly significant work because Sleeman himself led the campaign against 'Thuggee', and Philip Meadows Taylor's *Confessions of a Thug* (1839), in which an imprisoned 'Thug' leader relates the story of his life to a British interlocutor.

Interesting in Masters's fictionalised version is the assertive way in which he associates the suppression of 'Thuggee' with the complex of values which

I earlier described as 'good colonialism'. The central character, William Savage is the father of Rodney from the previous book. He is a district officer in a rural area of India and, in the early part of the narrative, takes it upon himself to go undercover and join a 'Thug' gang with the aim of investigating their activities. Prior to this, William has been presented as at odds with the colonial hierarchy: a little too slow, not especially ambitious, a little too fond of Indians in the opinion of his superiors. But it is exactly his sense of detachment from the British elite and his 'love of Indian India' which enable him to act successfully as a secret agent – his knowledge of local languages and ways of life is so perfect that he is undetectable in his assumed role. Thus, Masters offers 'liberal' readers the first type of reassurance mentioned above. Far from constructing the action of the book in terms of an officially sanctioned regime of surveillance, he makes this traditional trope of colonial legitimation into a function of William's more admirable qualities: his curiosity, his openness and his lack of arrogance.

Masters again places a personal moral struggle at the centre of his narrative. The issue here is the sheer allure of 'Thuggee' as a way of life. William almost finds himself drawn into this violent but fascinating way of being and it takes some effort for him to disentangle himself and return to a life with which we know that he is not entirely at ease. Masters later said that he had the rise of Nazism in mind here: the question of how seemingly ordinary people were prepared to turn a blind eye to, and even participate in, atrocities.[21] However, if that was his inspiration it is handled in a very restrained way. Rather than constructing the 'Thugs' as proto-Nazis, he uses them to make a case for the attractions of a life 'outside' and so, when William breaks cover and rejects that life, his decision is distanced from the fastidious disdain with which Victorian moralists often spoke about the 'customs' of the 'natives'. William emerges as one whose moral awareness is firmly grounded in the realities of experience. And once again the moral journey of the central character effectively masks the question of where his authority as a colonial agent is located. Just as the policeman's response to the 'terrorist' is complicated by the personal grudge he bears him, so William's situation is complicated by his sense that he is caught between his colonial superiors and the extraordinary lives which are led in the world immediately around him.

Aspects of the novels

Having looked at the relationship between characterisation and moral complexity in Masters's fiction, I want to deepen the discussion by examining his debt to E.M. Forster's writings on the novel. In a discussion of critical reactions to the fiction of Gustave Flaubert, Diana Knight notes that for a long time Anglo-American critics remained doubtful about the value of Flaubert's writing, a response which she attributes to the dominance of 'moral' criticism.[22] Her point is that Flaubert's central characters were often seen as 'weak vessels', ineffectual figures incapable of the levels of moral experience which were 'really' the stuff of narrative fiction. In this context Knight comments on characterisation as 'the traditional focus for the defence of the novel as a humanizing influence', and points to Forster's comments in *Aspects of the Novel* as a definitive statement of this view. When Forster comes to discuss characterisation in the two chapters of his work entitled 'People', these are his opening words:

> Having discussed the story – that simple and fundamental aspect of the novel – we can turn to a more interesting topic: the actors. We need not ask what happened next, but to whom did it happen; the novelist will be appealing to our intelligence and imagination, not merely to our curiosity. A new emphasis enters his voice: emphasis upon value.[23]

Thus for Forster the moral focus of the novel as a genre is located in its handling of character: the actors are more 'interesting' than the story; they demand that we engage the higher faculties of 'intelligence' and 'imagination'; and, for the first time, questions of 'value' become important. This conviction that the real significance of the novel lies in characterisation is unfashionable today but for Forster it was central.[24]

In his autobiography Masters explains that *Aspects of the Novel* was the text he relied on when he first began to write fiction.[25] He found it 'brilliant', he says, not least because of its 'stereoscopic clarity of insight'.[26] Furthermore, as he describes the process of writing *Nightrunners of Bengal*, he does so with reference to Forster's ideas of characterisation:

> The creation of the book began: the formation of the major characters to achieve my object; how many should there be? Must be at least two, one for the British and one for the Indian points of view. How shape the secondary characters (according to Forster's Law) to reflect light on the major ones?[27]

Rather than 'major' and 'secondary', Forster actually talks about 'round' and 'flat' characters, the latter susceptible to summary in a single sentence and the former conceived in a sufficiently complex fashion that they are capable of surprising the reader without becoming unconvincing. The process of creating supporting characters who serve to 'reflect light' on the central ones is very much part of Masters's practice and it's often gendered, a good example appearing in *Nightrunners*. There, both Rodney's wife, Joanna, and the woman he turns to after Joanna's death, Caroline, can be read as 'flat' in Forster's sense. The former is materialistic, snobbish and self-serving, the latter intellectually curious, morally earnest, and courageous. At no point does either 'surprise' the reader. However, the two together represent different attitudes to colonial life, in relation to both of which Rodney himself emerges as a more complex figure. Although his intellectual sympathies lie with Caroline, he nevertheless loves Joanna. Indeed, his descent into cynicism and mistrust is largely caused by the experience of witnessing her death at the hands of the sepoys. And this change in Rodney's behaviour does – I think – come as a 'surprise', not to the extent that it seems inexplicable, given what has happened, but in the sense that it is a far cry from the reaction of the stock adventure hero who can pass through crisis without sustaining any real psychic damage. The fact that for a time Rodney seems to become a wholly different person provides a plausible sense of his having experienced trauma, and represents a significant contrast to figures such as Ian Fleming's Bond.

Forster's categories do not reveal much about Masters's fiction which would not be apparent to any observant reader. But they do reveal something of Masters's practice of building moral complexity into his stories. Not only does this represent a response to the reactions of 'liberal' editors; it also constitutes a strategy derived from reading a particular tradition of literary interpretation in rather schematic terms. If the novel is the genre which 'would express values',[28] and if characterisation is the aspect of fiction that makes most demands on the reader's ethical faculties, then for readers with even a passing knowledge of it Masters's allusions to the Forster tradition function both as a signal of moral seriousness and of literary value. For a conventional distinction separating genre fiction from 'serious' writing turned on the use of the formulaic. I'm not suggesting that Masters's appropriation of Forster was cynical. As Bryden understood, the 'liberal' reader's ability to accept each of the Savages as a hero depended on the fact that 'Masters presents him with conscientious good faith'.[29]

Bryden himself was a great admirer of Masters's literary guru – 'If post-imperial Britain contains Alf Garnett, it also, and gloriously, contains E.M. Forster'[30] – and Forster's characterisation of colonialism certainly possessed the kind of critical qualities of which Bryden himself approved. In *A Passage to India* (1924) Forster considered whether the liberal virtue of friendship could extend across the fault lines of colonial society and intimated that it could not. But in Masters's novels personal connections are exactly what the protagonists seek to forge and the possibility that they will succeed is left much more open. Indeed, this is another aspect of the escapism which the books offered to readers such as Bryden. As well as respite from the shame of the post-imperial condition they also evoke a world in which, despite the political and social divisions that lie between them, people can really 'connect'.

Masters's temporality

I shall close my discussion by relating these issues of characterisation to the specific temporality of Masters's fiction and return to the point with which I began – the debt he acknowledges to his confrontations with 'American Liberals'. Bryden raised the issue of temporality in his description of the collective character of Masters's heroes, remarking that each is 'a slight imperial anachronism'.[31] When I first read this comment – speaking personally for a moment – I took it to mean that all the Savages seem to come from the *earliest* phase of British imperialism in India, the later eighteenth century, when conventional doctrines of 'orientalism' were dominant. In whatever period a novel is set, Masters's characterisation of his protagonist seems to hark back to the age of Warren Hastings, when imperial policy had principally been based on the acculturation of British imperial agents rather than on, as later, the 'anglicisation' of an indigenous elite. The Savages speak Indian languages with near-native fluency; they have a deep appreciation of South Asian cultures; as Bryden says, they are 'devoted to Indian India'. Of course, they are also anachronistic in that they seem aware – at least to an extent – of later critiques of imperialism. But either way not one of them embodies the attitudes which flourished in moments of reaction such as during the Governor-Generalship of Lord Macaulay or in the years immediately following the 'Mutiny'.

None of this would matter much if the family relationship among Masters's heroes did not itself invite interpretation in figurative terms. That all the books feature central characters with the same name and similar attributes encourages us to view them as more than a collection of individuals. Certainly Masters gestures towards this idea when he describes how he originally conceived of the work.[32] By his own account, he sat down and made a list of thirty-five moments of conflict in the history of British India, each of which might form the subject-matter of a book. He suggests that, even then, he saw all of these potential novels as elements of a single project: 'The whole would be larger and nobler than the sum of its parts, if I could complete it. At that moment I knew that I would like to.' And he comments specifically on his decision to unify 'the whole' by making it into a family saga:

> The family should have dominant, recognizable characteristics, which in turn should resemble the characteristics of the British as they showed themselves in India. The tragedies and dramas of my stories would not happen to 'the British' but to human-size people, who would also stand as measuring rods by which readers could judge the size of events.[33]

This statement asserts what the novels themselves imply – that the British collectively conformed to some kind of transhistorical persona over centuries of activity in South Asia. The qualities which Masters presents as elements of this persona are the ones that even Bryden's leftwing, literary friends could find it in their hearts to admire. Of course, other perspectives and other versions of imperial policy are represented, but usually by 'flat' characters arranged to 'reflect light' on the Savages themselves. Thus the qualities of the Savages emerge as a representation of what the British in India were 'really' like in opposition to the aberrations represented by the characters around them.

Masters was not the only writer who, in the early 1950s, took it upon himself to produce a survey of the history of British India. In 1953 and 1954 – the years in which *The Lotus and the Wind* and *Bhowani Junction* appeared – Philip Mason, formerly of the Indian Civil Service and then Director of Studies in Race Relations at Chatham House, published his two-volume historical work, *The Men Who Ruled India*.[34] In the introduction to the first volume, Mason indicated that the aim of the work was to consider the entire history of the Indian empire taken as a single 'achievement'. In doing so he often referred to 'the English' as a single character, and compared his task of discovering the meaning of the colonial encounter to the impulse of individuals – of men – to evaluate their own accomplishments:

> There comes a time in a man's life when he may well stand back and consider what he has built, planted, written or begotten and whether it was worth doing. If in such a mood the English ... look back on their varied history, the long connection with India will be an achievement that cannot be ignored.[35]

In his introduction to the second volume Mason began to employ theatrical imagery:

> The three hundred and fifty years the English spent in India make one story, but a story which unfolds itself like a stage play in a series of acts. The curtain falls for the interval after the third act; the fourth and fifth remain to be played. The third act has shown the hero – who is not one man but a thousand – at the height of his glory, but the contradiction in his own character and the conflict in the whole situation are already apparent; he has triumphed for the moment but the conflict is unresolved.[36]

Mason acknowledged the differences of attitude and policy among the British, using a second metaphor – one of different strains in a piece of music – to express his point. But he also asserted that when 'English rule in India' came to be judged, certain aspects of it would need to be prioritised, and he again compared the actions of 'the English' to those of an individual:

> To one invincible prejudice which runs through this book I will confess in advance. It is a belief in the Christian doctrine that a man must be judged not by his worst so much as by his best, and in the end not even by his best but by what he aimed at. And so English rule in India is to be judged by the conscious will of England expressed in Parliament and by the aims of a good district officer .... 'Not what thou art, nor what thou hast been, does God consider, but what thou wouldst be.'[37]

The resemblance to Masters's project is striking. Both Mason's history and Masters's sequence of novels aim to encompass the whole of British Indian history within the scope of a multi-volume work. Both find in the story of British India a certain continuity, one which can be expressed by figuring the British in India either as a single character, or in terms of successive generations of characters connected by family resemblance. Underwriting this homogenising strategy was the belief that it was possible to identify the 'true' character of British rule in India. If the end of the Raj prompted in the British a totalising response – an impulse to grasp the meaning of the entire experience – this is oddly akin to the way in which existentialist thought posits the totalising properties of the death of an individual. In both Masters and Mason the idea of 'character', organised in the figure of the representative individual, was decisive. And if – to follow the existentialist premise – it only becomes possible to say who a person really was once their life is rendered a closed totality by death, then the idea of the individual person provides a powerful figurative resource for writers whose concern was to explore the meaning of the imperial experience at the moment of its dissolution.

And this brings us back to the point at which we started. The 'liberal' position as Masters described it would also subsume his characters into a single transhistorical category – that of the 'imperialist oppressor'. But his fiction invites the reader to reimagine the historical figure as a moral actor, a being with an insatiable level of curiosity and a hunger for experience which in itself becomes a virtue. For Masters this radical openness could only be satisfied in a place which offered opportunities of the sort which India did. Yet in 1962 he published the last volume in his saga, *To the Coral Strand*, which depicts the experiences of another Rodney Savage in the years immediately following Indian independence. Like Masters himself, Rodney chooses not to return to England; but unlike Masters he stays in India struggling – and in large part failing – to find a role for himself. Read with reference to the autobiography *Pilgrim Son*, *To the Coral Strand* suggests that, in post-imperial times the hunger for experience which Masters believed characterised the British in India needed new places to inhabit – a real or figurative 'America', perhaps. To use Forster's terms, the 'liberal' critic functions in *Pilgrim Son* as a 'flat' character, casting light on the 'round' character which is the author himself, and what is revealed by this interaction is exactly the openness that Masters wishes to portray as the transhistorical virtue of the British in India, still going strong in a new world and among new people. Thus in his own autobiography his encounter with the 'liberal' critic and the becoming which it led to – becoming a writer, becoming American – in a strange way emerge as signs of the very continuity which is signalled in the structure of his Savage saga. This openness is offered to the reader as that which – beyond the politics – was the most significant feature of the empire.

Notes

1 John Masters, *Pilgrim Son* (London: Michael Joseph, 1971), p. 392.
2 John Masters, *Nightrunners of Bengal* (1951), *The Deceivers* (1952), *The Lotus and the Wind* (1953), *Bhowani Junction* (1954), *Coromandel!* (1955), *Far, Far The Mountain Peak* (1957), *To the Coral Strand* (1962), all published in the UK by Michael Joseph and in the USA by Viking, except *To the Coral Strand*, which was published by Harper in the USA.
3 An important source for this phase of Masters's life is his third volume of autobiography, *Pilgrim Son* (London: Michael Joseph, 1971). See also John

Clay, *John Masters: A regimented life* (London: Michael Joseph, 1992).

4   Clay, *John Masters*, p. 187.

5   On the 'Mutiny' in British literature and policy up to 1947 see Gautam Chakravarty, *The Indian Mutiny and the British Imagination* (Cambridge: Cambridge University Press, 2005).

6   Ronald Bryden, 'The last golden moustache' in Bryden (ed.), *The Unfinished Hero and Other Essays* (London: Faber and Faber, 1969), p. 223.

7   Bryden, 'Golden moustache', p. 224.

8   Bevan's speech has been included in the *Guardian*'s list of 'great speeches of the 20th century' and is available at the *Guardian* website as an audio file, www.guardian.co.uk/greatspeeches/bevan/ (accessed 11 August 2010).

9   Bryden, 'Moustache', p. 223.

10 Bryden, 'Moustache', pp. 226–7.

11 Masters, *Pilgrim Son*, pp. 110–11.

12 Masters, *Pilgrim Son*, pp. 191–3.

13 Masters, *Pilgrim Son*, p. 191.

14 Edith Efron, 'Dreamer at the edge of a swamp', *New York Times*, 18 January 1953.

15 Cited in Masters, *Pilgrim Son*, p. 295.

16 Edith Efron, 'A Reply', *New York Times*, 22 February 1953.

17 Masters, *Pilgrim Son*, p. 111.

18 Masters, *Pilgrim Son*, p. 151.

19 See Tapti Roy, *Raj of the Rani* (New Delhi: Penguin India, 2006).

20 A number of scholars have reassessed the evidence in an attempt to establish what kind of phenomenon 'thuggee' really was. See Martine van Woerkens, *The Strangled Traveler: Colonial imaginings and the Thugs of India* (Chicago: University of Chicago Press, 2002), translated by Catherine Tihanyi; Mike Dash, *Thug: The true story of India's murderous religion* (London: Granta, 2005); and Kim A. Wagner, *Thugee: Banditry and the British in early nineteenth-century India* (Basingstoke: Palgrave Macmillan, 2007).

21 Masters, *Pilgrim Son*, p. 202.

22 Diana Knight, *Flaubert's Characters: The language of illusion* (Cambridge: Cambridge University Press, 1985), pp. 1–6.

23 E.M. Forster, *Aspects of the Novel* (Harmondsworth: Penguin, 1962; first published 1927), p. 54.

24 See also Forster, *Aspects*, p. 103.

25 Masters, *Pilgrim Son*, p. 146.

26 Masters attributes the same clarity to *Passage to India* but says that this is a shortcoming of the novel since there is no clarity in India.

27 Masters, *Pilgrim Son*, p. 152.

28 Forster, *Aspects*, p. 53.

29 Bryden, 'Moustache', p. 224–5.

30 Bryden, *Unfinished Hero*, pp. 17–18.

31 Bryden, 'Moustache', p. 224.

32 Masters, *Pilgrim Son*, pp. 145–6.

33 Masters, *Pilgrim Son*, p. 146.

34 Philip Mason, *The Men Who Ruled India*, volume 1, *The Founders*, volume 2, *The Guardians* (London: Jonathan Cape, 1953 and 1954), originally published under the pseudonym, Philip Woodruff.

35 Mason, *The Founders*, p. 11.

36 Mason, *The Guardians*, p. 13.

37 Mason, *The Founders*, p. 16. The quotation is from *The Cloud of Unknowing*.

4

The entropy of Englishness: reading empire's absence in the novels of William Golding

Rachael Gilmour

In his 1983 Nobel lecture, William Golding, perhaps a little disingenuously, expressed concern at the international reach of his writing. As an English novelist, he said, one assumed a shared language and history with one's readership – a certain intimacy in which

> a man may think he is addressing a small, distinguished audience, or his family or his friends, perhaps; he is brooding aloud or talking in his sleep. Later he finds that without meaning to he has been addressing a large segment of the world.[1]

Universality is a claim often made for Golding's novels. He is frequently regarded as perhaps one of the last exemplars of the English novel's hubristic claim to speak for 'the human condition', to quote the 1983 Nobel Prize committee, among so many others.[2] Other obvious objections aside, this reputation has done much to obscure the unapologetic, if deeply troubled, Englishness of his writing. Although writing at an allegorical remove from many of his contemporaries, Golding's 'human condition' is very much an English condition, diagnosed amid the historical upheavals of the mid-twentieth century.

Although imperial allusions are to be found in much of his writing, it is the second world war which Golding most frequently cited as a context for the pessimism of his novels, particularly the early ones, and most critics have taken him at his word: postcolonial readings of Golding are thin on the ground, leaving aside his first and most well-known novel, *Lord of the Flies* (1954), with its intertextual relationship to R.M. Ballantyne's imperialist boys' adventure *The Coral Island* (1857). Here, critical responses are fairly polarised – *Lord of the Flies* has been regarded variously as a 'readjusted' articulation of imperialist ideology, or as 'an attack on the imperialist myth'.[3] Neither of these positions seems quite right, yet their divergence testifies to an ambivalence in the novel, and in Golding's writing more generally, which this chapter sets out to explore. Examining two groups of his novels, from two different moments in the empire's demise, we find in both a vision of Englishness indivisible from imperialism. Golding's first three novels, published in the mid-1950s amid the first phase of imperial collapse, allegorise imperialism in a mood of melancholy. The horrors of the war had demonstrated to Golding the parallels between imperialism and fascism, yet his vision of Englishness is so indivisible from the empire that its passing cannot but be mourned. Returning to post-imperial Englishness in the late 1970s and 1980s, in an increasingly comic mode, Golding tentatively explores the flaws and blind spots in a shared imaginative landscape forged through the history of imperialism. In a period characterised by mainstream English nostalgia for a lost empire, his later novels send up the English parochialism, obsession with race and unthinking sense of superiority which are imperialism's legacies. Never immune from the nostalgia they disdain, however, these novels retain a commitment to a historically rooted, culturally homogeneous – and by implication, exclusionary – vision of Englishness and English literary culture.

In the essay 'Fable', based on a lecture given at UCLA and published in his 1965 collection *The Hot Gates*, Golding offered a rationale for the bleak moral vision of *Lord of the Flies*. The book had been conceived, he wrote, both as a universalist fable about the 'diseased', 'fallen nature' of humanity, and as a riposte to the vision of Englishness exemplified in 'the literary convention of boys on an island', developed 'at the height of Victorian smugness, ignorance, and prosperity', and demonstrating the key virtues of imperialist boyhood: pluck, ingenuity, racial superiority, Christian virtue, moral sense.[4] Golding's source for *Lord of the Flies* was 'the great original' of the boys-on-an-island tradition, Ballantyne's *The Coral Island*, with its intrepid boy-heroes, sure of their position in the racial order of things:[5]

> We've got an island all to ourselves. We'll take possession in the name of the King; we'll go and enter the service of its black inhabitants. Of course we'll rise, naturally, to the top of affairs. White men always do in savage countries.[6]

Like so many boys growing up in England at the start of the twentieth century, Golding had been raised on a juvenile literature of islands, sea voyages and tales of colonial encounter. As a child he read G.A. Henty, Rider Haggard and Edgar Rice Burroughs, among a host of others; as John Carey's recent biography reveals, for a long time his favourite novel was George Manville Fenn's *Nat the Naturalist, or a Boy's Adventures in the Eastern Seas,* a once-popular tale of travels in the Malay archipelago, of hunting scientific specimens and of encountering 'treacherous savages'.[7] To the adult Golding, writing in the aftermath of the second world war and in the moment of decolonisation, such writing appeared hopelessly naïve, with its 'paper-cutout goodies and baddies and everything for the best in the best of all possible worlds' (although, as Carey's biography also reveals, this did not prevent him from reading *Nat the Naturalist* to his grandson in the 1980s).[8] Yet Golding's argument, in 'Fable' and elsewhere, is that a key to the English psyche is to be found in the narratives of imperialism and colonial encounter, the island stories which had 'always and for good reason bulked large in the British consciousness'.[9]

'Fable' emphasises *The Coral Island* as a source for *Lord of the Flies,* and underlines the imperialist conceits which the novel endeavours to subvert, but – although Golding's novel had been written amid the early phase of decolonisation, and 'Fable' in the aftermath of Suez – it never directly mentions the empire. Instead, the second world war forms the primary context for *Lord of the Flies.* The English considered themselves immune to the disease of Nazism, wrote Golding, but

> I condemn and detest my country's faults precisely because I am so proud of her many virtues. One of our faults is to believe that evil is somewhere else and inherent in another nation. My book was to say: you think that now the war is over and an evil thing destroyed, you are safe because you are naturally kind and decent. But I know why the thing rose in Germany. I know it could happen in any country. It could happen here.

Beneath the war's sickening horrors recalled in 'Fable', the memory of empire rises up, since imperialism's investment in racial hierarchy is belied by the lessons of the Holocaust. Yet Golding's challenge to English triumphalism at once disavows and reinscribes imperialist logic, by turning to the language of colonialist literature – to 'headhunters' and 'primitive tribes' – in order to register the perversity of European atrocity.

> [T]here were things done during that period from which I still have to avert my mind less I should be physically sick. They were not done

by the headhunters of New Guinea, or by some primitive tribe in the Amazon. They were done, skillfully, coldly, by educated men, doctors, lawyers, by men with a tradition of civilization behind them, to beings of their own kind.[10]

In the end, the lesson of Lord of the Flies turns out to be that of the British empire after all:

> The overall picture was to be the tragic lesson that the English have had to learn over a period of one hundred years; that one lot of people is inherently like any other lot of people; and that the only enemy of man is inside him.[11]

While Golding sets out to undermine imperialist certainties, there is a sense of melancholy in his invocation of the empire's 'tragic', if necessary, ending. Again discussing Lord of the Flies in an interview in the late 1960s, he suggested a parallel between the English preoccupation with race, and the 'boil' of Nazism in Germany. Lord of the Flies had been

> simply what it seemed sensible for me to write after the war, when everybody was thanking God they weren't Nazis. And I'd seen enough and thought enough to realize that every single one of us could be Nazis; you take, for example, this bust-up in England over coloured people – there were coloured people in some suburban part of one of our cities; there really was a bust-up over this ....[12]

Elements of Englishness, in other words – a racial chauvinism, forged in the empire – looked, in certain lights, a lot like Nazism. Yet it is also Englishness that Golding invokes, at the end of this interview, as a bulwark *against* the kind of chaos he explores in Lord of the Flies: that England of the 'ordered society' which, stable and peaceable, alone 'enables us to show our bright side'. If imperialism's role in the English psyche is troubling, then equally it must be seen as part and parcel of England's special status as an island of 'light'; and – in the following, hand-wringing reassertion of imperialist logic – a peculiar and unique emanation of the character of its people:

> I suppose what we are getting round to, finally, is the hopeless admission, in the middle of the twentieth century, that there is a hierarchy of society. The hierarchy of society must be based ultimately on a hierarchy of people. One can say that it is only by desperate

efforts in one or two fortunate, or perhaps unfortunate, places on the surface of the globe that the bright side of man has been enabled to emerge even as dimly as it has, and this must be because of the nature of the people who build that society. Which is against everything we are now taught, is it not?[13]

On the one hand, the lessons of 'Belsen and Hiroshima' surely make investment in notions of racial hierarchy unthinkable; and to look at a waning and morally bankrupt imperialism in the light of the war is to see all too clearly its irrationality and viciousness.[14] On the other, however, Golding cannot help himself lamenting the loss of an old order which, grounded as it is in the certainty of England's special status as the best of humanity, founders not just on the war's lessons, but on the empire's ending. Although himself no son of the empire, Golding's troubled wrestling with these questions is reminiscent of Orwell, who also combines a clear-sighted critique of imperialism's status in the English psyche with a deep investment in a historically rooted, unique and apparently homogeneous Englishness which is not easily separated from its imperialist origins. And, like Orwell, he remains unresolved on this question. Even at the end of his writing career, in the late 1980s, he could satirise the cruelties and absurdities, and expose the parochialism, of imperialist culture: yet it remains at the heart of his conception of Englishness.

Anatomies of imperialism: *Lord of the Flies* (1954), *The Inheritors* (1955), *Pincher Martin* (1956)

Golding's bleak and disturbing first three novels, removed as they are from historical time altogether – into the dystopian near-future, the prehistoric past or the delusions of a single dying mind – invite reading as universal allegories of a brutal and irrational 'human nature' laid bare. Yet, drawing as they do on an English literature of colonial encounter whose triumphalist logic looked so naïve in the war's aftermath, these allegorical studies of violence and cruelty blend the horrors of Nazism with the 'tragic lesson' of the declining empire, deriving not only their narrative form, but also their lexicon of cruelty, from the culture of English imperialism.

By the time Peregrine Worsthorne came to ask what might happen to 'a public school system designed to produce a race of colonial administrators without any colonies to administer?', Golding had already offered, in his first novel *Lord of the Flies*, arguably the bleakest conceivable answer. The boys stranded on his island are products of the English public school system and the imperialist cult of boyhood, still invoking their place at the pinnacle of a global order that lies, far behind them, in ruins.

We've got to have rules and obey them. After all, we're not savages. We're English; and the English are best at everything. So we've got to do the right things.[15]

As Golding is at pains to make clear, the seeds of the chaos and violence which engulf the boys are already contained within the imperialist culture which has forged them. Even their games and jokes revolve around the threat of brutality, or the domination of the weak by the strong.[16] The boys' choice of the motifs of 'savagery' is informed by their reading of colonialist juvenile literature: their spear-carrying, war-paint, war dances, ululation and often random violence, are for imperial boys the signifiers of '"pretending to be a tribe"' – '"I'd like to put on war-paint and be a savage"', says Ralph.[17] Golding repeatedly nods toward Baden-Powell's scouting movement, vital to the training of young imperialists: while the boys are hazy on the specifics of fire-making and shelter-building, they are certainly keen to put their knowledge of pig-sticking to immediate use. And, as Crawford points out, pig-sticking was significant to the scouting ethic – Baden-Powell devoted a book to its practice – because it was considered to provide important training, and the requisite brutalisation, for the pursuit of human quarry in imperial warfare.[18] This is a connection echoed in the violence of the pig hunt in *Lord of the Flies,* with its sexual and sadistic overtones, which moves with terrifying ease from the hunt for pig meat to the hunt for human prey with a 'stick sharpened at both ends'.[19] At the novel's implicitly cannibalistic crescendo, Ralph appears about to share the sow's fate in becoming both sacrifice and feast.

The distillation of violence into the motif of cannibalism recalls *Robinson Crusoe;* yet while for Defoe and his literary successors, cannibalism was the defining feature of 'savagery', in *Lord of the Flies* it becomes the logical endpoint of an imperialism turned in on itself. Similarly, in Golding's second published novel, *The Inheritors,* it is an act of cannibalism which serves as the most powerful emblem of the drive to colonise. The novel is mostly written from the perspective of Lok, one of a small group of Neanderthals, and culminates with their first meeting with early humans, the 'New People' or Cro-Magnons, whose response to the gentle Neanderthals is genocidal. Much as *Lord of the Flies* opposes the naïve imperialist logic of Ballantyne's *Coral Island,* this novel takes as its touchstone H.G. Wells's characterisation of Neanderthal man's 'repulsive strangeness':

Says Sir Harry Johnston, in a survey of the rise of modern man in his *Views and Reviews*: 'The dim racial remembrance of such gorilla-like monsters, with cunning brains, shambling gait, hairy bodies, strong teeth, and possibly cannibalistic tendencies, may be the germ of the ogre in folk-lore.'[20]

Golding reverses Wells's vision to give us Neanderthals who are socially cohesive, matriarchal goddess-worshippers, with a revulsion against killing. The technologically advanced, culturally sophisticated, aggressive 'New People', by contrast, more closely resemble 'monsters', and it is they who are the 'cannibals', killing, roasting and eating the Neanderthal child Liku in the novel's defining, off-stage act of brutality. Colonisation here becomes not a bulwark against cannibalism but the ultimate, catastrophic act of consumption. The novel's many echoes of colonial encounter narratives are reinforced by the emphasis placed on the New People's whiteness.[21] Bernard Bergonzi, for one, places *The Inheritors* as the last in 'a line of descent' of novels analysing 'the colonialist state of mind', from Kipling through Conrad to Burgess's *Malayan Trilogy*.[22]

Similarly, for the Crusoe-esque protagonist of Golding's third novel *Pincher Martin*, cannibalism is a 'superbly direct' expression of the drive to conquer.[23] Christopher 'Pincher' Martin is the sole survivor of a warship sunk in the North Atlantic during the war, washed up on a tiny, barren island which, as the novel's ending reveals, has been the purgatorial illusion of his dying mind all along. A Crusoe stripped of imperialism's illusions of order, and Christianity's consoling optimism, he is a particularly brutal example of what Crawford calls the 'colonizing personality' – cruel, controlling, sexually aggressive, 'born with his mouth and his flies open and both hands out to grab.'[24] Identifying his own drives with those of the cannibal, he muses that

Eating with the mouth was only the gross expression of what was a universal process. You could eat with your cock or with your fists, or with your voice. You could eat with hobnailed boots or buying and selling or marrying and begetting or cuckolding ...[25]

If imperialist drives, in Golding's early novels, are inherently cannibalistic, then equally they are founded on fear. When, in a revealing passage in *Pincher Martin*, like Crusoe naming Friday, Christopher Martin invokes the power of naming as possession, he simultaneously reveals both the colonising bent of his drive to survive and dominate, and the terror of obliteration which underlies it:

I am busy surviving. I am netting down this rock with names and taming it. Some people would be incapable of understanding the importance of that. What is given a name is given a seal, a chain. If this rock tries to adapt me to its ways I will refuse and adapt it to mine. I will impose my routine on it, my geography. I will tie it down with names. If it tries to annihilate me with blotting-paper, then I will speak in here where my words resound and significant sounds assure me of my own identity.[26]

The Inheritors, similarly, emphasises the 'fear' which drives the violence of the New People.[27]

Taken together, Golding's early novels offer an anatomisation of the imperialist psyche rooted in cruelty, fear and the urge to dominate, which despite the universalising power of their allegories, remain deeply and irrefutably English. This is so, not only in terms of the national identity of the protagonists of *Lord of the Flies* and *Pincher Martin*, but also in their invocation of an English literary tradition interwoven with the history of empire. *Robinson Crusoe* is, after all, the founding scene both of Englishness and imperialism in literature, and of the English novel itself.

At the end of *The Inheritors*, Golding installs the first, catastrophic encounter with otherness which is the novel's subject, as the primal scene for the forging of the New People's consciousness. The novel concludes with a dizzying shift to the perspective of Tuami, one of the leaders of the New People, as they sail away from the scene of genocide through the dawn light. Through his eyes, we see the New People transformed by what they have just experienced – 'haunted, bedevilled, full of strange irrational grief', 'as different from the group of bold hunters and magicians who had sailed up the river towards the fall as a soaked feather is from a dry one.'[28] In the boat sits the woman Vivani, nursing the young Neanderthal who has been stolen for her to replace the baby she has recently lost. The presence of the baby, and the people's involuntary responses to him, of 'love' as well as 'fear', contains a hint at the possibility of accommodating, as well as exterminating, otherness.[29] It is the unsettling complexity of these responses which contains, as Tuami recognizes, a 'password', an 'answer' to their own natures.[30] The novel concludes with an echo of the opening of *Heart of Darkness*, recalling Marlow on the imperial Thames, telling how England was once 'one of the dark places of the earth':

Marlan spoke in the silence.
'They live in the darkness under the trees.'

Holding the ivory firmly in his hands, feeling the onset of sleep, Tuami looked at the line of darkness. It was far away and there was plenty of water in between. He peered forward past the sail to see what lay at the other end of the lake, but it was so long, and there was such a flashing from the water that he could not see if the line of darkness had an ending.[31]

While Marlow recalls England's own history as a distant, subaltern outpost of a past empire, The Inheritors installs this primal scene of proto-colonial genocide as the origin of the 'line of darkness' which stretches ahead, past Conrad, to an indeterminate endpoint. And it is this indeterminacy which contributes, perhaps, to the uncertainty and pessimism which characterise Golding's early novels. While exposing the brutality and irrationality of imperialist drives, they abstract them from any specific historical juncture into a timeless, almost elemental force at the heart of English identity. And so, even with the 'tragic lesson' of the waning empire learned, what hope for imagining a post-imperial Englishness?

Post-imperial Englishness and the 'great Caucasian sentence': Darkness Visible (1979) and To The Ends of the Earth: A sea trilogy (1980–89)

As it turned out, there was not long to wait for an answer to that question. By the time Golding published his 'condition of England' novel, Darkness Visible, in 1979, he was addressing the condition of a post-imperial England in decline. Darkness Visible charts the changes wrought between the 1940s and the 1970s in the almost parodic English everytown of Greenfield, on the outskirts of London. The book offers a decidedly bleak take on an England in the grip of entropy, spiralling into postmodern chaos and cultural and economic decline, with an elaborate subtext on the theme of race.[32] The novel's action takes place against a backdrop of increasingly toxic domestic racial politics through the 1960s and 1970s, including escalating racist violence, and a burgeoning National Front. The third-person narrative, meanwhile, moves into and out of the consciousness of a series of white characters – Matty, Sophy, Sim Goodchild – who each, in varying ways, exemplify the English obsession with race. It is Matty, the novel's flawed hero, who encapsulates this when he speaks aloud what the narrator calls 'the great Caucasian sentence' itself: "'They all look the same to me.'"[33]

The 'great Caucasian sentence' dominates aspects of the narrative in Darkness Visible. In the mid-1960s we see the little Stanhope twins, Sophy and

Toni, walking 'primly in the High Street, conscious of difference among the black and yellow and brown'.[34] As an adult, Sophy becomes overtly racist: targeting 'Paki shops' for robbery, constantly aware of racial difference, which inspires in her alternating reactions of amusement, disgust and sexual desire.[35] Toni, meanwhile, becomes 'the perfect terrorist', 'talk[ing] wildly about imperialism'.[36] That, for all her talk of international anti-imperialist struggle, Toni remains Sophy's 'twin', is evident in the Conradian echoes when TV footage shows

> Toni and Gerry and Mansfield and Kurtz, herding their hostages towards the plane; and again, ... there was Toni in Africa, broadcasting, beautiful and remote, the long aria in that silvery voice about freedom and justice.[37]

Sim Goodchild, meanwhile, tries to espouse liberal values, but is haunted by guilty and compulsive, secret Powellite visions of 'swarming':

> Get a Paki, a lad, he'll work. Have to keep an eye on him though.
> *Don't* think that! Race relations.
> All the same they swarm. With the best will in the world I must say they swarm. They are not what I think, they are what I feel. Nobody knows what I feel, thank God.[38]

As the narrative moves from Matty's perspective, to Sophy's, to Sim's, it returns again and again like a tic to the 'black and brown men and women' who increasingly throng the High Street, to the new mosques and temples, the shops whose names register a changing England. Particularly for Sim, representative of the older generation, anxieties about race are bound up with nostalgia for an idealised Greenfield past, with its village green and church – which, as Edwin points out, is a fantasy of a homogeneous culture which was only ever visible 'if you shut one eye.'[39] This mournful nostalgia for a fictional English past is satirised, too, in the pub called the Copper Kettle, with its 'fake eighteenth-century furniture and fake horse brasses.'[40] That these are not neutral or harmless fictions, but instead fantasies of a past built on the order of empire, is clear when the ex-soldier and petty criminal Gerry contrasts the unruliness of a posting in Ulster with past colonial wars in which one's black combatants knew their place:

> Time was, you used not to get wounded or captured. Nigs had a decent sense of who was who. Now you get shot like these poor bastards.[41]

In many ways, Golding's novel sets its face against such nostalgia. Its iconic opening scene, of a firestorm in the Blitz from which the child Matty walks, badly burned but miraculously alive, is set in the firebombed docks east of the Isle of Dogs – an area 'where there had been as many languages spoken as families that lived there'.[42] This remembrance of an ancient, polyglot London fights shy of the homogenising tendencies particularly prevalent, as Gilroy has observed, in invocations of the second world war in mainstream English culture.[43] Yet *Darkness Visible*, condemning as it does so much of contemporary English life, hardly remains immune from the nostalgia it satirises. As S.J. Boyd points out, when Sebastian Pedigree looks out of his schoolroom window to the horizon 'where the suburbs of London were now visible like some sort of growth', this growth 'is in one sense a burgeoning of life', but in another it is 'a tumour ... expanding outwards to engulf the Greenfields of England.'[44] At times, the novel comes close to sounding an elegy for a lost historical and cultural unity which it neither wholly believes in, nor can bring itself entirely to discard. This tone of nostalgic longing is at its keenest in relation to the English culture of letters, symbolised in Sim Goodchild's antiquarian bookshop: 'Here were only the silent books waiting faithfully on their shelves, their words unchanged, century after century from incunabula down to paperbacks.'[45] Lamenting the bookshop's spiralling decay under the pressure of cultural decline, Sim wonders

What to do? How to bring in the Pakis? How the Blacks? What brilliant and unique stroke of the antiquarian bookseller's craft would prise that crowd of white people away from the telly and persuade them to read old books again? How to persuade people of the essential beauty, lovableness, humanity even, of a beautifully bound book?[46]

That the new immigrants are somehow inimical to the culture of letters which the bookshop represents is highlighted as a 'small black boy pressed his face to the plate glass, looked into the impenetrable innards of the shop and ran away.'[47]

The relationship between the 'small black boy' and the bookshop represents a genuine conundrum in *Darkness Visible*, which appears torn between nostalgia for a lost cultural wholeness, and a longing to encompass new forms of Englishness which might themselves constitute a new unity in a postwar, post-imperial England increasingly lost to meaninglessness and 'entropy'. The novel's central symbol of unity, after all, is the Arab schoolboy who, according to the flawed prophet Matty, will herald a new Pentecost, bringing 'the spiritual language into the world and nation shall speak unto nation.'[48] Yet it is the 'great Caucasian sentence' which dominates the novel and defines its limits. As it tackles the plight of the ethnically English, the lives of the new multiculture remain beyond its powers of representation.

> High walls, less penetrable than brick, than steel, walls of adamant lay everywhere between everything and everything. Mouths opened and spoke and nothing came back but an echo from the wall. It was a fact so profound and agonizing, the wonder is there was no concert of screaming from the people who lived with the fact and did not know that they endured it. Only Sim Goodchild in his bookshop whimpered occasionally. The others, Muriel Stanhope, Robert Mellion Stanhope, Sebastian Pedigree, thought it was their individual and uniquely unfair treatment by a world that was different for everyone else. But for the Pakistanis, the men in their sharp suits, the women in gaudy colours with a corner snatched across the face, but for the Blacks, the world *was* different.[49]

The communicative entropy with which the novel wrestles is the malaise of the novel's white characters, condemned to a silence they do not even recognise; yet the most profound silence in *Darkness Visible* surrounds not the white English behind their 'walls of adamant', but the immigrants and their children. The world may well be 'different' for these deindividuated, generic 'Pakistanis' and 'Blacks', but Golding's novel proves itself entirely incapable of telling us *how* this might be so.

On one level, the ceaseless objectification of 'Pakistanis' and 'Blacks', taken together with its tendency to treat immigration as a harbinger of cultural decline, gives *Darkness Visible* a troublingly reactionary air. On another, however, it must be acknowledged that the novel self-consciously dramatises its own failures of perspective, suggesting how it is itself trammelled by the 'great Caucasian sentence'. In this sense, *Darkness Visible* makes an important confession: that it is a post-imperial English novel hampered by its own inadequacy, faced with a new England and a set of new experiences of Englishness seemingly beyond its capacities of representation.

Rites of Passage, published the year after *Darkness Visible* and winning the 1980 Booker Prize, marked Golding's final return to the narratives of sea travel and colonial adventure from which he had set out. Two sequels were published over the next nine years, *Close Quarters* (1987) and *Fire Down Below* (1989), and the three were collected and reissued in 1991 as *To The Ends of the Earth: a sea trilogy.* Highly intertextual, the *Sea Trilogy* draws upon a range of sources including eighteenth- and nineteenth-century nautical travel literature, and novels such as those of Captain Marryatt, of which the narrator Talbot's account is, among other things, a sophisticated pastiche.[50] The title of the *Trilogy* itself recalls Kipling's 'A Song of the English', with its vision of a flawed but ultimately redemptive God-given imperialist Englishness, defined through the motif of the sea journey:

> Fair is our lot – O goodly is our heritage!
> (Humble ye, my people, and be fearful in your mirth!)
> For the Lord our God Most High
> He hath made the deep as dry,
> He hath smote for us a pathway to the ends of all the Earth!

While the popularity of the *Sea Trilogy* may have had some connection to the invocations of imperial memory and romanticisation of empire so pivotal to 'official Englishness', as Simon Gikandi terms it, from the 1970s onward, it bears little outward resemblance to the soft-focus Raj nostalgia of the 1980s.[51] Golding's is a distinctive and ironic take on Kipling's vision: God's favour is little in evidence on this particular sea journey, and he has certainly not 'made the deep as dry'. The poem's final stanza offers an interesting counterpoint to the *Trilogy*, both as a comment on its unreliable narrator, and in its implication that it is in the nature of English imperialism, however flawed, to reveal any kind of 'truth':

> Hear now a song – a song of broken interludes –
> A song of little cunning; of a singer nothing worth.
> Through the naked words and mean
> May ye see the truth between
> As the singer knew and touched it in the ends of all the Earth![52]

The *Trilogy* is set on board an unnamed English ship-of-the-line carrying colonists to Australia towards the end of the Napoleonic Wars, that pivotal moment in imperial mythology which paved the way for the expansion of the Victorian empire. The whole three-volume narrative takes place almost entirely at sea, in the indeterminate space between metropole and colony, making landfall only in the closing pages of the final book. This is a journey which Golding describes tellingly in his Foreword to the *Trilogy* as 'more like a memory than an imagination', recalling how 'the scene of Talbot boarding the ship, the ship herself and her people, emigrants and passengers' came to him so effortlessly.[53] Crossing the globe 'from the south of Old England to the

Antipodes', the 'ship herself and her people' are a microcosm of the English imperial order being exported to the colonies.[54] The narrator, Edmund Talbot, is a vain young man travelling to take up a post in colonial administration, and his fellow passengers comprise every stratum of white colonial society. The ship, meanwhile, is a warship, built of 'English oak', recently returned from the West Indies, which has in its twilight years been pressed into service to transport emigrants to the new colonies in Australia.[55] The travelling world of the ship tells a story of empire as journey rather than destination, while the destinations themselves – India, the Caribbean, even Australia itself – are banished to the margins of the narrative. Indeed Golding's *Sea Trilogy* fits with that tradition of empire writing which treats the rest of the world as a backdrop to England's self-imagining; yet it is far from reproducing the kind of confident and apparently coherent self-image which that tradition implies. As a metaphor for imperialist Englishness, the ship and its passengers reveal a topsy-turvy world of violence, chaos and irrationality, concealed beneath a slowly eroding veneer of order. There is a serious import to Talbot's flippant exclamation, "'Long live illusion, say I. Let us export it to our colonies with all the other benefits of civilization!'"[56] Images of decay, corruption and collapse abound; the passengers, and especially Talbot, struggle to maintain the illusion of order as sexual, social and physical boundaries break down, while the ship itself threatens to disintegrate beneath them.

For all that, imperialist rhetoric is mostly played for laughs in the *Trilogy*. On the very first page of *Rites of Passage*, Talbot's young brothers fantasise about his colonial adventures, drawing promiscuously on their vague knowledge of 'savages' gleefully to imagine his fate in a cannibal's cooking pot:

> Young Lionel performed what he conceived to be an Aborigine's war dance. Young Percy lay on his back and rubbed his belly, meanwhile venting horrid groans to convey the awful results of eating me![57]

Yet their vision of colonial encounter is no more ludicrous than the moment in *Close Quarters* where Talbot announces

> Mark me ..., in this century I am convinced the civilized nations will more and more take over the administration of the backwards parts of the world.[58]

The humour here comes in part from the emptiness of Talbot's rhetoric: he is in the middle of explaining to Charles that he sees his role as a colonial administrator – for 'a few years – a very few years' – merely as a stepping-stone to a career in parliament, thanks to his godfather's control of a rotten borough. With post-imperial hindsight, Golding gently mocks the pretensions of nineteenth-century imperialism to be a beneficent order of global administration of the 'backwards' by the 'civilised'.

There is a serious edge to Golding's satire of empire, however. If the ship is a floating metaphor for all the illusions which make up English imperialism, then it is also haunted by the disavowed realities of the empire which these illusions conceal. Its physical structure sustains increasing damage as the narrative progresses; carrying its familiar Golding cargo of cruelty, irrationality, fear and desire, the disintegrating ship becomes impossible to control, floating directionless and threatening to fall apart completely.[59] This physical damage to the ship originates with some unseen corruption clinging to the hull, sustained in its previous service in the West Indies – although the nature of its involvement, presumably in the protection of the recently abolished British slave trade, is a subject about which Talbot's narrative is silent.[60] When in desperation the crew attempt to remove this corruption with a dragrope, what they dislodge is not the anticipated coral, but a giant and unidentifiable 'thing', which obtrudes in Talbot's rational, Augustan prose in a moment of unparalleled horror. The 'thing' is 'black and streaming', both horrifyingly alien and strangely human, with 'something like the crown of a head pushing up through the weed'. This 'apparition' haunts Talbot, returning to him over and again 'in nightmare':

> My dreaming spirit fears as my waking spirit fears that one night the thing will emerge, bringing with it a load of weed that only half conceals a face.[61]

This unnamed and terrifying 'thing' object may be, perhaps, a fragment of the hull – we never learn for certain. Yet Talbot's anthropomorphised imagining of the 'apparition' as a black figure appearing from the waves, suggests the 'haunting' of the text by the threat of alterity which its imperialist illusions conceal.[62]

When, in *Fire Down Below*, the ship finally makes landfall, the scene that greets the colonists is another kind of illusion: a domesticated Australia which 'seemed to cry us a welcome in our own tongue'.

> So seeing those bald lumps of land and hearing their names, King Island, Flinders Island, Cape Howe, I felt, even if I did not cry, 'England for ever!'[63]

In this final section of the *Trilogy*, Golding satirises the domesticating conventions of English colonialism. The penal settlement of Sydney Cove itself is already adopting a veneer of English respectability, with a party and fireworks in the Residency gardens to honour the king's birthday, and convicts renamed 'government men'. It is, nevertheless, a shabby simulacrum of home – its pub already well established, yet its church still unbuilt – and as Talbot drily observes to Miss Chumley:

> Our only proper road goes out to Paramatta. Our principal view or prospect is thought to be the harbour with its shipping. In the circumstances, I do understand your disinclination for it. What else? Our buildings, as you see, are not metropolitan.[64]

But if Talbot is unimpressed with colonial life, he is almost entirely blind to what lies beyond it: omission and evasion characterise his colonial gaze. Through him, Golding both reproduces and satirises the solipsism of colonialist writing which, as Elleke Boehmer argues, excluded the indigenous in favour of

> a world in which British rule was accepted as part of the order of things: the natives were governed as they should be; the Queen Empress was on her throne; there was no question that her people occupied a central place in history. In this world, it almost goes without saying, British meanings and values were paramount.[65]

Talbot closes his eyes so effectively to Australia that, as an old man looking back on his time there, he is haunted by the sense that, save for 'glimpses', he never actually saw it at all.[66] When, on a drive along the coast from Sydney Cove, Miss Chumley exclaims delightedly, "'Oh, what pretty birds!'", Talbot does not respond, merely instructing her that

> We must go this way. There are savages down *there* and their appearance is not to be borne, the women in particular.[67]

As she comments on "'the strangeness of things – the trees, the plants, the air – Oh, what a butterfly! Look, look! And what flies!'", he can only reply that "'One endures them, that is all, I am afraid.'"[68] Soon after, he is discomforted by the appearance of two aboriginal Australian men, whose apparent indifference and troubling unreadability disrupt his narrative composure:

An aboriginal was following us. He was stark naked and he carried a wicked-looking spear. I shouted at him repeatedly and at last he turned aside and vanished into the scrub. I do not think it was because I shouted. I think he had lost interest in us, as they do after a while.

A wooden seat had been set there for weary travellers and I welcomed it, though an aboriginal stood by it, gazing out over the harbour as if he owned the place! The horse stopped by the seat. The native wandered off without a backward glance.[69]

There is a strand of post-imperial comedy at work in the *Trilogy* which relies for effect on the distance between Talbot's understanding and the reader's. We see, as he does not, the irony in his outrage at the aboriginal man's 'gazing out over the harbour as though he owned the place', since this man does indeed 'own the place', more than Talbot can ever do. At the same time, however, the *Trilogy*'s humour is at a far remove from the despairing irony of Golding's early novels: Talbot is a comic figure, but Golding treats him with sympathy, for all his callow snobbery and often misplaced self-belief. As first-person narrator, it is his consciousness through which the *Trilogy* is filtered, and his set of cultural meanings which define the limits of the narrative, despite its tacitly acknowledging its confinement by 'the great Caucasian sentence'. We might even be tempted to read a measure of Golding himself, in the maturing Talbot's exclamation that:

> I have been brought to see ... the defects of England. I will not subscribe to the furious rubbish of 'My country right or wrong!' But nevertheless, when I search my heart, among all the prejudices of my nature and upbringing, among all the new ideas, the acceptance of necessary change, ... the deepest note of my heart-strings sounds now as it will to my dying day – 'England for ever!'[70]

At the very end of *Fire Down Below*, Talbot completes his journal as a legacy for his descendants, turning the narrative into family history, and asserting his intimate connection to his future readers, five generations hence. Yet as Talbot's story reaches its conclusion – fulfilling, as he insists his readers require, the conventions of colonial romance – there remains a comic gap between his perspective and those of his 'unborn readers':

> Yet I divine in my unborn readers an unease. Something is missing, is it not? The bishop could not consent to our journeying from India to England while still unmarried. It would be an extremely bad example

to set in a part of the world only too open to licence of every kind!
He himself very cordially offered to perform the ceremony! So, my
dear readers may rest contentedly assured: there did come a day
when I leapt ashore in India from a pinnacle. A 'young person' under
a rosy parasol stood, as it might be, twenty yards away. Valuable
Janet was behind her and a group of dark servants. ... I swept off my
hat – she broke into a run – and your great-great-great-great-great-
grandmother fairly sprang into my arms![71]

Coming from Talbot, it is hard to miss the hypocrisy of imperialist sexual
codes which suggest that it is *Indian* impropriety which is to be guarded
against by his swift marriage to Miss Chumley – reminding us that the 'part
of the world only too open to licence of every kind' is the imperial ship itself.
His post-imperial great-great-great-great-great-grandchildren may also be
inclined to notice, unlike Talbot, the jarring presence of the 'group of dark
servants' in the background.

The *Trilogy*, and particularly the final novel *Fire Down Below*, fits with a
particular strand of later twentieth-century English comic writing sending
up the pretensions and inconsistencies of imperialism, and Golding's vision
is perhaps more clear-sighted, not to mention jaundiced, than many.[72]
Nevertheless, while acknowledging the evasions and illusions which constitute
imperialist thought, Golding's *Trilogy* is oddly reticent – particularly given
the violence of his earlier novels – on the brutality of empire itself. And
one effect of this reticence is to more easily assert the history of empire as
the heart of the kind of collective memory which itself, in Golding's vision,
constitutes Englishness. In this sense, the *Trilogy*'s conclusion works to 'keep
it in the family' all too clearly.

In an essay from *The Hot Gates* entitled 'In My Ark', originally published
in 1960, Golding turned to the originary scene of imperialism in English
literature, the encounter with the single footprint in the sand, in order
to register both the genealogical connection, and the unbridgeable divide,
between the certainties of an old order and the chaos of the present. The
Englishman stands on the shore, he writes,

not as our Victorian fathers stood, lassoing phenomena with Latin
names, listing, docketing and systematizing. Belsen and Hiroshima
have gone some way towards teaching us humility. We would take
help and a clue from anywhere we could. It is not the complete
specimen for the collector's cabinet that excites us. It is the fragment,
the hint. ... We stand among the flotsam, the odd shoes and tins,

hot-water bottles and skulls of sheep or deer. We know nothing. We look daily at the appalling mystery of plain stuff. We stand where any upright food-gatherer has stood, on the edge of our own unconscious, and hope, perhaps, for the terror and excitement of the print of a single foot.[73]

In place of the Victorian faith in systematisation, the surety of 'the collector's cabinet', all that is left is the 'fragment'. On one level, Golding's longing to return to the moment of encounter, to see afresh the single footprint in the sand, represents a yearning for an old imperial order which is forever lost. Yet, robbed of such consoling fictions, he is also able to dream of a way to experience this moment in all its 'terror and excitement', to face alterity without seeking to reduce it into sameness. Thirty years later, the *Sea Trilogy* turns the generational divide into post-imperial comedy, yet it demonstrates how far the English novel continues to fail the test of the footprint in the sand.

Notes

My thanks to all my fellow contributors – particularly to Suzanne Hobson, Huw Marsh, Patrick Parrinder, Michael Ross and Bill Schwarz – for their insightful comments on this chapter.

1 William Golding, 'Nobel Prize Lecture' [1983] in James R. Baker (ed.), *Critical Essays on William Golding* (Boston: Hall & Co., 1988), p. 152.

2 The dominant theme in the critical literature devoted to Golding has been, certainly until recently, the alleged timeless universality of his novels. See for example Samuel Hynes, 'William Golding's *Lord of the Flies*' in Baker, *Critical Essays*, pp. 13–21; Virginia Tiger, 'William Golding's "wooden world": religious rites in *Rites of Passage*' also in Baker, *Critical Essays*, pp. 135–49. For an alternate perspective see Paul Crawford, *Politics and History in William Golding: The world turned upside down* (Columbia: University of Missouri Press, 2002).

3 Alan Sinfield, *Literature, Politics and Culture in Postwar Britain*, 2nd edn (London: Continuum, 2004), p. 160; Frédérick Regard, '"Nothing more to say": William Golding's *Egyptian Journal* and the fate of the orientalist', *Études Anglaises* 58: 2 (2005), p. 141.

4 William Golding, 'Fable' [1962] in Golding, *The Hot Gates* (London: Faber, 1965), pp. 87–8. On the 'boys on an island' tradition see for example Joseph Bristow, *Empire Boys: Adventure in a man's world* (London: Harper Collins, 1991).

5 Golding, 'Fable', p. 88. Golding's novel refers repeatedly to Ballantyne's ('"Jolly good show. Like the *Coral Island*"', says the naval officer at the end

of the novel, with dreadful irony), echoes many of its central conceits, and two of its central characters – Jack and Ralph – are named after Ballantyne's protagonists.

6   R.M. Ballantyne, *The Coral Island* [1857] (Ware: Wordsworth Editions, 1993), p. 16.

7   John Carey, *William Golding: The man who wrote 'Lord of the Flies'* (London: Faber, 2009), pp. 27–8, 36; William Golding, 'Astronaut by gaslight' [1961] in *The Hot Gates*, p. 111; George Manville Fenn, *Nat the Naturalist, or a boy's adventures in the eastern seas* (London: Blackie, 1882).

8   William Golding, 'A moving target' [1976] in Golding, *A Moving Target* (New York: Farrar, Strauss, Giroux, 1982), p. 163; Carey, *William Golding*, p. 28. See also for example James R. Baker, 'Why it's no go' in Baker, *Critical Essays*, p. 23.

9   Golding, 'A moving target', p. 163.

10 Golding, 'Fable', pp. 86–7.

11 Golding, 'Fable', p. 89.

12 William Golding, quoted in Jack Biles, *Talk: Conversations with William Golding* (New York: Harcourt Brace Jovanovich, 1970), pp. 3–4.

13 Golding, quoted in Biles, *Talk*, pp. 44–5.

14 William Golding, 'In my ark' [1960] in *The Hot Gates*, p. 105.

15 William Golding, *Lord of the Flies* (London: Faber, 1970), p. 47. See also pp. 99, 188–9, 191, 199.

16 See for example *Lord of the Flies*, pp. 12, 30, 36–7. For a perceptive analysis of imperialism in *Lord of the Flies*, see Minnie Singh, 'The government of boys: Golding's *Lord of the Flies* and Ballantyne's *Coral Island*', *Children's Literature* 25 (1997), pp. 205–13.

17 Golding, *Lord of the Flies*, pp. 163, 156.

18 Crawford, *Politics and History in William Golding*, p. 55, Robert Baden-Powell, *Pig-Sticking or Hog-Hunting: A complete account for sportsmen and others* (London: Jenkins, 1924).

19 Golding, *Lord of the Flies*, p. 219.

20 H.G. Wells, *Outline of History*. Epigraph to William Golding, *The Inheritors* [1955] (London: Faber, 1961). When not musing on the nature of Neanderthal man, Johnston was best-known as one of the leading Victorian authorities on and agitators for the colonisation of Africa, having spent his career there as a colonial administrator, geographer, explorer and anthropologist.

21 Golding, *Inheritors*, pp. 138–9; 194.

22 Bernard Bergonzi, *Situation of the Novel*, 2nd edn (London: Macmillan, 1979), p. 179.

23 William Golding, *Pincher Martin* [1956] (London: Faber, 1962), p. 88.

24 Crawford, *Politics and History in William Golding*, p. 85; Golding, *Pincher Martin*, p. 120.

25 Golding, *Pincher Martin*, p. 88.

26 Golding, *Pincher Martin*, pp. 86–7.

27 See for example Golding, *Inheritors*, p. 209.

28 Golding, *Inheritors*, pp. 225, 231.

29 Golding, *Inheritors*, p. 231.

30 Golding, *Inheritors*, p. 233.

31 Golding, *Inheritors*, p. 233.

32 It is worth noting here that most critics have seen this simply as part and parcel of Golding's rendering of a 'modern urban wasteland'. See for example Don Crompton, 'Darkness Visible', in Baker, *Critical Essays*, p. 113.

33 William Golding, *Darkness Visible* [1979] (London: Faber, 1980), p. 67.

34 Golding, *Darkness Visible*, p. 118.

35 Golding, *Darkness Visible*, p. 158.

36 Golding, *Darkness Visible*, pp. 140, 253.

37 Golding, *Darkness Visible*, p. 261.

38 Golding, *Darkness Visible*, p. 218.

39 Golding, *Darkness Visible*, p. 203.

40 Golding, *Darkness Visible*, p. 168.

41 Golding, *Darkness Visible*, p. 153.

42 Golding, *Darkness Visible*, p. 9.

43 Paul Gilroy, *After Empire: Melancholia or convivial culture?* (London: Routledge, 2004), pp. 95–6.

44 Golding, *Darkness Visible*, p. 32; S.J. Boyd, *The Novels of William Golding*, revised edn (Hemel Hempstead: Harvester Wheatsheaf, 1990), p. 126.

45 Golding, *Darkness Visible*, p. 217.

46 Golding, *Darkness Visible*, p. 193.

47 Golding, *Darkness Visible*, p. 201.

48 Golding, *Darkness Visible*, p. 239.

49 Golding, *Darkness Visible*, p. 83.

50 See for example Tiger, 'Golding's "wooden world"', pp. 138–40.

51 Simon Gikandi, *Maps of Englishness: Writing identity in the culture of colonialism* (New York: Columbia University Press, 1996), p. 21.

52 Rudyard Kipling, 'A Song of the English', in Rudyard Kipling, *A Song of the English* (London: Hodder and Stoughton, 1912).

53 William Golding, 'Foreword', *To The Ends of the Earth: A sea trilogy* (London: Faber, 1991), p. viii.

54 William Golding, *Rites of Passage*, in *To The Ends of the Earth: A sea trilogy*, p. 3.

55 Golding, *Rites of Passage*, p. 196.

56 Golding, *Rites of Passage*, p. 108.

57 Golding, *Rites of Passage*, p. 3.

58 William Golding, *Close Quarters*, in *To The Ends of the Earth: A sea trilogy*, p. 252.

59 For a more detailed reading of the significance of the ship's disintegration see Tamas Benyei, *Acts of Attention: Figure and narrative in postwar British novels* (Frankfurt: Peter Lang, 1999), p. 167.

60 Golding, *Close Quarters*, p. 456.

61 Golding, *Close Quarters*, p. 464.

62 We might also argue that Talbot's vision carries echoes of more specific horrors which his fantasies of imperial beneficence obscure – memories, for example, of the infamous Zong massacre of 1781, in which 122 African slaves were thrown overboard en route to Jamaica.

63 William Golding, *Fire Down Below*, in *To The Ends of the Earth: A sea trilogy*, p. 716.

64 Golding, *Fire Down Below*, p. 746.

65 Elleke Boehmer, *Colonial and Postcolonial Literature: Migrant metaphors*, 2nd edn (Oxford: Oxford University Press, 2005), pp. 62–3.

66 Golding, *Fire Down Below*, p. 744.

67 Golding, *Fire Down Below*, p. 746.

68 Golding, *Fire Down Below*, p. 748.

69 Golding, *Fire Down Below*, p. 752.

70 Golding, *Fire Down Below*, p. 716.

71 Golding, *Fire Down Below*, pp. 758–9.

72 We might think, for example, of another Booker winner, J.G. Farrell's *The Siege of Krishnapur* (London: Weidenfeld and Nicolson, 1973). Thanks to Huw Marsh for pointing out this connection.

73 Golding, 'In my ark', p. 105.

5

The empire of romance:
love in a postcolonial climate

Deborah Philips

The rose of romance, the internationally recognised logo of the Mills &
Boon publishing house, might appear to be a very English rose, but its sales
are global and its readership multinational. In 1999, the official historian of
the company could write: 'Ninety years after its founding, Mills & Boon
is one of only two British publishers to have become a household name in
Britain and throughout the Commonwealth ... [it is] a worldwide publishing
empire.'[1] In 2008, it was estimated that Mills & Boon titles sold 200 million
books worldwide and the next year the company announced a search for new
authors in India.[2]

While 'love' is regularly claimed by the writers and editors of Mills
& Boon to be a universal, eternal concept – immune from the limitations
of geography and history – the forms and sites of romance visibly shift in
different contexts. The postwar heroine is a different creature from the
pre-war period and, indeed, from current incarnations, while the settings
for romance have now become rather different from those of 1945. Since
Mills & Boon began publishing, the 'exotic' romance had always been an
identifiable sub-genre of romance fiction, familiar to readers if not always
to publishers or to critics. The fantasy of true love has always involved a
measure of international travel, and Mills & Boon heroines have found their
heroes across the world. The current Mills & Boon list includes a subgenre of
the romance novel; the 'Modern' romance (a generic label in the catalogue)
promises, according to their website: 'Dramatic, contemporary, emotionally
intense love stories that take readers around the world ... romance set
against a backdrop of luxury, wealth and international locations.'[3] The
international locations for the romance novel in the aftermath of the second
world war, however, tend not to be a 'backdrop of luxury [and] wealth', but

rather the outposts of what had once been the British empire. The Mills & Boon view of the globe was expressed for most of the 1950s with a strap-line on the dust jackets asking: 'Are you reading this book in some place far away from London – in New Zealand or Australia, in South Africa or Canada or in Singapore?'

Both readers and writers of the popular romance were necessarily implicated in the transition from empire to Commonwealth in the aftermath of the second world war; many lived and worked in what had become the former British colonies and the Commonwealth countries represented a significant market for romance fiction. These novels were read by thousands throughout Britain and across the world, and can be understood as a constituent element in a postwar colonial discourse, a discourse which naturalised, for women readers, a continuing belief in England as the 'mother country'.

The 'exotic' romance could find a market among British settlers in the new Commonwealth, and also offered a form of armchair tourism for British readers dispirited by postwar rationing. The codification of the romance genre coincides with a postwar sensibility; Mills & Boon had established its reputation as a romance publisher during the war and it is the postwar period which saw 'Mills & Boon' developed as a brand. The Mills & Boon product became standardised, the brown bindings of the books were identical and strict editorial control ensured a consistency of length, of plot and of the moral rectitude of the story line. The romance novel is, necessarily, because of the strict conventions of its genre, a conservative form, but British authors could not remain immune to the shifts both in gender relations and in the international landscape which had followed two world wars. The world in which romance fiction was marketed, written and read had changed, and so too had the map of romance, and the hero's and heroine's place within it.[4]

British women had been active participants in the second world war, many working in fields which had previously only been open to men. The active citizen heroine, with career aspirations, is a standard feature of the postwar Mills & Boon novel.[5] McAleer has noted that these newly independent heroines are presented with opportunities for work and travel: 'A distinctive change in the Mills & Boon heroines in the 1950s is evident in the new emphasis on leaving home and family for a "career", often in a foreign setting.'[6] These 'foreign settings' had, before the war, been shaped by the fact of the British empire. In the nineteenth-century novel, the USA, South Africa, Australia and New Zealand had offered a narrative solution for unresolved contradictions and unassimilable characters who would neatly be displaced 'overseas'; Mills & Boon authors readily adopted the same convention.

According to Boots lending library, the hero of the postwar romance novel 'usually comes from a good family but owing to some misunderstanding has cut himself off from society to brood about in the outposts of the Empire'.[7] As the colonies of the British empire were becoming the newly independent states and territories of the Commonwealth, however, 'the outposts of the Empire' were no longer apparently straightforwardly distant places to send the wayward sons and daughters of 'good families'. The fictional construction of Englishness and its place in the world could no longer rely on England's status as the mother country of an empire.

jay dixon has described the categories within the romance genre from the beginnings of Mills & Boon, and identifies:

> the country novel, the city novel and the exotic novel. The first two of these are set in England, in the countryside or in a large town (usually London) respectively; the latter is set abroad, generally in a country belonging to the British Empire.[8]

In the 'exotic novel' there is a regular slippage between the terms 'Empire' and 'Commonwealth', which are frequently used interchangeably. Mills & Boon romances in the postwar decades were carried out under the skies of South Africa, Rhodesia, Malaya, the South Seas, Nigeria, Egypt, Tunisia, Morocco, New Zealand, Canada and Australia. The exoticism of these settings is largely generic rather than geographically specific: the location was not of particular importance to the authors themselves (many had never set foot in the country in which their fiction was set) or to the publishers, although Mills & Boon editors were concerned that their authors should get their facts right.[9] And while 'abroad' as a location for a romance narrative had once meant a region of empire, after 1945 some acknowledgement had to be made of the newly independent states of the Commonwealth; the 'foreign' was no longer a space in which the Englishman and woman could presume ascendancy.

A 1954 English school textbook tells 'The Story of the British Commonwealth and Empire', in which it is reluctantly conceded that:

> Great Britain is no longer the most powerful and the wealthiest country in the world as it was in our heyday. ... There is in these days a clearer recognition of the part a concerted economic policy can play in cementing the bonds between Great Britain and her partners in the Colonial Empire through the development of their joint resources in the interest of both.[10]

It is this 'Colonial Empire' which is the stage for the Mills & Boon exotic romance of the postwar world, a stage in which the hero and heroine have to engage with the problem of how to 'cement' these bonds in the new circumstances of the Commonwealth. The ideological construction of the new Commonwealth connected in some respects with the modernity and femininity of the romance heroine. The young and newly married Queen Elizabeth, who took up her career as monarch in 1952, was then of an age with the Mills & Boon heroine; she represented an embodiment of a modern womanliness, romance and a postwar optimism. As queen, Elizabeth was also the ceremonial leader of the Commonwealth. A broadcast, made from Cape Town to the British Commonwealth in 1948, however, suggests that the distinction between empire and Commonwealth was not yet one which was easily made. In her speech the young princess dedicated her life to 'the service of our great imperial family to which we all belong'.[11] The Commonwealth, like the young queen who headed it, seemed to stand for a resolution between an imperial past and a postwar modernity. As Christine Geraghty has put it: 'The post-war Commonwealth was strange and familiar, built out of the British Empire but with a new and more modern emphasis on self-government and multi-racial co-operation.'[12] In the figure of Queen Elizabeth, the modernity of the new Commonwealth was coupled with the trappings of tradition, secured by her royal status.[13] With a young woman as its figurehead, the Commonwealth was also feminised; the heroines of the postcolonial romance represent a parallel mythical resolution of modern femininity with the traditional values of the old 'mother country'.

There is a structural feature of these 'foreign romance novels' of this period in which the heroine arrives by train, ship or plane at a far-flung corner of the world, which is simultaneously familiar and strange. Her destination is known to her as a place of the imperial past, where a father, brother or uncle has been working on some business loosely connected to the 'British Empire'; but it is also represented as a space of unknown foreign adventure. The heroine is a personification of an ideal English femininity; she is frequently described as having the looks of an English rose, and her name is always emphatically English; Priscilla, Vanessa, Sandra, Sylvia, and often, with its royal associations, Elizabeth.[14]

As libraries purchased only a limited number of titles from a single author in any one season, Mills & Boon writers in this period often wrote under pseudonyms, using a range of pen-names in order to increase their output. Among the most prolific of the Mills & Boon 'Colonial' authors was Lilian Warren, herself based in South Africa, who wrote under three pseudonyms: Rosalind Brett, Kathryn Blair and Celine Conway.[15] The Rosalind Brett novels have been described by a current Mills & Boon author, Charlotte Lamb, in terms which demonstrate the familiar characteristics of the heroine and hero:

a hesitant, frightfully sensitive, not to say neurotic English girl and a hero who is an Empire building Englishman with a pipe in his mouth and a belief that the little woman should be protected and stay in the kitchen.[16]

This is not quite fair to Warren, whose heroines are always intrepid travellers, and who are clearly aware, as are their heroes, that empire building is not without its problems and that the Commonwealth itself also presented new challenges. The 1950 Kathryn Blair novel, *The House at Tegwani*, was set in South Africa. For Mills & Boon writers and readers of the 1950s, South Africa was not the country of apartheid, but rather – as the cover indicated – 'the colourful, romantic background of South Africa'. South Africa may have been presented as exotically 'colourful' to British readers of Mills & Boon, yet the writers were notably reticent on the subject of colour. Mills & Boon had a large market in South Africa, and the editors were careful of white South African sensibilities. A mixed race romance could not be countenanced in novels set in South Africa nor, indeed, anywhere else in the Mills & Boon world. As one editor expressed it: 'we have to think of our South African market ... and I don't believe they'd stand for it.'[17] The heroes and heroines of these novels were uncompromisingly white, as was their social world. Alan Paton's excoriating account of life in South Africa, *Cry the Beloved Country*, which had been published in 1948 (and filmed in 1951), made the iniquities of apartheid starkly apparent to a wide readership. Even so, the political context of contemporary South Africa was firmly positioned beyond the boundaries of what the romantic novel in the postwar world could discuss.

The heroine of *The House at Tegwani*, Sandra, is a motherless daughter who travels to 'romantic' South Africa in search of her father. We are told that she came to South Africa 'two years ago', which makes her date of arrival 1948, the year of the election of the National Party. The novel's setting is the 'easygoing, fair sized but clannish town of Pietsburg'; for Sandra and her father, the only clans which count are those of the white population. Sandra's father is a public schoolmaster, and his pupils white South Africans. While Sandra is an avowedly modern heroine, she runs her household in line with the expectations of pre-war upper-class England, able to afford to employ a houseful of servants, for as the narrator observes: 'everyone kept a coloured girl and most professional men ran to two and a houseboy.'[18] Throughout the story there is a clear nostalgia for a past England; South Africa offers the heroine (and readers) a fantasy of an upper-class English world as it was before the war, relocated to a warmer climate.

The few black characters whom Sandra does encounter are all servants, and these are, without exception, described as 'cheerful' and loyal to their white employers. A 'housegirl' is 'a cheerful worker, honest, and very much attached to young missus'; the 'houseboy', John, is 'a small Basuto boy of immense strength and enthusiasm, [who] never ceased to smile'. There is, too, a Boer manservant who is presented as an old and loyal family retainer, rather than a member of the group whom Eric Hobsbawm has described as the 'architects of the Apartheid regime of 1948'.[19] Sandra's task is to train all these 'foreign' domestic workers into British standards of cleanliness and into appropriate behaviour and so rescue them from their own 'primitive' (a term which persistently recurs) natures. Here the narrator describes, with a knowing authority, the difference between black and white South African households:

> In her own abode a native will hoard rags and bottles, but the house in which she works must be uncluttered and spotless ... [Sandra liked] her maid's amiable bronze plumpness in starched blue cotton, white cap and apron.[20]

The heroine insists that in her house British customs and timetables are to be adhered to, and so, 'fairy cakes appear for elevenses and tea'. The colonialisation of the South African people moves here onto the domestic front, and becomes the white woman's burden.

The hero of the novel is a white South African who is represented as a man of the African land. He is 'hardened from contact with the primitive and untamed' and 'owns a citrus farm – he has thousands of acres.'[21] Like the heroine, he simultaneously represents conservative English values and modernity; he is a gentleman farmer, but is bringing new farming methods to South Africa. He is a man of the soil, but reassuringly reveals himself to be of English parentage, and to have been a student at Cambridge, where he acquired a taste for poetry. Despite this education, the hero is described as having a 'primitive masculinity' which must be 'tamed' and domesticated; this is achieved, as it is with the African servants, through the heroine's love and patience. It is thus the spheres of the feminine and the domestic which are shown to sustain English values and to bring 'civilisation' to the new South Africa. The hero and heroine together are seen as the benign and progressive future for South Africa. African land was not, as Paton's novel vividly demonstrated, an uncontested space, but it appears so in these novels; any political resistance to apartheid or to white settlement is firmly absent. One Mills & Boon author, Alex Stuart, was taken to task for writing a sympathetic anti-apartheid character and was told by the publisher: 'We feel it undesirable that the heroine's father should have written this book which brings him into conflict with South Africa. ... What worries us is the colour question.'[22]

The 'abodes' of the black South Africans themselves, their 'native dwellings', are kept remote and at a safe distance from Sandra and from the small white settler town of Pietsburg. This geographical distance would conform to the segregated racial areas which had become ever more rigid after the 1948 election, although these developments are never mentioned. The 'native shacks' instead become picturesque elements in an exoticised and distant South African landscape:

> Shrub-crusted veld, with here and there a few cattle gathered at a waterhole or a huddle of native shacks in the midst of which a fire burned and a hanging pot boiled, so that steam merged with the twig smoke and rose into the richly coloured evening sky.[23]

Here, the 'natives' are rendered invisible, their own domestic lives literally turned into smoke.

Moon Over Africa (1955) is a later novel in which an Englishwoman, who shares her name, Elizabeth, with the new British queen, comes to South Africa, like Sandra, to join an expatriate father. Cape Town is described in the glowing terms of a travel brochure: 'one of the loveliest cities in the world ... with the unbelievably blue sea piling on to the golden beaches, awakes a feeling of breathless astonishment in the heart of every traveller.'[24] Despite its un-English climate and scenery, the region reassuringly displays some of the familiar flora found in England, flourishing happily alongside more exotic blooms: 'the sight of hollyhocks and dahlias – flowers which she had believed belonged exclusively to England – blooming side by side with bougainvillea and hibiscus.'[25] The heroine – like the flowers – can, it is suggested, also be successfully transplanted from her English roots and adapt to South Africa. The hero's capacious garden has 'a tiny secluded corner where some of the choicest roses that bloom in English rose-gardens opened velvet petals beneath the exciting kiss of the sun'.[26] The South African landscape, it is also implied here, will come to embrace Englishness and English values and could become a utopian England in a foreign land.

Elizabeth's father, like Sandra's, is a professional man who had moved to the 'colonies' to make his fortune, and has failed. Elizabeth's idea of Africa has been shaped by her father's speculative travels across the continent in search of profit: 'There must be magic in Africa, she thought, even in Central Africa ... he wrote to her about the Gold Coast ... the Belgian Congo ... and Northern Rhodesia ... finally he had taken root on a little fruit farm ... investing unsuccessfully in a citrus farm.'[27] The Africa of the old empire had promised the English wealth and riches which the new Commonwealth could not deliver. But Africa has dangers. As a doctor involved in 'medical missions [in] disease ridden corners of the globe', her father is fading fast because he has contracted a germ from 'disease ridden' Central Africa.[28] Medicine has proved too dangerous for him so he has turned to fruit farming. Nonetheless, like Sandra's father, he dies; the older generation cannot survive the rigours of the new Africa, and it is left to the next generation to reinvent British values overseas.

The tension between Britain and white South African settlers is embodied in the hero, who has business interests in Britain, but who is also rooted in the South African land. His name is a combination of English uprightness and Dutch Boer heritage: Nigel Van Kane. His house is 'old Cape Dutch', but its furnishings speak of aristocratic English tastes; a rosewood clock, curtains of 'highly glazed chintz, little pink rosebuds and delicate blue harebells', a 'handsome carved oak staircase'. The narrative is at pains to emphasise that Nigel's Dutch ancestry is more European than Boer. A Dutch landscape painting hanging in his house evokes the journey of the Pilgrim Fathers, as if to suggest that white travellers have been triumphant in South Africa, as they had once been in America:

> a placid, smiling landscape of the Holland the early settlers knew – and must often have recalled with pangs of homesickness when they were striving to eke out an existence in the strange, new land that was Africa.[29]

Africa remains, in the second half of the twentieth century, a 'dark continent' open to colonial exploration, mysterious and dangerous, as the hero explains to the naïve heroine: 'the vast continent was still a map that was only half unfurled, and much of it still lay well below the level of occidental thought and reasoning.'[30]

Africans themselves are present (once again) in the narrative only as servants. Like the African landscape, they are both exotically beautiful and potentially threatening. The manservant 'Muemba' is described as 'a magnificent specimen, so black that he appeared as if he was polished ... he had large gold rings in his ears, a little ivory tusk through his nose.'[31] He appears to have accepted English domesticity and so represents no threat: 'he wore shorts and a tunic that were always superbly laundered', he is 'soft footed', and he knows how to be 'invisible and discreet' and to call his employer 'Baas'. Nonetheless, there is a disquieting sense throughout the novel that black South Africa may not be so easily silenced or integrated into the hero and heroine's 'civilised' values, for 'Muemba cast his shadow upon the cool, cream-coloured walls'.[32]

If the South Africa of the early 1950s could be presented as reassuringly white, and native Africans were apparently kept safely at bay, by the 1960s, it had become a more uneasy setting for a British heroine. South Africa continued to represent an important market for Mills & Boon – and the company was anxious not to alienate its readers. Alan Boon, managing editor of Mills & Boon, described a concern among editors of women's magazines of the period – Mills & Boon novels were often sold as magazine serialisations – that politics might intrude upon romance:

> I find there is a certain nervousness in some serial quarters about using the African background. I think some of the editors may be worried that there might be political trouble just as they are running the serial. In my view, it would not matter if that did occur.[33]

One of the Mills & Boon stable of authors, Wynne May, was advised by Alan Boon to set her novels somewhere other than South Africa. She cheerfully moved her locations to other African settings, interchangeable in their exoticism and foreignness: 'I went from island to island backgrounds. Then, I used Namibia, Kenya, Mombasa and Zanzibar.'[34]

Anne Vinton's 1957 novel The Hospital in Bulwambo is set in West Africa. This was the first Mills & Boon novel to be taken up by the Canadian publishers, Harlequin, and was to set the precedent for an exchange of medical romances between Britain and the North American publishers.[35] Anne Vinton had herself worked as a nurse in West Africa (and in the Sudan), and she does demonstrate an uncomfortable awareness of white privilege. The 'natives', as black characters nonetheless continue to be named, are more present here than in the earlier romances, and their roles do extend beyond those of servants. The city where the heroine first arrives, Lagos, is described as:

> a study in contradictions. ... Across the way was an elegant penthouse with balconies ... a roof garden with striped awnings. ... Immediately

below this scene of opulence and comfort a cluster of natives were fishing edible refuse out of the gutters.[36]

Like *Moon Over Africa,* in which the heroine's father contracts a mysterious, fatal disease, the narrative is dominated by the strangeness and dangers of West Africa. The descriptions of the perils of the region in this and other African romance novels are echoed in the account of a 1951 geography textbook:

> Few white settlers have made their homes in West Africa; for many years malaria, yellow fever, sleeping sickness and other tropical diseases caused much ill-health and even loss of life, and Nigeria and other parts were sometimes spoken of as the 'white man's grave'.[37]

The narrative puts its heroine, Sylvia, through most of these trials; those which she does not directly experience herself she encounters in her role as a doctor. Sylvia suffers from malaria, comes close to contracting leprosy, and nurses the doctor hero through a venomous snake bite. Despite its dangers, Africa represents an attractive challenge to Sylvia; depressed by austerity Britain, and bruised by a broken relationship, it holds out an appealing exoticism far removed from the gloom of the rationing, the 'make do and mend' ethos of postwar London and the betrayals of unmanly men. Sylvia, like many of the heroines of these novels, is a newly qualified and highly trained young woman, but the lure of the foreign appeals more than the rebuilding of England.

Sylvia does not discriminate between the different regions or cities of Africa, all of which are interchangeable to her in their mystery and strangeness (as they were for the writer Wynne May): 'There were hospitals in places with magic names like Aden, Adis Ababa, Buwambo.'[38] Sylvia's family have had some direct experience of Africa; her brother had undertaken 'tours of duty' there (of what remains obscure) – until, like many a male relation in these fictions, he fatally succumbs to 'an obscure fever'. Mervyn's reports of his travels encapsulate an idea of Africa which combines both wonder and fear:

> Her brother, Mervyn, had spent a good deal of time on the African continent and he used to say: 'God put all the torments of hell into latitude nought, and nine-tenths of those are concentrated in Africa. But he put something indefinably grand there too.'[39]

Africa thus represents a mystique and excitement for the postwar new woman, in contrast to the dullness of 'home'. Even its potential dangers are an attraction; the advertisement which draws Sylvia to the fictional 'Buwambo' reads: 'West African Bush hospital, ninety miles from the nearest township. Plagues, wild life and atrocious climate thrown in. Only the genuinely interested please apply.'[40] Throughout the plot there is a recurrent suggestion that West Africa is dangerous, particularly so for a white woman. Refuge and protection from danger are however to be found in the space of the hospital: 'the neat hospital compound beyond a screen of flowering loquats, and invisible to the rest of the village'.[41] The hospital – a place where life and death dramas are enacted, and a space where the vulnerable need the expertise of trained medical professionals – became so popular a setting for romance novels as to constitute a genre in its own right. In the context of the 'exotic' romance, it becomes a paradigm for an Africa in need of education and technological enlightenment, and it is British expertise which is shown to provide it.

The British hero and heroine are inevitably the key professional authorities in the running of the hospital; all the senior employees are clearly indicated as white, but the wards are also staffed by qualified Nigerian nurses and doctors. The white ward sister proudly describes her staff as: 'All colours you know – tawny to black'.[42] If black Africans may now themselves be qualified and trained, the novel makes it clear that they still need to remain deferential to their white associates, who behave as their masters rather than their colleagues. The nurses may be Nigerian, but the hospital's expectation is that their professional skills should be entirely modelled on Western practices, and that it is the British who will teach them: 'Two nurses, both black as ebony ... were girls from Buwambo village, and this was the only nursing they had done, but Sister was a Training Hospital in herself, and when she had finished with them her staff could go anywhere.'[43] It is made clear that the 'girls from Buwambo village' have not brought any suitable knowledge or skills from their own community, and that they will not be taking their training back into that community. Sister's nurses are trained to go 'anywhere'; their qualifications are intended not for the benefit of their own locality, but for the 'world'. The British National Health Service had made use of trained staff from the 'colonies' since its inception in 1948, and, by the time of this novel, was reliant on trained medical staff from the Caribbean, Africa and India. The Buwambo hospital itself is described as very basic; it is clearly in need of Western investment and of medical expertise. Sylvia is appalled at a building 'where the very sick lay. Some would die, there, in horror, having come too late for treatment.'[44] Africans could not be trusted to run the hospital or to diagnose illness in themselves or in the patients.

Respect for educated Nigerians is nonetheless a quality associated with the hero and heroine; a sense of racial superiority is invariably a characteristic of the unsympathetic white characters, most notably the ward sister, and is clearly condemned within the narrative:

> Dr Kalengo ... had always stood in awe of Sister since the day he had arrived, five years ago from Ibadan University. She had never let him forget that his skin was black and therefore inferior to her own: though it was a word she never employed, she implied 'Nigger' whenever she addressed him.[45]

The liberal carapace of both the hero and the narrative is exposed, however, in the hero's reaction when this Nigerian doctor makes a slight medical error, and thus needs to be taken in hand by the white doctor. The surgeon hero rebukes his junior 'in a native dialect ... the coloured man replied "Yes, sir. But I speak English very well, as you know". ... "The devil you do! After this business you have reverted to the native as far as I am concerned".'[46] There is an uneasy distinction made here between the educated African and the 'native' – the latter understood to be a constant threat who could undermine the incomplete Westernisation of educated black people. The word 'native' is used recurrently in these novels as a means of referring to indigenous customs and traditions, whether these are African, Indian or Arabic. It is a term which carries connotations of danger and it suggests that however educated and 'civilised' a black African may appear to be, the 'primitive native' lurks behind his or her 'white mask': 'Kalengo bridled immediately. An alarming primeval anger swept over him so that the leopard-skins of his ancestors almost showed through the white drill suiting he wore.'[47]

Despite the best efforts of the hero and heroine to impose their training and values, this 'alarming primeval anger' is constantly threatening to escape from the restraints of British conduct. It is 'primeval', rather than political. There is no reference in these novels to any kind of independence movement; while there are rumours of resistance at a convenient distance, it is never perceived as political, but rather is characterised as irrational and primitive. The heroine regularly encounters a mild form of resentment, which emerges from incomprehension on the part of her servants. Although less formally educated than the medical staff of the hospital, domestic workers are no less subject to the imposition of British codes of behaviour. The 'house boy', Festus, is a source of ostensibly affectionate humour, as black servants repeatedly are in these texts. He is unfamiliar with British dining and social etiquette: 'flowers as a house-decoration were obviously beyond his comprehension, as was "eating grass" which a green salad appeared to be to him.'[48] The 'native' does not have the sophistication to understand the complexities of English customs and table manners; it is up to the white mistress to civilise the natives, and to teach them how things are done in Britain. Her role is also to act as a gentle curb on the potential racism of the hero, in chiding his impatience with black Africans who are slow, or resistant, to accept the ways of their master and mistress.

The hero and heroine end the novel about to establish a leper hospital – taking with them the loyal black doctor, who has come to embrace Christian values, Western practices and the authority of his medical mentor: 'he would follow his star and David Carroll to the Ebe Mula leper settlement as its resident Medical officer ... as a devout Christian, he asked Heaven's protection for his body that he might be spared to help the sick.'[49]

It is not only the African continent which can offer mystery and adventure to the postwar romance heroine; Arab countries provide a similar exoticism, and Arab 'natives' are in as much need of a heroine's civilising authority as their African counterparts. Jean Herbert's 1955 novel *The Desert's a Woman* is set in 'the Lateral East', an unidentified Middle Eastern region.[50] The narrative opens with an archaeologist heroine who is keen to work with an adult embodiment of the values of the *Boy's Own* imperial hero: 'the famous Keith Trevor! – the explorer of the desert, the discoverer of cities hidden in the sand.'[51] For much of the narrative, the hero appears to be a postwar version of Lord Carnarvon (who financed the 1922 British expedition to excavate the Valley of the Kings), as an archaeologist and explorer. Like Rider Haggard's late nineteenth-century hero, Allan Quartermain, Colonel Trevor is unremittingly English, but displays a knowledge of, and familiarity with, other cultures: 'English to the core ... he fitted into the part of an Oriental Sheikh so well ... she longed to see him with the men of the real desert.'[52] Trevor has 'an unerring desert sense', he refers to 'my Arabs', and he 'is friends with all the Bedouin and knows them thoroughly'. We are told that he speaks fluent Arabic, but, in a manner also reminiscent of Haggard, throughout the novel this 'fluency' is rendered as cod biblical language: 'it is the noble camel that hath been told the Hundredth Name of Allah' – a form of language which firmly locates 'his' Arabs in an Old Testament past.[53]

The heroine, Priscilla, is emphatically English; she has an 'English wild rose prettiness' and she hails from a 'very English scene, rural and reposeful' – a world where 'gentle lives [are] completed under the circle of the softly billowing sky with its attentive fields and trees'.[54] This rural and fertile landscape is in constant opposition to the desert heat and barren landscape of the 'Lateral East'. The 'gentle' English world is also set against the dangers which lurk in this inhospitable place, where the heroine's brother, a charter pilot, has disappeared, a regular fate of so many male relatives in these novels. The East is Orientalised, both in the title of the novel and in the text, as a dangerously seductive woman: 'the desert's a woman: winning, capricious, unpredictable, self-obsessed, dangerous and cunning'.[55] Despite its perils, the seductive East, interchangeable in its alien exoticism with Africa, promises the mystery and excitement which postwar England lacks. It represents a classic place for imperial adventurers: 'Like Africa ... the fantastic Lateral East; the birthplace of so many legends, the grave of so many hopes ... this was indeed Asia, and Priscilla, seeing the dark faces, knew that the great adventure had begun.'[56]

It is significant that the heroine and hero are both archaeologists; their interest lies (initially), in the past rather than in the present of the 'Lateral East'. The contemporary Middle East is portrayed as fly-ridden; it is populated with 'Arab menials and labourers' and filled with 'truly Eastern smells and no ventilation'. It is only the ancient civilisation which is of any concern to the European archaeological party. This concern with antiquity in the region is rendered secondary once the expedition comes upon oil, at which point the imperatives of modern colonialism intervene more immediately. While the narrative at first appears to be a romance of Egyptology, it turns into an affirmation of Britain's continuing rights to the world's resources. The romantic resolution finally hinges on the discovery of oil; the contemporary importance of ownership and control is made explicit: 'Oil, for which the world was crying out! – to set running all peace-time machinery and in the right hands to stave off the threat of war!'[57]

The novel makes it clear that the 'right hands' are British rather than Arab. The Arabs throughout are represented as childlike, 'primitive peoples' who – like their African counterparts – need to be managed by the British. The Arab characters are not to be trusted, and replicate the Arab grave robbers of contemporary popular imagination.[58] The hero complains: 'For us menfolk, there is the strain of supervising native labour and watching with eagle eye to see that nothing is stolen or destroyed.'[59] With the experience of archaeological expeditions behind him, he takes on 'the strain' of negotiating oil rights, and becomes successful as a deal-maker in securing the rights for Britain. He works to secure a 'Treaty of Concession', by which Britain and the fictitious region will drill the oil together, to their mutual benefit (although how this is to be managed remains unclear). Colonel Trevor's resolution is 'to develop the bonds between Great Britain and her partners in the Colonial Empire thorough the development of their joint resources in the interest of both', just as E.H. Carter had recommended in his 1954 school textbook. The nineteenth-century imperial adventurer has here acquired a patina of modernity; as the archaeologist forgoes historical digging for digging for oil, he becomes a contemporary ideal of masculinity. A male colleague comments: "'Foreigners have been manoeuvring for similar rights for months. [I]f he pulls off this Treaty and if the stuff is there in quantity, he'll be something of a national hero".[60]

The romantic resolution reassures that in their home together, the hero and heroine will ensure that the Arabs will be taught how to serve tea at the appropriate hour and Christian values will prevail. When proposing to the heroine, Colonel Trevor declares: "'What a good thing we are both steady C. of E."[61] Priscilla is not alone in her affiliation to the Church of England; there is a recurrent insistence in the exotic romance on the heroine's Christian values. Priscilla gives thanks for her brother's survival in an Anglican monastery, Elizabeth wears no adornment but a 'tiny gold cross', while Sylvia visits the 'nearby Anglican church'. The heroine of the postwar romance ensures that English and Anglican values will prevail wherever she may find herself – whether in the Lateral East, in South Africa or in West Africa.

There is a recurrent narrative pattern in these romances, in which the heroine goes in search of a male relative who has been drawn to the colonies by the mysterious masculine world of commerce. Older brothers or fathers are repeatedly lost, dead or enfeebled in an erstwhile British colony, remnants of a faded empire.[62] In contrast, the youthful heroine is drawn overseas by a spirit of adventure; she is (to a limited degree) accepted by the community, and her marriage represents a narrative future that promises reconciliation and partnership in the shape of the new Commonwealth. The romance heroine thus provides an ideological resolution to postcolonial tensions; she appears to bring modernity, understanding and a fascination for foreign cultures to her new environment, but ultimately her role is to domesticate and to feminise the unfamiliar.

There is one unbreakable proscription in the novels: romantic relationships can never be between partners of different races.[63] It is a fixed convention that the heroine is a variant of an 'English Rose' and the hero always emphatically 'English', born and educated in England. Mixed relationships are throughout 'taboo', the term used by the writer of a manual for aspiring writers in 1960. Potential romance writers were told that:

> editorial policy contains a number of taboos concerning subjects which might offend readers. ... There is ... a colour bar. ... To make

a mixed marriage the central situation in a story is to invite a definite rejection at the present time.[64]

In the colonial romance, the white heroine is subject to unsuitable advances from white or (even more dangerously) mixed race characters – but never from a black man. Black male characters are rendered entirely subservient; they are largely present as comic servants, or else rendered as passive (often childlike) recipients awaiting the skills and superior knowledge of white professionals. An educated black doctor can make a fleeting appearance in hospital romances, but he remains respectfully aloof from the heroine, in awe of her Western training as a nurse or doctor herself. The possibility that a white woman could feel desire for a black man is not brooked in these novels, nor is the possibility that an adult black man could approach a white woman in any other mode than the deferential. The fear of miscegenation is clear from the conspicuous absence of any interracial relationships. Minor black characters are regularly employed in a comic subplot, but romance is strictly limited to members of one's own race, and it exists always in the shadow of the blinding passion of the central white hero and heroine. Bill Schwarz has argued that:

> In the England of the 1940s and 1950s the language of miscegenation was the central issue in terms of white perceptions of race, defining the boundaries of England and signifying its inviolate centre which could brook no impurity.[65]

In the world of the postwar romance, the 'boundaries of England' continued to be sustained in the former colonies; however far the heroine may have travelled, she will ensure that there will always be an England. Together she and the hero maintain an 'inviolate centre' in which their Englishness remains unchallenged and untouched by the foreign world around them. Well into the late 1950s, these narratives were shaped by a colonial frame which was uneasy about a new Commonwealth and which could not entirely accept the demise of the empire. The romance novel is centred on the private and domestic, but the dramas of an English heroine dealing with her servants in Africa or in the Middle East cannot but have a political and racial edge. Gayatri Spivak has suggested that:

> If the fabric of the so-called public life is woven of the so-called private, the definition of the private is marked by a public potential, since it *is* the weave, or texture, of public activity.[66]

This quotation comes from an essay which Spivak has subtitled 'Marginalia'. These romances are themselves marginalia; their authors and titles are largely forgotten, they have been collected by but remain almost entirely unread in the British Library. The novels nonetheless have had a long life; many of the titles published in the 1950s remained in print throughout the decades of the 1960s and 1970s, and some (including *The Hospital in Bulwambo*) continue to appear in catalogues of popular fiction, as 'vintage' romances.

Homi Bhabha has argued that:

> The objective of colonial discourse is to construe the colonized as a population of degenerate types on the basis of racial origin, in order to justify conquest and to establish systems of administration and instruction ... a form of governmentality that in marking out a 'subject nation', appropriates, directs and dominates its various spheres of activity.[67]

These novels are replete with what Bhabha terms the concept of 'fixity'; the 'natives' are repeatedly represented as childlike and potentially dangerous – still a threat of disorder and degeneracy. The English heroine appears to be a representative of a new and modern order but continues to demand the standards of a past England in her domestic sphere. The hero and heroine are found to be literally appropriating, directing and dominating spheres of activity; in running hospitals, uncovering oil in the Middle East, or in farming large estates in Africa they establish their own 'systems of administration and instruction'. The romance fiction written during the period of decolonisation, despite its insistence on the heroine's modernity, was inevitably implicated in this colonial discourse; it is feminised and located in the private world of love, but it remains a colonial discourse. These novels set out to reconcile the end of empire with nostalgia for the pre-war world, in which the romantic resolution reassures the reader that wherever a Mills & Boon heroine may travel, there will always be an England.

Notes

Thanks are due to my co-authors, especially to Rachael Gilmour, Bill Schwarz, Richard Steadman-Jones, Cora Kaplan and Michael Ross.

1   Joseph McAleer, *Passion's Fortune: The story of Mills & Boon* (Oxford: Oxford University Press, 1999), p. 2. The other publisher is Penguin Books.
2   Archana Venkatraman, 'Romance with a modern twist', *Marketing Week,* 15 January 2009.

3 Mills & Boon website, www.millsandboon.co.uk (accessed 25 May 2011).

4 For an account of the postwar development of Mills & Boon as a publishing house and its relationship with North American publishing companies, see Deborah Philips, 'The marketing of moonshine' in Alan Tomlinson (ed.), *Consumption / Identity / Style* (London: Routledge, 1990), pp. 139–53.

5 Deborah Philips and Ian Haywood discuss the postwar romance heroine in *Brave New Causes* (London: Cassell, 1998).

6 McAleer, *Passion's Fortune*, p. 200.

7 Cited in McAleer, *Passion's Fortune*, p. 174. Boots the Chemist was the most successful commercial lending library in Britain, until it ceased trading in 1966.

8 jay dixon, *The Romance Fiction of Mills & Boon, 1909–1990s* (London: UCL Press, 1999), p. 5.

9 According to McAleer: 'Although … *Romantic Fiction: The New Writers' Guide* urged authors "*Never* set a whole book in a country you have not visited …", many successful Mills & Boon authors did just that'. *Passion's Fortune*, p. 260.

10 E.H. Carter, *Across the Seven Seas: The story of the British Commonwealth and empire* (London: Thomas Nelson and Sons, 1954, pp. v–vi).

11 Official website of the British Monarchy, www.royal.gov.uk (accessed November 2009).

12 Christine Geraghty, *British Cinema in the Fifties: Gender, genre and the 'New Look'* (London: Routledge, 2000), p. 112.

13 The Commonwealth Institute, built in London in 1962, would later come to embody this paradox, with its modernist architecture housing displays of 'native cultures' which were close to the 'native village' displays of the world fairs of the empire.

14 Geraghty identifies very similar patterns in the romances of 'Commonwealth films' of the same period. *British Cinema in the Fifties*, pp. 112–32.

15 See McAleer, *Passion's Fortune*, p. 97.

16 Charlotte Lamb [Sheila Holland], quoted in McAleer, *Passion's Fortune*, p. 99.

17 Quoted in McAleer, *Passion's Fortune*, p. 208.

18 Kathryn Blair, *The House at Tegwani* (London: Mills & Boon, 1950), p. 10.

19 Hobsbawm explains that many Boers were sympathetic to Hitler during the war and re-emerged afterwards as key figures in the ruling National Party. Eric Hobsbawm, *Age of Extremes: The short twentieth century* (London: Michael Joseph, 1994), p. 40.

20 Blair, *The House at Tegwani*, p. 13.

21 Blair, *The House at Tegwani*, p. 15.

22 Alan Boon quoted in McAleer, *Passion's Fortune*, p. 270.

23 Blair, *The House at Tegwani*, p. 15.

24 Pamela Kent, *Moon over Africa* (London: Mills & Boon, 1955), p. 5.

25 Kent, *Moon over Africa*, p. 26.

26 Kent, *Moon over Africa*, p. 51.

27 Kent, *Moon over Africa*, p. 10.

28 Kent, *Moon over Africa*, p. 42.

29 Kent, *Moon over Africa*, p. 59.

30 Kent, *Moon over Africa*, p. 56.

31 Kent, *Moon over Africa*, p. 52.

32 Kent, *Moon over Africa*, p. 64.

33 Quoted in McAleer, *Passion's Fortune*, p. 245.

34 Wynne May, quoted in McAleer, *Passion's Fortune*, p. 268.

35 See Margaret Ann Jensen, *Love's Sweet Return: The Harlequin story* (Bowling Green: Bowling Green State University Press, 1984).

36 Anne Vinton, *The Hospital in Bulwambo* (London: Mills & Boon, 1957), p. 31.

37 Muriel Masefield, *The British Commonwealth and Empire* (London: G. Bell and Sons, 1951), p. 120.

38 Vinton, *The Hospital in Bulwambo*, p. 10.

39 Vinton, *The Hospital in Bulwambo*, p. 16.

40 Vinton, *The Hospital in Bulwambo*, p. 15.

41 Vinton, *The Hospital in Bulwambo*, p. 117.

42 Vinton, *The Hospital in Bulwambo*, p. 21.

43 Vinton, *The Hospital in Bulwambo*, p. 39.

44 Vinton, *The Hospital in Bulwambo*, p. 117.

45 Vinton, *The Hospital in Bulwambo*, p. 68.

46 Vinton, *The Hospital in Bulwambo*, p. 39.

47 Vinton, *The Hospital in Bulwambo*, p. 69.

48 Vinton, *The Hospital in Bulwambo*, p. 54.

49 Vinton, *The Hospital in Bulwambo*, p. 164.

50 Most Mills & Boon writers of this period were highly educated professional women, but Jean Herbert was particularly so; Herbert was the pseudonym of an English Literature lecturer, Dr Mary Isabel Leslie.

51 Jean Herbert, *The Desert's a Woman* (London: Mills & Boon), 1955, p. 5.

52 Herbert, *The Desert's a Woman*, p. 44.

53 Herbert, *The Desert's a Woman*, p. 37.

54 Herbert, *The Desert's a Woman*, p. 5.

55 Herbert, *The Desert's a Woman*, p. 20.

56 Herbert, *The Desert's a Woman*, p. 32.

57 Herbert, *The Desert's a Woman*, p. 173.

58 The grave robber is a figure in popular culture who dates from the first European excavations in Egypt, and is still to be found in contemporary theme parks: at Chessington World of Adventures, The Terror Tomb centres on a greedy Arab figure who is subjected to a series of grizzly punitive attacks for his trespass into a mummy's tomb.

59 Herbert, *The Desert's a Woman*, p. 85.

60 Herbert, *The Desert's a Woman*, p. 172.

61 Herbert, *The Desert's a Woman*, p. 175.

62 It is interesting to note a similar trope in John Osborne's *Look Back in Anger*,

in which Jimmy Porter and Alison's father, Colonel Redfern, share a nostalgia for the old days of Empire.

63 dixon, writing in 1999, could maintain: 'There are still no black heroines or heroes in Mills & Boon', *The Romance Fiction of Mills & Boon*, p. 53.

64 Anne Britton and Marion Collin, *Romantic Fiction* (London: T.V. Boardman & Company, 1960), p. 17.

65 Bill Schwarz, 'Black metropolis, white England' in Mica Nava and Alan O'Shea (eds), *Modern Times: Reflections on a century of English modernity* (London: Routledge, 1996).

66 Gayatri Chakravorty Spivak, 'Explanation and culture: marginalia' in Gayatri Chakravorty Spivak, *In Other Worlds: Essays in cultural politics* (London: Methuen, 1987), pp. 103–17.

67 Homi Bhabha, 'The other question: stereotype, discrimination and the discourse of colonialism', in Homi Bhabha, *The Location of Culture* (London: Routledge, 2009), pp. 94–120.

6

Passage from Kinjanja to Pimlico: William Boyd's comedy of imperial decline

Michael L. Ross

William Boyd is a writer with a distinctively mixed heritage, combining the colonial and the metropolitan.[1] He was born to Scottish parents in the Gold Coast, soon to become the independent nation of Ghana. Not surprisingly, his fiction displays a marked alertness to the repercussions of fading imperial grandeur and the mutating significations of Britishness. His 1981 debut novel, *A Good Man in Africa*, explores the comic possibilities of Kinjanja, a fictional country based on Nigeria, where the writer spent part of his childhood. Not until 1998, after producing five other, mainly non-comic novels, did Boyd return to the comic mode in *Armadillo*, shifting the scene from Africa to the erstwhile imperial capital, London. Where in *A Good Man* the springboard for comedy had been Britain's lingering colonialist aspirations, humour now arises from the metropole's diminished, colony-less present. It is insular anxiety rather than imperial nostalgia that is the major source of laughter.

Both novels follow familiar precedents of British comic fiction. In *A Good Man* the obvious model is Kingsley Amis's *Lucky Jim*. Like Amis's Jim Dixon, Boyd's protagonist, Morgan Leafy, is comic largely because of the incongruity between his inner promptings and his outward demeanour. 'Morgan smiled and raised his own glass. I hate you, you smug bastard! he screamed inwardly. You shit, you little turd, you've ruined my life! But all he said was, "Congratulations. She's a fabulous girl".'[2] The dissonance stems from the pressures to which Leafy's official position subjects him. His superior, Deputy Commissioner Arthur Fanshawe, is a bumbling, senescent authority figure like Amis's overbearing Professor Welch. In more important ways, however, *A Good Man* recalls two earlier novelists whom Boyd greatly admires, Evelyn Waugh and Joyce Cary.[3] Boyd's African characters, like those in Waugh's *Black Mischief* or Cary's African novels, cling to superstitions which provoke Europeans to exasperated laughter. They are stereotyped in other ways as well: they are obsequious like the diminutive office worker Kojo, or mendacious like Leafy's mistress Hazel, or conniving like the politician Sam Adekunle. The signal instance of 'African' waywardness is the occult 'Shango killing' by lightning of the Fanshawes' maid, Innocence, which occasions the portentous *double-entendre*, 'Innocence is dead'. The mishap embroils Leafy in a macabre farce of body snatching and replacing. The Commission staff refuse to move the awkwardly situated corpse: '"We cannot totch her, sah",' the normally compliant Isaac tells Leafy. '"Please, I beg you once more. Ifn you totch her before, you will bring yourself trouble. Bringing everyone wahallah"' (75). Here, as in Waugh and Cary, 'native' irrationality is rendered more risible by the irregular English usage.

Yet *A Good Man* does not merely replicate earlier paradigms. The brunt of the humour falls not on African 'backwardness' but on the fatuousness of the British, above all their failure to register their loss of hegemony. Such willed obtuseness calls to mind a syndrome Paul Gilroy terms postcolonial melancholia, 'an anxious, melancholic mood [which] has become part of the cultural infrastructure of [Britain], an immovable ontological counterpart to the nation-defining ramparts of the white cliffs of Dover'.[4] The melancholy, for Gilroy, derives from 'an inability even to face, never mind actually mourn, the profound change in circumstances and moods that followed the end of the empire and consequent loss of imperial prestige'.[5] When relocated from the white cliffs of Dover to the supposed 'periphery' this denial of historical fact becomes even more dispiriting, but at the same time potentially funnier. Lee Wan, a British citizen of Malay birth, claims that he has '"[n]ever seen a more neurotic, glum bunch in [his] life"' (90) than the British expatriates. Gilroy writes of the need to 'break laughter's complicity with postcolonial melancholia and to locate new sources of comedy in a remade relationship with our heterogeneous selves'.[6] Boyd's comic treatment of his glum British misfits elegantly accomplishes Gilroy's imperative.

Yet Gilroy's postcolonial melancholia is too much of a catch-all to fit the diverse array of Boyd's melancholics. Fanshawe and Leafy, for example, are quite distinct cases. The Deputy Commissioner personifies to a tee the post-imperial penchant for denial. A walking anachronism, he hopes to infuse 'civilisation' into Kinjanja by screening a film about the domestic life of the British royals, 'a gentle but potent reminder to all the non-British present of precisely just what it was that they didn't possess and why, therefore, they just weren't quite such special people' (111). Predictably, Fanshawe fears that the scandal of Innocence's unburied body will make the Commission appear 'totally and unacceptably non-British' (253). In order to bolster the British presence he endeavours to influence the course of Kinjanjan politics, betting on the KNP, Adekunle's party and 'a possible friend to Britain' (100) to prevail in the upcoming elections while cultivating Adekunle himself. The humour hinges on British officialdom's floundering inability to comprehend postcolonial nuances. Fanshawe proposes to beguile Adekunle with a trip to London: '"Offer it to him as a kind of reward: you know, first-class tickets, couple of nights at Claridges"' (133). Leafy reflects that 'Fanshawe's approach seemed to belong to another age, as if plane tickets and hotel reservations were an updated version of beads and blankets' (133). As expected, Fanshawe's manoeuvring laughably backfires. Adekunle himself finds the offer hilarious: '"My good God," he said. "You British are indeed astonishing." ... He wheezed with laughter' (142). The media-savvy politician exploits the trip by contriving to make the invitation appear an outright British endorsement. Innocence, in the geopolitical sense, is indeed dead, but Fanshawe never registers its demise.

Leafy, younger and less fixated on the past, has a keener awareness of African realities, or is at least more alive to the limits of his awareness. His peculiar brand of melancholia, however, issues in opportunistic game-playing. If Fanshawe tries fruitlessly to pursue the old imperial Great Game, courting Adekunle through what he lamely calls 'Operation Kingpin', Leafy becomes involved in games that are less grandiose but equally futile. Ensnared by Adekunle he is obliged to play a round of golf with the upstanding Dr Alex Murray; his losing stroke is his desperate bid to bribe Murray into compliance with Adekunle's interests. Adekunle sends Leafy a gift of resplendent golf clubs 'newly minted, like lethal weapons', along with a sardonic note: 'Have a good game. Sam' (249) – the line between gamesmanship and warfare is slender. Even relatively innocuous games humiliate Leafy, like his recruitment by the Fanshawes as a Father Christmas performing a preposterous yuletide charade amid the animist tropics.

More typically Leafy's African games are sexual in nature. He sleeps with his African mistress Hazel while pursuing the white English Priscilla, Fanshawe's daughter, in the hope of scoring a career breakthrough. To abet his wooing of Priscilla he takes her on a fishing trip into the bush: '"Real Heart of Darkness stuff don't you think?" he asks her. "What's that?" she replies blankly (125). The girl's ignorance of Conrad's classic exposé of colonialism ironically points up that text's relevance to Leafy's predicament. In Heart of Darkness Kurtz's engagement to the ethereal European woman identified only as the Intended is thwarted by his immersion in destructive African elements. These include Kurtz's extravagantly 'savage' African paramour, who is not named but who might aptly be called the Unintended. In Boyd's novel the

Unintended is represented by the African girl Hazel, who by transmitting gonorrhea to Leafy inadvertently thwarts the consummation of his amour with the Intended white Priscilla. Predictably, the parallels with Conrad's novel collapse into parody. Priscilla's missing of Leafy's allusion betrays her remoteness from Conrad's moral terrain. She may figure as Leafy's Intended in embodying the horizon of his careerism, but she is no exalted Conradian female, merely a pert British bachelorette. Nor is Hazel a tumultuously primitive Unintended; she is rather a citified opportunist whose 'two main interests in life' are clothes and status (39) and who uses her charms for material advantage. Ultimately the two women mirror each other more than they differ, a likeness conspicuous in their common sexual availability. By deconstructing 'dark woman / fair woman' dichotomies Boyd's novel subverts Manichean commonplaces of Eurocentric comedy, making the humour unsettlingly double-edged.

In his relations with Africans even Leafy favours practices recalling a bygone era. He bullies his house-boy Friday, whose name mordantly comments on the nature of his terms of employment. He also sexually exploits and on one occasion slaps the unreliable Hazel. She, however, covertly turns the colonialist tables on Leafy – he senses 'that it was *he* not her who was being exploited' (39) – living in the flat he provides while surreptitiously seeing other men. This reversal epitomises the outcome of British efforts to micro-manage Kinjanjan affairs. Adekunle, whom Fanshawe and Leafy aspire to manipulate, turns out, like Hazel, to be himself the manipulator, cunningly using both men to further his own questionable aims. Among the British characters only Dr Murray, an unofficial *médecin sans frontières,* stays clear of the machinations of both Africans and Europeans until his death amid the post-election rioting that is the lamentable aftermath of decolonisation.

Leafy, for all his scheming, is at bottom a detached and solitary figure. He shares this condition with later Boyd protagonists; as Douglas Dunn has observed, 'Boyd's cosmopolitan reach is one largely of a comic restlessness, round pegs in square holes, unlikely people in unlikely places'.[7] Leafy feels marooned in Kinjanja, for him not just a square hole but a 'stinking hot frustrating shit-hole of a country' (12). Local children call after him 'Oyibo!' (white man), 'a persistent reminder that he was a stranger in their country' (36–7). Yet he feels similarly estranged from his fellow Britons. Toward those who are not English, like his Welsh colleague Denzil Jones or the Scottish Murray, he displays harsher animus than toward the local Africans. He detests 'the sight of [Jones's] fat little Welsh knees peeking out between the hem of his shorts and the top of his socks like two bald, wrinkled babies' heads' (13). Ultimately his alienation from his countrymen matches his sense of distance from the Kinjanjan natives. At a moment of acute irritation, he equates his rage against the obtuse Fanshawe with his bafflement at the crowd surrounding Innocence's body: 'They might have been waxworks, moon-men or zombies for all the understanding their minds shared with his. But there again, he thought, the same could be said about the gulf that existed between him and Fanshawe' (235). The residual British presence in Africa has generated two solitudes, and Leafy feels locked in a third, anomalous solitude, distinct from the other two.

There is, however, a force working to mitigate Leafy's estrangement: the agency Gilroy labels conviviality. Gilroy identifies this force with 'the processes of cohabitation and interaction that have made multiculture an ordinary feature of social life in Britain's urban areas'.[8] In the Kinjanjan backwater Boyd evokes such cohabitation and interaction are not ordinary. While the 'good man' of the novel's title may suggest bonhomie, comradeship among the British Commission personnel seldom goes beyond perfunctory joviality, like the 'Good man' young Dalmire bestows on Leafy when accepting a drink in the novel's opening line – 'If he had a tail he'd be wagging it' (11), Leafy reflects. Yet such canine heartiness is offset by more genuinely convivial moments, as when the office worker Kojo visits Leafy with his family to offer him the present of a live Christmas turkey. Though amusingly unorthodox, the gift is heartfelt. Again, a knockabout comradeship evolves between Leafy and Friday during their slapstick struggles to dispose of Innocence's remains. An incipient fellowship also develops between Leafy and the regrettably Scottish but courageous and dedicated Dr Murray, only to be curtailed by Murray's death, an event which impresses upon Leafy the futility of his own presence in Africa.

Ultimately, Africa remains alien to Leafy. At best, he intuits the breadth of his own ignorance: 'Kinjanja was a mystery to him, he realized, he knew next to nothing about the way its inhabitants' minds worked, the way its colonially imposed institutional superstructure related with the traditional tribal background; he knew nothing of the ethnic, racial and religious pressures surreptitiously influencing events' (138). Far from being unique to Leafy, the incomprehension afflicts all the forlorn British exiles who stay on, absurdly hoping to steer history in the wake of a vanished imperium. Finally, after the fiasco of the Kinjanjan election and British meddling in it, 'Shango, that mysterious and incomprehensible god, flashed and capered happily above the silent dripping jungle' (312). The supernal victory-dance symbolises all that the white interlopers cannot hope to bend to their designs. Such a finale contrasts tellingly with the endings of comic antecedents like Waugh's *Black*

Mischief or Cary's *Mister Johnson*, where 'European' orderliness, at whatever cost in vivacity, gets re-imposed on the unkempt African scene. If *A Good Man in Africa* retains elements of such earlier fiction its governing impulse is to overturn that fiction's constitutive premises, humorously puncturing the melancholia which still clings to them.

In *Armadillo* the scene shifts to a *fin-de-siècle* London replete with raffish eccentrics, like the vapid manager Torquil Helvoir-Jayne, who recall not Waugh and Cary but rather Anthony Powell or even P.G. Wodehouse. The protagonist, Lorimer Black, is not, like Leafy, an Englishman out of his native element, but rather a Londoner of diasporic descent – a Gypsy – 'passing' as indigenous by altering his birth name (Milomre Blocj) and professing a spurious Scottish ancestry. The imperial past is not here directly confronted; the key issue is not command over events in an ex-colony but control of one's life amid the complexities of a globalised metropolis. Apart from their comic mode the two books have little obviously in common.

What links them is their shared concern with the uncertainties which cluster around British identity. In *A Good Man* Leafy, bent on consulting Murray about his sexual ailment, refuses to see either of the two physicians on duty, Dr Obayemi or Dr Rathmanatathan. Although he has 'absolutely no objection' to them, he explains to Murray, 'they aren't British – I assume – and you are' (93). Late in *Armadillo*, Lorimer Black requires medical attention of a different sort. A collector of antique armour, he has managed to get his head ludicrously wedged inside a rare Greek helmet. He is rescued by a physician named, not coincidentally, Dr Rathmanatathan, about whose nationality he too jumps to conclusions. "'Are you from Ceylon?"' he asks her. "'Doncaster," she said in a flat Northern accent. "And it's currently known as Sri Lanka these days, not Ceylon".'[9] Despite his own unusual origins and his important recognition that '[l]ike himself ... there were many types of Englishmen' (124), Black turns out to share Leafy's naivety concerning what defines Britishness. Whether in England or abroad, Boyd intimates, this myopia remains a disabling national deficit. And while the perplexingly British Rathmanatathan has only a walk-on part her role is crucial, for it is she who symbolically liberates Black – the 'little armed man' of the title – from the grip of his outmoded, constricting psychological armour.

Black's compulsive self-protectiveness is imbricated with issues of nationality. Unlike the complacently English Leafy, Black finds his family origins a cause for anxiety. He is not visibly other; nobody points at him and calls him Oyibo, but he keeps his Roma antecedents to himself. He presents himself ordinarily as Lorimer Black, a 'normal' insurance loss adjuster, but on visits to his family home he becomes again Milomre Blocj. The stress caused by this split obviously contributes to the sleep disorder from which he suffers, and for which he is receiving experimental therapy from his researcher friend Alan Kenbarry. Boyd has declared that 'I am not an autobiographical writer. ... [M]y fiction will provide no handy keys to unlock the door to my personal history', but elements of his history connect with the unease afflicting his fictional Gypsy-turned-faux-Scot.[10] Boyd's life has featured Gypsyish wanderings, and while his ancestry is authentically Scottish, he has written that as an African-bred child at a Scottish school he felt an impostor. Of his early life he recalls, 'We were always in transit, welcomed, but always "just visiting"'.[11] He admits to feeling 'somewhere, deep inside me, the private hollow of fear and insecurity that all aliens (however legal) carry within them. My passport was British, so why was I uneasy?'[12]

It is a query Boyd's insomniac adjuster might well put to himself. But the hollow of fear and insecurity that Lorimer Black carries within him is not his exclusive possession. In *Armadillo* the multiform malaise of Gilroy's postcolonial melancholia spreads to affect ensconced insiders and displaced outsiders alike; it fosters a perception of existence in modern London as unnervingly contingent. The *coup de théâtre* of the opening, in which Black discovers the hanged body of a despairing client, a Mr Dupree, strikes the keynote. Afterward, Black feels 'a depression settle on him like a shawl' (5) – a mood endemic in this treacherous urban milieu. Nick Rennison has observed that in *Armadillo* Boyd 'seems curiously ill at ease with a story set in contemporary London',[13] but it would be truer to say that the London of *Armadillo* is a place in which it is perfectly natural to feel ill at ease.[14]

Where Leafy is oppressed by the heavy-handedness of British authority abroad, Black suffers from the homeland equivalent. Louring over Boyd's metropolitan landscape is the insurance colossus Fortress Sure, parent company of the loss adjustment firm for which Black works, GHH Ltd. In the absence of the empire, Fortress Sure operates as the epicentre of control and entitlement. The corpse of the defeated client Black starts his day by confronting serves as a *memento mori* testifying to its dour efficiency. Within its insular boundaries the company behaves like a ruthless colonial power. George Orwell's famous summation of imperial England as 'a family with the wrong members in control'[15] perfectly fits Fortress Sure, guided by men like the pettifogging Sir Simon Sherriffmuir and Black's superior, George Hogg. In Hogg Black must placate not a bumbling fogey like Fanshawe but a bullying manipulator more akin to the cutthroat Sam Adekunle. Hegemonic in its *modus operandi*, the firm crushes the hopes both of agents like Black and clients like the luckless Dupree. The company name blazons a monumentally established order. Approaching 'the Fort', Black observes 'the aquamarine neon sign. Solid, emphatic, classical roman font – FORTRESS SURE' (13). Even the orthography stirs recollections of empire.

The recollections turn out, however, to be ironic. Where the empire had once projected a sense of impregnable collective safety like an administrative Rock of Gibraltar, Fortress Sure offers only a specious promise of security to a chronically endangered populace. As Hogg explains, the loss adjuster's calling is to subvert the very premises of the company name: '"We act out in our small way one of the great unbending principles of life: nothing is sure, nothing is certain, nothing is risk-free, nothing is fully covered, nothing is forever"' (149). According to Hogg's mantra, his team carry out a sacred mission: 'to "disturb all anticipation"' (262). Rather than maintaining the safe imperial past enshrined in the national imaginary, the insurance company aggravates the pitfalls of the seditious present.

If Fortress Sure projects melancholia on a broad public level, it is a private citizen, the flower vendor Marlobe – tangential to *Armadillo*'s plot but central to its moral universe – who is that distemper's loudest voice. Orwell notes 'a minor English trait which is extremely well marked ... and that is a love of flowers'.[16] Boyd's portrayal of his florist cancels any complacency regarding the national fondness. Morose and profane, Marlobe vents sentiments by no means cheerfully horticultural. In his view, it is cheerfulness itself that has humbled Britain: '"Always looking on the stinking bright side. ... That's why this nation is on its knees. On its knees in the gutter looking for scraps"' (301). He has little use for the nation's lawmakers: '"You know," Marlobe went on ... "if I had a Uzi, if I had a fucking Uzi, I'd fucking go into that place [the Houses of Parliament] and fucking line them up against the wall"' (30). His response to Lorimer's report that his car has been torched by vandals runs true to form: '"I'd castrate them," Marlobe said reasonably. "I'd castrate them and then I'd cut their right hands off. Wouldn't do much vandalizing after that. Fancy a nice bunch of carnations?"' (229). An apostle of the free market, he cites neoliberal bromides to justify the ethnic cleansing of uncompetitive newcomers: '"You cannot buck the market. I mean, face it, we are all, like it or not, capitalists. And the amount I pay in fucking taxes justifies me, personally, in saying to those whingeing, fucking scroungers – PISS OFF. And you, matey, fuck right off to your own sad fucking stinking country, wherever it is"' (112). The florist is a minor Enoch Powell, brandishing an angry garland of carnations.

Marlobe's conviction of national loss is shared by capitalists on a grander scale. Sitting with Hogg beside the bowling green in Finsbury Circus, Black registers his superior's morose nostalgia: 'All around the neat central garden were the leafless plane trees with their backdrop of solid, ornate buildings with a few frozen workers smoking and shivering in doorways. The old city, Hogg always said, as it used to be in the great days' (85). Unfazed by the discomfort of the workers who toil to preserve the city's *beaux restes*, Hogg is entranced by a juggler keeping three red balls in the air. '"Bloody marvellous," Hogg said, "sort of mesmerizing. Run over there and give him a pound, there's a good lad"' (86). It is a stunt of trivial control, not the gritty round of quotidian labour, that elicits Hogg's gesture of patronising largesse.

Control of a more sinister kind feeds into Boyd's comedy by exacerbating melancholia. The dominant ethos, as Hogg's name bluntly suggests, is brutish. To quote Marlobe's apothegm, '"It's dog eat fucking dog, my friend"' (112). Struggling to survive in this capitalist jungle Lorimer Black incurs afflictions unknown in Leafy's Africa; his pretentious title of loss adjuster veils the ironic subtext that he himself holds a losing hand. The name of the Pimlico street on which he lives, Lupus Crescent, blatantly evokes the wasting disease. His insomnia, which he terms 'indigestion of the soul' (19–20), has similarly morbid associations. He views himself as a 'bystander who can only see glimpses of the race and cannot tell who's winning or who's being lapped; he felt the buffeting, burly power of forces he did not comprehend or welcome, pushing at and shaping his destiny' (335). Leafy in Kinjanja had felt a dismaying sense of uncontrol, but instead of the temperamental Shango the god presiding over Black's urban trajectory is the dour impersonal Moloch of market forces.

Where literal facts of geography loom over *A Good Man*, a more figurative geography dominates *Armadillo*. In his Book of Transfigurations, where he jots down random reflections, Lorimer frames his predicament as a clash between two countries of the spirit: Serendip, 'a southern land of spice and warmth', and Zembla, 'another world in the far north, barren, ice-bound, cold, a world of flint and stone' (234). The first land signifies happy, spontaneous accident; the second, dogged but unrewarding calculation. Zembla contains Black's workaday life, in which he meticulously calibrates his professional and personal moves yet still feels swept hopelessly along like a box tossed by the Thames. Yet even Zemblan Britain is visited by warming currents from Serendip. These flow principally from the ecumenical impulse of Gilroy's conviviality. Its workings are as capricious in Black's London as they were in Leafy's Kinjanja. According to Gilroy, 'The radical openness that brings conviviality alive makes a nonsense of closed, fixed and reified identity and turns attention toward the always unpredictable mechanisms of identification'.[17] 'Unpredictable' is a fitting word for Lorimer's elderly neighbour, Lady Haigh. Unlike the profit-obsessed Marlobe she genuinely evinces the celebrated 'English' love of flowers. An avid but unfussy gardener, she turns her tiny plot into an oasis within arid Pimlico; her 'little verdant rectangle' extends 'a form of wild invitation' (66). She proudly displays her precocious fritillaries; to Black the flowers seem to thrive in their own 'little micro-climate' (67). Lady Haigh's gardening prowess is abetted by Nigel the Santafurian, 'a thin black man with waist-length dreadlocks, thick as coaxial cables' (100), who seems emphatically 'other' vis-a-vis the aged white aristocrat but who supplies the compost her plot of ground requires. After her death, Nigel turns out to have been on a first-name basis with her, an intimacy Lorimer regrets never having enjoyed. But Black's jealousy soon yields to a more convivial impulse; in a decisive gesture of rapprochement he grasps the Santafurian's raised hand. 'Unthinkingly Lorimer gripped it, shoulder-high, thumbs interlocking, like two centurions taking their leave at the frontiers of some distant province, far from Rome' (338). Beleaguered survivors of empire, the black man and the white join hands in a ritual salute to their dead friend. The moment of contact enacts a bridging of the fissures of race, class and origin riddling the social topography of contemporary Britain.

Such conviviality, a growth as rare as Lady Haigh's fritillaries, may invite reflexive scepticism. Learning of Lady Haigh's death Black's sleep-researcher friend Alan alleges that she has been prejudiced against him because of his race. (Boyd cagily withholds until the eleventh hour the information that Alan is not white.) Believing her to have been 'always a bit suspicious' of him, he concludes, '"Once an old colonial always an old colonial"'. '"Because you're black?"' Lorimer snaps back. '"Ridiculous"' (336). Alan errs in attributing what Gilroy calls a fixed and reified identity to the old woman, but in the prevailing smog of suspicion such conditioned responses become inevitable. The tired wisdom of the imperium still haunts the transmuted cityscape of contemporary London.

Such wisdom can no longer provide a secure basis for action – even for safety. Black himself is exposed to reprisals (like the torching of his car) by those his professional judgements have damaged. Apart from fugitive moments of conviviality he must deal each day with a climate of institutionalised enmity. The trope of warfare punctuates the novel; Hogg even characterises his squad of adjusters as 'specialist élite units' (89). An intruder into this armed camp like Black, feeling 'the hollow of fear and insecurity that all aliens carry within them', is understandably driven to devise protective stratagems. According to Gilroy the arrival of migrants from the imploding empire 'even when they were protected by their tenure of formal citizenship, was … understood to be an act of invasive warfare'.[18] Lorimer, whose suppressed origins affiliate him with such invaders, adapts by transforming himself into the titular little armed man. Overtly he does this by collecting armour, but he accoutres himself in less tangible ways as well.

Gilroy notes that newcomers 'will seek salvation by trying to embrace and inflate the ebbing privileges of whiteness'.[19] Although Lorimer is black only by courtesy of his assumed surname, he too seeks salvation through replicating British normativity. As a child he was exposed to 'the constant incantation', '"Now you are English boy, Milo. This is your country, this is your home"' (40). As an adult he feels a compulsion to perform Britishness, a task he necessarily finds confusing. To quote Stuart Hall, 'What it means to be "British" or "Russian" or "Jamaican" cannot be entirely controlled by the British, Russians or Jamaicans, but is always up for grabs, always being negotiated, in the dialogue between these national cultures and their "others"'.[20] The man who has dubbed himself Lorimer Black is continually obliged to negotiate his British persona in the face of conflicting signals from his habitat. As he reminds himself, after a youthful, shaming episode in Scotland he had had his new name registered in all official records and had made sure his old name was expunged, because '[o]nly in this way could you truly possess your different identity' (121). What he neglects to ask is whether he can ever truly possess that identity – whether instead it is the identity that possesses him.

In reality, rather than 'possessing' a unitary new identity Black fabricates an identity which is a work in progress, slipping heuristically out of one constructed persona and into another. This morphology reflects not simply the dodges of the migrant uneasy in his own skin but a more general postmodern crux regarding identity formation. According to Hall, an adequate concept of identity accepts 'that identities are never unified and, in late modern times, [are] increasingly fragmented and fractured; never singular but multiply constructed across different, often intersecting and antagonistic, discourses, practices and positions'.[21] In the contemporary London of *Armadillo* conventional markers of identity are becoming cryptic: a restaurant off Tottenham Court Road called O'Riley's is run by a Moroccan named Pedro.

Lorimer Black, however, takes adaptive self-transformation to a maladaptive extreme. One of his self-protective ruses is to dress for business appointments by minutely calculating the persona he thinks it expedient to present. He thus confirms the commonplace that 'fashion and clothing are used to send messages about oneself to others'.[22] Paradoxically, though, the message sent by Lorimer's sartorial fine-tuning is that there is no message.

Once again, the secret motive behind his exacting fashion statements is to convince himself of his invulnerability: 'And this was what he was after, really: the minute alterations in his appearance were designed primarily for himself ... encouraging confidence in the persona he had decided to wear. They functioned ... as a form of almost invisible armour and, thus protected, he was ready to do battle' (122). The adjuster, preparing for the single combat of business, is perpetually adjusting himself.

Some of the novel's funniest moments arise from the exposure Black invites through his very efforts to maintain his carapace of a fabricated identity. Trading on his ersatz Scottishness, he wears a hired kilt to a social gathering at Torquil Helvoir-Jayne's country house. 'He was pleased to be wearing a kilt again after so many years and surprised, as he always was, by the transformation it wrought on him – he almost didn't recognize himself. ... This was, to his mind, as close to the Platonic "Lorimer Black" as he had ever desired, as complete a metamorphosis as he could ever have wished for' (153–4). Transfigured into a Platonic idea of himself, his invented name shielded by inverted commas, he feels equipped to assert himself before assembled strangers. An implied element of the figure he hopes to cut is virility; Malcolm Barnard refers to the 'obviously manly attractions of the kilt'.[23] Black's narcissistic expectations are punctured by a female prankster named Potts: '"Och aye, he's a true Scot," Potts said, standing behind him, the pleated hem of his kilt held high in her hands, "he's no wearing knickers"' (155). The joke depends on Potts's whimsically reading the absence of undergarments as the presence of authentic ethnicity. In fact, of course, Lorimer is no more a 'true Scot' than the young woman's music hall stab at dialect is a true duplication of Scottish speech. The kilt, instead of affording Black a triumphant flourishing of his masculinity, inflicts upon him an emasculating sense of exposure: 'Somehow Lorimer's smile stayed pasted to his face, his scorching embarrassment was covered by the explosion of nervous laughter that followed' (156). Discarding the 'unpresentable' stereotype of the Gypsy, Lorimer eagerly embraces the stereotype of the Scot, which putatively conforms more closely to normative Britishness. He discovers that there is no safety in stereotypes; any may invite ridicule and exclusion, rather than fluent conviviality.

What above all spurs Black to fabricate a Platonic simulacrum of himself is his rejection of his inherited ethnicity and his family's domestic culture. His filial visits cause him mental and even physical upset. 'One hundred yards from his family home, and it kicked in, the stomach acids started to bubble and seethe' (31–2). Yet curiously, while shunning Roma cultural traditions Lorimer/Milomre is the sole Blocj who still obeys migratory promptings.

Rather than settling down in Pimlico he restlessly procures a back-up residence in a Zemblan suburb: 'It seemed a different, pioneering city out here in the east, with its emptiness and flatness, its chill, refulgent space. ... Snow coming, he thought, all the way from Siberia' (78). Such a frigid urban *tabula rasa* is an apt setting for one who has wiped his own slate clean. It ratifies his severance from his personal past, releasing him from determinate nationality: '[E]verything was new here, and he felt new also ... as if he were in a newer city, different altogether, more anonymously European' (200). To the woman he loves he gives a predictable explanation of his need for such a place: '"It makes me feel – I don't know – safe. Safer, I suppose. It's my insurance. There's always somewhere I can go and start again".' She responds pertinently, '"Sounds more like a place to go and hide. What are you hiding from, Lorimer Black?"' (313). It is a question which he cannot as yet answer.

Nevertheless, Lorimer is open to forces that counter his panicky urge to cower within his armour, chief among them his fascination with African music. In his essay 'Music and identity' Simon Frith argues, like Hall, 'that identity is *mobile*, a process not a thing, a becoming not a being', adding 'that our experience of music – of music making and music listening – is best understood as an experience of this *self-in-process*'.[24] Unlike his Scottish fantasies, Black's exploration of non-Western musical modes has the potential to enhance his self-formation. Troubled by the daily dissimulation his job entails, he rejects contemporary rock music because he finds it 'fatally bogus ... a conspiracy of manipulated tastes, faddery and expert marketing' (192). He turns instead to recordings by artists from former colonies: King Johnson Adewale and his Ghana-beat Millionaires, or Emperor Bola Osanjo and his Viva Africa Ensemble. Such music represents a distillation of 'southern' conviviality, a sonic Serendip, countering the mercantile sterility of late twentieth-century London. The Africa that witnessed Morgan Leafy's estrangement resurfaces here as an antidote to the disaffecting homeland: a spectacular case of the return of the repressed. Colonies whose loss engendered melancholia undergo a metamorphosis into an energising source of emotional renewal. If Lorimer is unblushingly appropriating a tradition not his own, his predicament as a displaced person hungering for viable traditions goes far toward justifying him.

John Chernoff's observation about Ghanaian drumming applies to the recordings Black relishes: 'African music is a cultural activity which reveals a group of people organizing and involving themselves with their own communal relationships – a participant-observer's comment, so to speak, on the processes of living together.'[25] Such music supplies a convivial antidote to the armoured solipsism within which Black customarily dwells. Late in the

novel he begins listening to some 'meditative' Monteverdi, then 'change[s] it
for Bola Folarin and Accra 57' (309). (Bola 'was renowned for his excessive
use of drummers'.) His second-thought is more than casual; it signifies a
considered shift from the depleted Western atomistic to the jubilant African
communal. His Fortress Sure associates react in character to his 'eccentric'
tastes. Torquil, sprawling drink in hand on Lorimer's sofa, is baffled by Bola
Osanjo: '"What the hell is this crap you're playing?"' (193). Hogg responds
even more vehemently: '"You know, Lorimer, sometimes I think you're
fucking barking mad"' (135). What by Fortress Sure standards is deviancy
becomes for Black a pathway to restored sanity.

But there are limits even to the life-transforming potency of music; Black
needs a more enveloping 'southern' magic to exorcise Zemblan melancholia.
He finds it in his new love interest, the elusive actress Flavia Malinverno. In
Armadillo, as in *A Good Man*, the protagonist's dilemma lies between opposed
erotic alternatives; but Black's options carry a more decisive weight than
Leafy's. Both in her Italianate name ('Malinverno' or 'bad winter' intimates
that cold is to be shunned) and in her flamboyant temperament Flavia is
the polar opposite of Lorimer's current sexual partner, Stella Bull, whose
surname pegs her as irremediably English. Unlike Stella, whom Lorimer
has met through his work, Flavia has aroused his interest through the most
serendipitous of glimpses. Stella offers Black partnership in a fish farm near
Guildford, a damp prospect calculated to send Flavia into gales of Latin
mirth. A piquant blend of caprice and candour, the actress inveigles Lorimer
out of his self-protective shell into a subtropical emotional climate. A turning
point is their tryst at the Sole di Napoli (Sun of Naples) restaurant, redolent
of 'the warm south' (214) in contrast to the snow falling outside. The pair's
parting kiss on the threshold is theatrically saluted by the 'applause of Sole
di Napoli's serving staff standing ... in the window whooping and clapping'
(219). The comedy here hinges on Lorimer's besetting dread of exposure,
but the incident also marks a serious step in his progress from isolationism
to conviviality. Farcical moments like the scene at the Sole di Napoli disperse
the clouds normally shrouding Lorimer's London life, confronting him with
the possibility of sunnier psychic weather systems. Here again, the action
obeys the imperative, stated by Gilroy, to 'break laughter's complicity with
postcolonial melancholia'.

With her nonconformist laughter Flavia helps to demolish that complicity,
obliging Black to face up to realities he normally evades. '"You've got to name
things",' she lectures him. '"Name things in your life from now on, Lorimer
Black. I insist. It makes everything more ... more real"' (216–17). Lorimer's
progress can be gauged by his growing consent to name things, himself

included. He becomes 'more real' to Flavia when, provoked by her taunt 'What are you hiding from, Lorimer Black?' he drops his habitual lying and reveals his 'foreign' birth name: '"My real name is Milomre Blocj. I was born here but in fact I'm a Transnistrian. I come from a family of Transnistrian Gypsies"' (313). Flavia greets this avowal with scepticism ('"And I come from a planet called Zog in a far-flung galaxy"'), but the disclosure marks a milestone in their relationship and in Black's sense of himself. 'He felt like weeping: something important had happened – tonight he had told someone else about the existence of Milomre Blocj' (315). His revelation signifies his readiness to shed his psychological armour, as does his presentation to Flavia of a key to his new house in the Siberian hinterlands. When he later discovers her there taking refuge from her violently jealous husband, she acknowledges their intimacy by pronouncing his real name: '"Milo," she said, and chuckled. He could hear her laugh reverberate through her body, vibrations on his face' (368). Once again, her laughter levels barriers, signalling her acceptance of the unreconstructed man behind the Platonic construct. It is fitting that, hoping to join her at Heathrow en route to Vienna, Lorimer has himself paged as Milo: 'He heard his new name – his old name – echo out among the bright shops and bars, the cafeterias and the burger franchises. She would hear it, he knew, and she would come' (374). By reclaiming his originary identity he enables a selfhood no longer confined by the warping mask of impersonation.

Black's climactic assertion of that new selfhood targets the Ground Zero of melancholia, the flower stall of the Enoch Powell understudy Marlobe. Smarting from his brusque banishment by the Fortress Sure mob, Lorimer vents his anger on the flimsy structure: '[H]e stepped forward and took a grip of the lower rim of Marlobe's flower shack and heaved. ... [T]he whole trolley went over with a dull but satisfyingly heavy bang and a great rushing of water as the metal vases and buckets voided themselves' (352–3). The act of violence is (as Boyd's word-choice implies) truly purgative. Its effective cause is Marlobe's insulting banter with a female bystander, but its resonance extends further. By this point Marlobe and his shack have accumulated powerful associations with the whole late-capitalist system which Black has diligently served and which has trashed him. As both exemplar and apostle of cutthroat competition, the florist makes an irresistible scapegoat.

However impulsive, Black's act of vandalism marks his new willingness to jettison his shell and take risks. Hitherto he has been loath to accept Hogg's maxim that 'all endeavours were hazardous in the extreme and life was ... a cycle of happenstance and rotten luck' (319). By now, however, he has experienced enough happenstance and rotten luck to know that if he is to live fully he will have to acknowledge them. According to Zygmunt Bauman, 'The mark of postmodern adulthood is the willingness to embrace the game wholeheartedly, as children do'.[26] By this standard Black qualifies as a childlike postmodern adult. Where Leafy had been caught up in games largely of other people's devising, Black is now beginning to play by his own rules. If the high command of Fortress Sure 'had cut him loose and he was drifting away' (372), he recognises that drift holds more promise than their rigged games of disguise and manipulation. Hoping to join Flavia in Vienna he reflects, 'This shaky formula for his future happiness was as solid as anything else in this world, after all' (370). The woman he follows may be a footloose professional actor who lives by role-playing, but her artifices have a transparency which the convoluted designs of Fortress Sure lack. They offer the hope that innocence, of a more fruitful sort than can be found in Leafy's Kinjanja, is not after all dead.

By drifting away from his meticulously constructed fortifications, Black may at last discover whom he really wishes to become. If, as Bauman claims, '[t]he hub of postmodern life strategy is not identity building, but avoidance of fixation',[27] then Black is accepting such a strategy. While he may still seek a more viable identity, he must first abjure the fixed positions he has up to now occupied. His experience bears out Hall's dictum that identity is about 'not "who we are" or "where we came from", so much as what we might become … not the so-called return to roots but a coming-to-terms with our "routes"'.[28] Unlike even so fantastic a creation as Salman Rushdie's Saladin Chamcha in *The Satanic Verses*, Black has no homeland, real or imaginary, to which he can return. His junket to Vienna does not aim to retrace the faltering footsteps of his Gypsy ancestors. Lorimer may have resumed calling himself Milo, but he will never hanker after the acrid aroma of his grandmother's boiled pork. Rather than a recovery of Roma roots, his sortie to the Continent signifies a pursuing of his own idiosyncratic routes.

In pragmatic terms, however, the distinction between 'roots' and 'routes' is perhaps more complicated than Hall's binary formulation would allow. Unlike the predicaments of more typical migrants Black's is at bottom existential rather than positional: he is a 'stranger' in the sense defined by Camus rather than by the British Home Office. Because he bears no visible marks of minority affiliation he is free to mimic the nation's 'mainstream' majority; his alien status springs from his perception of himself, not other people's perceptions of him. In this respect he has more in common with Morgan Leafy than with the diasporic adventurers in novels by writers like Salman Rushdie, Hanif Kureishi or Andrea Levy. In their haunting sense of estrangement both Leafy and Black reflect the feelings of difference and exposure Boyd recalls from his own early years. Rather than highlighting the challenges facing migrants in often unfriendly latter-day Britain, Black's Roma origins function primarily as a trope for the alienation of the generic outsider in the modern world. Like Leafy's, his situation is inherently comic by virtue of his dislocation amid a horde of seekers after values that are outmoded or debased. One could argue that *Armadillo* is itself an act of impersonation: a postmodern novel by a white British writer masquerading as a migrant narrative. In broad terms, however, both *Armadillo* and its predecessor, *A Good Man in Africa*, evoke a Britain shorn of its global pretensions and ludicrously in denial of that fact. As a child both of the periphery and of the homeland, Boyd was peculiarly well situated to produce such a pair of comic epitaphs for empire.[29]

Notes

1 I would like to thank my fellow contributors to this volume, and particularly Sarah Brophy, for their valuable criticisms of this chapter.

2 William Boyd, *A Good Man in Africa* (London: Penguin, 1981), p. 11. Subsequent references to this work will be inserted parenthetically within the text.

3 Boyd has written a number of appreciative pieces on Waugh; see *Bamboo*. He has done an adaptation for television (1988) of *Scoop*, the comic novel by Waugh he most admires. More recently (2001) he has produced an adaptation of Waugh's *Sword of Honour* trilogy. He provided an enthusiastic introduction (1985) to a Penguin reprint of Cary's *Mister Johnson*, and several years later (1990) wrote the screenplay for a film version of that novel.

4 Paul Gilroy, *Postcolonial Melancholia* (New York: Columbia University Press, 2005), p. 14. British editions bear the title: *After Empire: Melancholia or convivial culture?*

5 Gilroy, *Postcolonial Melancholia*, p. 90.

6 Gilroy, *Postcolonial Melancholia*, p. 135.

7 Douglas Dunn, 'Divergent Scottishness: William Boyd, Allan Massie, Ronald Frame'. Gavin Wallace and Randall Stevenson (eds), *The Scottish Novel since the Seventies: New visions, old dreams* (Edinburgh: Edinburgh University Press, 1993), p. 152.

8 Gilroy, *Postcolonial Melancholia*, p. xv.

9 William Boyd, *Armadillo* (London: Penguin, 2009; first published 1998), p. 358. Subsequent references to this work will be inserted parenthetically within the text.

10 William Boyd, *Bamboo: Essays and criticism* (New York: Bloomsbury, 2007), p. 1.

11 Boyd, *Bamboo*, p. 11.

12 Boyd, *Bamboo*, p. 13.

13 Nick Rennison, *Contemporary British Novelists* (Abingdon: Routledge, 2005), p. 29.

14 Some other recent British fiction manifests a comparable sense of acute civic endangerment. A particularly salient example is Ian McEwan's 2005 novel *Saturday*.

15 George Orwell, *Collected Essays, Journalism and Letters*, vol. 2 (Harmondsworth: Penguin, 1968), p. 88.

16 Orwell, *Collected Essays*, vol. 2, p. 77.

17 Gilroy, *Postcolonial Melancholia*, p. xv.

18 Gilroy, *Postcolonial Melancholia*, p. 101.

19 Gilroy, *Postcolonial Melancholia*, p. 101.

20 Stuart Hall, 'The Spectacle of the "Other"' in Stuart Hall (ed.), *Representation: Cultural representations and signifying practices* (London: Sage, 1997), p. 236.

21 Stuart Hall, 'Introduction: who needs "identity"?', in Stuart Hall and Paul Du Gay (eds), *Questions of Cultural Identity* (London: Sage, 1996), p. 4.

22 Malcolm Barnard, *Fashion as Communication*, 2nd edn (London: Routledge, 2002), p. 31.

23 Barnard, *Fashion as Communication*, p. 118.

24 Simon Frith, 'Music and identity' in Hall and Du Gay, *Questions of Cultural Identity*, p. 109 (emphasis in original).

25 Quoted by Frith, 'Music and identity' in Hall and Du Gay, *Questions of Cultural Identity*, p. 111.

26 Zygmunt Bauman, 'From pilgrim to tourist – or a short history of identity', in Hall and Du Gay, *Questions of Cultural Identity*, p. 32.

27 Bauman, 'From pilgrim to tourist', p. 24.

28 Hall, 'Introduction: who needs "identity"?', p. 4.

29 Boyd's most recent novel, *Ordinary Thunderstorms* (London: Bloomsbury, 2009), might qualify as another such epitaph for empire. Like *Armadillo* it is set in a treacherous, globalised metropolis, which exposes the protagonist, Adam Kindred, to murky cross-currents of corporate malfeasance. Like Lorimer Black, Kindred is obliged to take on fabricated identities in order to survive in the post-imperial metropolitan jungle.

7

Unlearning empire:
Penelope Lively's *Moon Tiger*

Huw Marsh

In the opening lines of Salman Rushdie's *Midnight's Children* (1981), the novel's narrator, Saleem Sinai, famously describes himself as 'mysteriously handcuffed to history', his 'destinies indissolubly chained to those of [his] country'.[1] In the opening lines of Penelope Lively's *Moon Tiger* (1987), the novel's narrator, Claudia Hampton, less famously describes her relationship with the history of her times: 'The bit of the twentieth century to which I've been shackled, willy-nilly, like it or not.'[2] In Lively's 1993 novel *Cleopatra's Sister*, the bonds are looser yet still binding, and the heroine, Lucy Faulkner, is 'hitched to events'.[3] In *Oleander, Jacaranda* (1994), Lively's memoir of her early years, the same metaphor describes the author's uncertain relationship with England during a Cairo childhood: 'we were all of us in some mysterious way hitched up to this distant and inconceivable place of which I knew so little.'[4] In Rushdie's novel and throughout Lively's work, handcuffs, hitches and shackles are used as metaphors for the historical – and *historicised* – nature of private lives. Each demonstrates a deep scepticism towards the precise nature of these bonds, describing them in playful and self-aware ways which probe at the boundaries between fact and fabulation, but each suggests a significant interplay between public and private histories.

Yet whilst much of the criticism of *Midnight's Children* has justifiably focused on its depiction of empire and its end, this has not formed the context for discussions of Lively's most famous novel, *Moon Tiger*. Instead *Moon Tiger* has been read for its challenge to the orthodoxies of realist fiction and conventional historiography, with little sense of how it might speak to its own historical moment. Although not always explicitly engaging with these ideas, Linda Hutcheon's category of 'historiographic metafiction' is an important touchstone for discussions which emphasise *Moon Tiger*'s postmodernist or feminist credentials in terms of its non-linear structure and self-aware narration.[5] Influenced most prominently by Michel Foucault and Hayden White, Hutcheon developed these ideas in *A Poetics of Postmodernism* and then in more detail in *The Politics of Postmodernism*, in which she describes a characteristically postmodern form of fiction which, drawing on developments in philosophy and historiography, reflects on its own status as fiction, on the relationship between history and narrative and on the significance of these to questions of ethics and authority.[6] Novels such as John Berger's *G.* (1972), Graham Swift's *Waterland* (1983) and Julian Barnes's *Flaubert's Parrot* (1984) look to history in order to suggest how the 'past really did exist, but we can only know it today through its textual traces'. They challenge 'received notions about the process of representing the actual in narrative' by emphasising the means through which the past is known and, like the histories which began to be written during the same period, they often give an alternative perspective on familiar narratives: 'we now get the histories (in the plural) of the losers as well as the winners, of the regional (and colonial) as well as the centrist, of the unsung many as well as the much sung few, and … of women as well as men.'[7]

These ideas provide a significant and useful framework for approaching *Moon Tiger*, a poioumenon in which Claudia Hampton, a popular historian, embarks upon a history of the world which becomes the book itself. As Claudia lies in hospital dying of bowel cancer she recounts fragments of her life as well as observations about historiography and world history. Alternating between first and third person narration, past and present tenses and different, contradictory, viewpoints, it is a fragmentary history which Claudia describes as 'kaleidoscopic', or as akin to a pack of cards being forever shuffled.[8] Details from Claudia's life including her (possibly incestuous) relationship with her brother, Gordon, her time in Egypt during the second world war and her taking in of Laszlo, a refugee from the 1956 Hungarian Revolution, are linked to meditations on the nature of history and asides on historical events related to the books she has written. Claudia concludes that history is 'disorder', it is 'death and muddle and waste', a view reflected in the history she writes.[9] *Moon Tiger* describes a non-chronological, disorderly and, in Foucauldian terms, discontinuous history which is both reflective of Claudia's 'presumption' at embarking upon such a project and conscious of its inevitable shortcomings and biases.[10] As is persuasively argued by Hutcheon, these types of narrative fireworks are not merely play and also have a political dimension which serves to '"de-doxify" our cultural representations and their undeniable political import'.[11] However, there remains more to be said.

Hutcheon's theory of postmodernism is useful in framing *Moon Tiger* and challenging too-easy assumptions about the realism or parochialism of Lively's fiction. It also helps to establish a political context within which the novel can be read. But the category of historiographic metafiction has its limitations and Hutcheon's readings too often overlook the very specific histories in which these novels are imbricated. As Steven Connor has suggested, Hutcheon's work relies on 'too ready an acquiescence to the manner in which history and fiction have traditionally been contrasted, namely in terms of the degree of their respective truthfulness or capacity to refer accurately to the real'. Consequently Hutcheon – and many of those who have since drawn upon her work – does not fully take account of 'the different ways in which novels may address historical material, be historical and act in history'.[12] Similarly, whilst Stephen Baker broadly agrees with Hutcheon, he suggests in *The Fiction of Postmodernity* that she 'insists on postmodern fiction's interrogation of history and historical discourses, without ever really offering a historicised analysis of the forms that interrogation might take'. According to Baker, Hutcheon focuses on the challenge postmodern fiction presents to received ideologies but 'neglects to study in any depth the ideology of that very critique beyond acknowledging the often contradictory stance which postmodern cultural texts adopt in relation to the societies in which they are produced'.[13] What these arguments reveal are both the significance and limitations of Hutcheon's ideas. Historiographic metafiction remains a useful formulation and suggests a political context for novels too often dismissed as pastiche or apolitical play, but there are historical dimensions to this fiction which are in danger of being lost under too generalised notions of anti-authoritarianism, scepticism and revisionism.[14] In *Moon Tiger* this is clearly linked to notions of nationhood and, inextricably, to Britain's imperial history.[15]

Piecing together the history – and historical critique – in *Moon Tiger* is a case of reading in the margins and identifying the links between chronologically and paginally disparate elements. But Lively's tangential approach to writing about empire should not be read as avoidance or acceptance, and instead suggests ambivalence and uncertainty about how to represent a colonial past which is both recent and firmly entrenched in ideas of national identity. In *Oleander, Jacaranda*, she reflects on the processes of time, memory and history to reimagine her childhood self and the values she learnt during lessons with her nanny, Lucy:

> England was pink. I knew that from Bartholomew's atlas. Pink was good. And there was plenty of it, too, a global rash .... I learned

history from a book called *Our Island Story*, much approved by Lucy. It had glossy romantic pictures of national heroes, with potted accounts of the finer moments of the nation's rise to pink glory. Boadicea and King Arthur and Sir Walter Raleigh and Kitchener and Queen Victoria all somehow rolled into one to produce essence of Englishness. The atlas reinforced this triumphant digest of the Whig interpretation of history .... I imbibed it all with a whisper of unease: did I truly have a claim to all this?

From her later vantage point she looks back in 'dismay' and suggests that there 'has been a lot of unlearning to do'.[16] What once seemed natural had to be denaturalised and Lively had to learn new stories about England and its role in the world; to find a voice and way of representing the past which did not rely on an orderly Whig version of things. In part Lively responds to empire by turning her back on it and seeking to avoid the reinscription of the same tales she was told as a child, yet its presence can still be traced. Lively felt she was 'going into exile' when she returned to her putative home in England, a country which 'bore no resemblance whatsoever' to the 'glowing nirvana' she was told about abroad and to whose culture she was 'alien'.[17] She has described 'a sense of not quite belonging, of finding it difficult to ever feel a paid-up member of anything', which instilled in her a persistent 'feeling of being an outsider, of standing on the outside looking in, observing, watching'.[18] In *Moon Tiger* she, like George Orwell or J.G. Ballard, casts an outsider's glance on the history of her own – and Claudia Hampton's – times and, more ambitiously, on the history of the world.[19]

Archaeologists, palaeontologists and historians of various stripes populate Lively's novels.[20] She has never written what would, in the strictest sense, be called an historical novel but suggests that 'instead, a preoccupation with history, time and the operation of memory has generated narrative themes and sometimes the characters themselves'.[21] Her work demonstrates an abiding interest in the operations of history and memory and, like the other novels featuring historians outlined in Bill Schwarz's introduction to this volume, *Moon Tiger* suggests associations between the interpretation of the past and present-day questions of nationhood and identity.[22] Echoing Lively's own reflections on her education, *Moon Tiger*'s Claudia Hampton is mindful of the uses and abuses of history:

'Please, Miss Lavenham,' I said, when I was fourteen, all guile and innocence. 'Why is it a good thing to learn about history?' We have got to the Indian Mutiny now, and the Black Hole of Calcutta, and are suitably appalled. ... 'Because that is how you can understand why England became a great nation.' Well done, Miss Lavenham. I'm sure you never heard of the Whig interpretation of history, and wouldn't have known what it meant, but breeding will out.[23]

This is the type of historiographic critique outlined by Hutcheon, but it is a critique which draws upon a very specific context. Claudia's irony undercuts the rhetoric of expansion and progress, with the modern reader supplying a degree of knowingness about changes in Britain's global position since this classroom scene of 1924. The passing references to the Indian Mutiny and to the Black Hole of Calcutta also subvert any sense that England's status as a 'great nation' was built on sound principles and indicate how it is no longer acceptable – or *should* no longer be acceptable – to base notions of national identity and pride on these dubious foundations.

Moon Tiger is, in fact, a novel concerned with origins, but its disruption of chronology and its presentation of unstable, ever-shifting boundaries between eras offer a challenge to the telos of imperialist rhetoric. It is a novel which begins with an ending of sorts when, as Claudia lies dying in the hospital, a nurse and doctor speak as if she were not there: '"Was she someone?" enquires the nurse. ... yes, the records do suggest she was someone, probably.'[24] Claudia has already been relegated to the past tense, but the stories she narrates undermine this dismissiveness and show that she both *was* and *is* 'someone'. At the same time it is clear that Claudia is dying and that, in a novel in which her life is so self-consciously 'hitched' to world history, her imminent death has wider implications. Francis Fukuyama's thesis on the 'end of history' was still a few years away when *Moon Tiger* was published, but there is a similar sense of eras ending. In contrast to Fukuyama's triumphalist and apocalyptic view, however, Lively describes cycles of history rather than teleological narratives of end times and sees precedents and new beginnings everywhere. Claudia is aware that people are 'sleeping histories of the world' and sets down her thoughts and experiences for posterity – 'The history of the world as selected by Claudia: fact and fiction, myth and evidence, images and documents' – but her death is not the end.[25]

The final chapter of *Moon Tiger* seemingly describes Claudia's death, at which point she experiences a moment of illumination in which the tree outside her hospital window is bathed in sunlight.[26] Claudia 'is filled with elation, a surge of joy, of well-being, of wonder' which is quickly extinguished as the sun fades, leaving her room 'empty', a 'void' in which there is 'no life'. But outside her window the 'world moves on'; life continues and on the radio 'a voice starts to read the six o'clock news'.[27] There is a sense of an ending here, but also of continuation, and when Gordon earlier expresses his resentment at dying and '"being axed from the narrative"' it is clear that he has had a role to play but that the drama will continue nonetheless.[28] The death of Claudia and others of her generation is seen as reflective of the end of a certain era, but it is not an especially mournful death and Lively seems more interested in understanding processes and new beginnings rather than clearly bounded end times.

Claudia says that she has 'always been interested in beginnings'. She suggests that 'we all scrutinise our childhoods, go about the interesting business of apportioning blame' and that she is similarly fascinated by 'those innocent dawn moments from which history accelerates'.[29] Under scrutiny these moments are less innocent than they at first appear – again there is some apportioning of blame to be done – but repeatedly she turns to the exploits of explorers and conquerors of one sort or another, and particularly to the first European settlers in North America. Claudia is fascinated by the motivations and endurance of these early settlers and addresses them as 'innocents at large in that Garden of Eden'.[30] She is also aware of the environmental and humanitarian impact their colonisation will have on the continent and is interested in the way these beginnings have shaped her own life as well as the course of world history: 'what I am doing is to slot myself into the historical process, hitch myself to its coat tails .... The axes and muskets of Plymouth in 1620 reverberate dimly in my own slice of time.'[31] The idea of being hitched to history once again resurfaces to describe the ongoing processes which shape one's time and the dimly perceptible links between individuals separated by unbridgeable divides in experience and ideology: '[I] am as imprisoned by my time as you were by yours,' Claudia tells those Pilgrims on the Mayflower.[32]

For Claudia, moments always recall other moments, both from her life and from the history of the world. The coexistence of these moments is described in terms of 'strata', a geological model suggesting layers which are discrete yet linked, ordered by chronology yet present simultaneously, as in the Blue Lias formations where Claudia hunted for fossils as a child. When she speaks of the island of Lindisfarne, for example, Claudia thinks of the Viking raids of the eighth century as well as her visits there with Gordon. She and Gordon visited the island as children and again in the 1930s, when the prospect of invasion once more seemed very real – 'it was as though the Vikings were here again, the blood-red sails on the horizon, the tread of men heavy with weapons'.[33] This in turn recalls Claudia's earlier discussion of the form her history should take:

Perhaps I should write like the scribes of the *Anglo-Saxon Chronicle*, saying in the same breath that an archbishop passed away, a synod was held, and fiery dragons were seen flying in the air. Why not, after all? Beliefs are relative.[34]

The flying dragons are recorded in the *Chronicle*'s entry for 793, which describes the portents preceding the Viking raids of that year: 'This year came dreadful fore-warnings over the land of the Northumbrians, terrifying the people most woefully: these were immense sheets of light rushing through the air, and whirlwinds, and fiery dragons flying across the firmament.' A famine ensued, followed by the arrival on Lindisfarne of the invaders: 'the harrowing inroads of heathen men made lamentable havoc in the church of God in Holy-island, by rapine and slaughter.'[35] Claudia's history links twentieth-century fears of invasion to those of the eighth century, which are in her mind bound up with her daughter Lisa's childhood questions about the existence of dragons. This recollection is in turn linked to the occasion at the Ashmolean museum when Claudia announced her pregnancy as she and Lisa's father, Jasper, stood in front of a Chinese dish bearing a picture of a dragon. The connections made between these strata – as well as Claudia's conclusion that beliefs are relative – emphasise *Moon Tiger*'s postmodernist challenge to orderly, chronological descriptions of the past and the empirical certainties of conventional histories. Yet once again this challenge is not simply addressed to debates in historiography and – in a way which develops Hutcheon's ideas – it can be situated within a specific historical moment: like Claudia's thoughts on American history, the references to the Viking invasion of Lindisfarne are suggestive of a broader meditation on beginnings and endings, discoveries, empire and its end.

Claudia is 'fascinated' by the individuals at the centre of these processes, who make their names capitalising on the moods of their times: 'the exploiters of historical circumstance. Political adventurers – Tito, Napoleon. Medieval popes; crusaders; colonisers.'[36] She has written a book on Tito and also one on Hernando Cortez about whose colonial exploits she dreams and, on waking, asks herself 'was I a Spaniard or an Aztec?'[37] Such questions of power and complicity pervade the novel but nowhere more so than in its depictions of Egypt, which are both literally and metaphorically at the centre of Claudia's narrative. The central chapters of the novel describe Claudia's time in Egypt as a war reporter and her subsequent return as a tourist. Although she takes the long view and sees the country as 'a continuous phenomenon, the kilted pharaonic population spilling out into the Nile valley of the twentieth century', Egypt's history is anything but an orderly tale of progress.[38] Again the various strata of the past are visible in the present, with the waves of empire and settlement – Persian, Roman, Ottoman – always apparent in 'polyglot and multi-racial' Cairo.[39] But it is the British presence which dominates.

Egypt was not formally part of the British empire (on Lively's atlas it was 'not pink but diagonally striped with pink – a worrying ambiguity'), but it was, as Peter Mansfield suggests in *The British in Egypt*, 'only with the dismantling of their Empire that the British relinquished what they had come to regard as their seigneurial rights' over the country.[40] Mansfield describes the 'imperial nostalgia' which converged around Egypt and which 'had still not finally disappeared' by the time of the 'ludicrous Suez adventure'.[41] And although Suez is a curiously marginal presence in *Moon Tiger*, Lively does not stint in describing the attitude of entitlement which contributed to the debacle.[42] Life in Anglo-Egyptian Cairo during the 1930s and 1940s was clearly seductive and functioned as a seemingly natural background for the young Lively, who describes in her memoir how she 'perceived it all as an immutable state of affairs, requiring observation but no explanation'. As a child she observed but did not comprehend in the way she later could: 'The notes taken are with me still; now, I can interpret them.'[43] In *Moon Tiger* Claudia takes a similar approach to revising her earlier perceptions and it is only later, when piecing her history together, that she can view it with any kind of critical distance. Interspersed with her wartime experiences are recollections of Claudia's return to Cairo as a tourist in later life and her realisation that the city is entirely changed: 'The egrets no longer roost by the English bridge and the polo grounds are gone.' She resists nostalgia and realises that the place she once knew has gone for a reason: 'I felt quite dispassionate about all this. I do not think I would have wished to find them.'[44]

Claudia does, however, allow her past happiness to inform her descriptions of Egypt as she remembers it from a wartime train ride with her lover, Tom Southern. The landscape is described in pastel shades and the people feature as picturesque ornaments to the vista: 'bare-legged fellaheen with their galabiehs looped up between their thighs, little figures of children in brilliant dresses – vermillion and crimson and lime.' But although she acknowledges this beauty, Claudia also comes to recognise the uncomfortable realities behind it: 'when you began to see it you saw also the sores round the mouths of children, the flies crawling on the sightless eyes of a baby, the bare ulcerated flesh on a donkey's back.'[45] The poverty she witnesses is not attributed solely to British exploitation, but it is seen to exist alongside a community in which people continue eating ice-creams in a café as a woman dies opposite them, and in which 'racial complacency' and indifference meant 'there was no social intercourse between English and Egyptians'.[46] Like Olivia Manning in the *Levant Trilogy* (1977–80), Lively describes how the genteel world of the British went on undisturbed even during wartime; how the lives of many were punctuated only by the 'sounds of ice clinking in glasses, the slap of the suffragis' slippers on the stone of the hotel terrace, the buzz of voices, laughter' at those bastions of Anglo-Egyptian culture the Gezira Sporting Club, the Turf Club and the terrace of Shepheard's Hotel.[47] As Caryl Philips suggests in a 2000 interview with Lively, such clubs had a role in the British imperial project because 'a club involves membership – some people are in it and some people are out of it'.[48]

Lively is not polemical in her condemnation of this society, but rather uses suggestion and irony to get beneath its genteel surface. She has praised J.G. Farrell's novel *The Singapore Grip* (1978) for its evocation of Singapore on the eve of the Japanese invasion – 'the defiant fiddling as the place began to burn' which was 'a manifestation of imperial confidence' – and sees this as analogous to her experience in Egypt.[49] Indeed, in *Moon Tiger* she describes a similarly deluded and defiant attitude and tacitly looks forward to the end which was to come. And when the revolution did come, the symbols of wealth and British authority were first to be attacked. Sparked off by a British assault on the Egyptian police barracks in Ismalia, Cairo rose up on 26 January 1952. On what came to be known as 'Black Saturday', the Shepheard's Hotel was razed to the ground as were Barclays Bank, the BOAC building, Thomas Cook's, W.H. Smith's, the British Council offices and the British Institute. Nine British citizens were also murdered at the Turf Club, 'the symbol of British Privilege in Cairo'.[50] This was the beginning of the revolution which would bring true independence to Egypt and it struck at the heart of the complacent society which, shortly before, had been bristling with 'imperial confidence'. Claudia's history undermines this sense of assurance, offering a postmodernist critique directed not simply at conventional historiography or at realist modes of narration. Rather it offers a history bound up with, but critical of, empire; a history which describes the rise and fall of empires and is aware of their ongoing presence.

On Claudia's return to Egypt the revolution and subsequent modernisation of the country have erased the sites of her memories, but she is not mournful of their passing. Instead she focuses on the positive changes which have taken place: 'The fellaheen are still there but their mud huts have electricity now and infant mortality is no longer forty per cent. The king is gone and so are the English; that society is as distant as Memphis or Thebes.'[51] Once again an historical analogy provides the context for Claudia's analysis of post-independence Egypt and it is a comparison which suggests distance rather than proximity, transition rather than loss. Britain's presence in Egypt cannot simply be forgotten – Claudia's recollections and the history she writes are testament to that – but it is something which should be consigned to the past rather than clung to for affirmation. Claudia's disorderly history of her own life and times – and of those of the world – demonstrates the living presence of the past, but also the need to turn to that past with an analytical, sceptical eye; not to use the past in order to constitute present identity, but rather to grasp processes and change, endings and beginnings.

Notes

1 Salman Rushdie, *Midnight's Children* (London: Picador, 1982), p. 9.
2 Penelope Lively, *Moon Tiger* (Harmondsworth: Penguin, 1988), p. 1.
3 Penelope Lively, *Cleopatra's Sister* (Harmondsworth: Penguin, 1993), p. 104.
4 Penelope Lively, *Oleander, Jacaranda: A childhood perceived* (Harmondsworth: Penguin, 1995), p. 18. This and similar metaphors recur in *Moon Tiger* and a number of Lively's other novels; as Mary Hurley Moran has suggested, 'Lively has become repetitive in some of her observations and phrasings' including 'her reflections on the palimpsest quality of people and places and her figurative use of the words *tethered*, *hitched*, and *kaleidoscopic*'. Mary Hurley Moran, *Penelope Lively* (New York: Twayne, 1993), p. 80.
5 See Christina Kotte, *Ethical Dimensions in British Historiographic Metafiction: Julian Barnes, Graham Swift, Penelope Lively* (Trier: WVT, 2001). And for discussions which situate Lively's work in the contexts of postmodernism and alternative history but do not explicitly engage with Hutcheon's ideas see Debrah Raschke, 'Penelope Lively's *Moon Tiger*: re-envisioning a "history of the world"', ARIEL 26: 4 (1995), 115–32; Mary Hurley Moran, '*Moon Tiger*: a feminist "history of the world"', *Frontiers* 11: 2/3 (1990), 89–95; and Mary Hurley Moran, 'The novels of Penelope Lively: a case for the continuity of the experimental impulse in postwar British fiction', *South Atlantic Review* 62: 1 (1997), 101–20.
6 Of particular significance is Foucault's description in *The Archaeology of Knowledge* (1969) of a movement away from 'vast unities like "periods" or "centuries" to the phenomena of rupture, of discontinuity'. The history he outlines emphasises uncertainty and difference rather than continuity or evolution. Michel Foucault, *The Archaeology of Knowledge*, trans. by A.M. Sheridan Smith (London: Routledge, 2002), p. 4. White's ideas about the role of narrative in historical writing are developed throughout his career. See, for example, 'The historical text as literary artifact' (1974), *Tropics of*

Discourse: Essays in cultural criticism (Baltimore: Johns Hopkins University Press, 1978), pp. 81–100, and a number of the essays in *The Content of the Form* (Baltimore: Johns Hopkins University Press, 1987).

7   Linda Hutcheon, *The Politics of Postmodernism*, 2nd edn (London: Routledge, 2002), pp. 75, 63.

8   Lively, *Moon Tiger*, p. 2. For a useful summary of Lively's use of tense see John Mullan, 'Week one: divided tenses', *Guardian Review*, 1 May 2010, www.guardian.co.uk/books/2010/may/01/penelope-lively-moon-tiger (accessed 21 June 2010); and for a discussion of voice and viewpoint in the novel see John Mullan, 'Week two: divided viewpoints', *Guardian Review*, 8 May 2010, www.guardian.co.uk/books/2010/may/08/penelope-lively-moon-tiger-bookclub (accessed 21 June 2010).

9   Lively, *Moon Tiger*, p. 152.

10 Lively, *Moon Tiger*, p. 2.

11 Hutcheon, *Politics of Postmodernism*, p. 3.

12 Steven Connor, *The English Novel in History, 1950–1995* (London: Routledge, 1996), pp. 131–2.

13 Stephen Baker, *The Fiction of Postmodernity* (Edinburgh: Edinburgh University Press, 2000), p. 4.

14 Most famously, Fredric Jameson has accused postmodernism of being depthless, prone to pastiche and uncritical nostalgia, and representative of a weakening of historicity. Fredric Jameson, *Postmodernism; or, the cultural logic of late capitalism* (London: Verso, 1991).

15 Amy Elias's *Sublime Desire* provides a useful touchstone here. It features a discussion of 'novels written by First World authors that attempt to look at their own Western history from the perspective of its Others'. Although her argument does not quite transfer to *Moon Tiger*, Elias does suggest a number of ways in which Hutcheon's ideas can be extended and developed. Amy J. Elias, *Sublime Desire: History and post-1960s fiction* (Baltimore: Johns Hopkins University Press, 2001), p. 219.

16 Lively, *Oleander, Jacaranda*, pp. 18–19.

17 Lively, *Oleander, Jacaranda*, pp. 163, 173, 170.

18 Penelope Lively and Caryl Phillips, 'End of empire and English literature' (2000), event at the British Library, www.fathom.com/feature/122056/index.html (accessed 22 June 2010).

19 As Bill Schwarz discusses in the introduction to this volume, both Orwell and Ballard spent their early years in colonial outposts and felt at odds with metropolitan culture.

20 *Treasures of Time* (1979) is concerned with the legacy of Hugh Paxton, a recently deceased archaeologist, while Howard in *Cleopatra's Sister* is a palaeontologist. One of the major characters in Lively's recent novel *The Photograph* (2003) is a landscape historian, and Lively has herself published an introduction to landscape history: *Presence of the Past* (London: Collins, 1976).

21 Penelope Lively, 'The presence of the past', *Oxford Today* 16: 1 (2003), www. oxfordtoday.ox.ac.uk/2003-04/v16n1/05.shtml (accessed 22 June 2010). Some sections of *Moon Tiger* conform to Avrom Fleishman's suggestion that those novels set beyond an (admittedly arbitrary) limit of forty to sixty years in the past should be considered historical. However, these sections comprise only about half the novel, the rest being set in the present day. Avrom Fleishman, *The English Historical Novel: Walter Scott to Virginia Woolf* (Baltimore: Johns Hopkins University Press, 1971), p. 3.

22 In Angus Wilson's *Anglo-Saxon Attitudes* (1956), for example, the Piltdown Man forgery which frames the novel had implications going far beyond the academy. As David Higdon suggests, the 1912 discovery of bones, seemingly from an unknown form of early man, 'raised questions of validity and nationalism' because 'with the discovery of Neanderthal man in Germany in 1856 and the cave paintings in France in 1878–79, England lagged far behind in offering signs of prehistoric inhabitation'. The 1953 revelation that it was a crude hoax made up from fragments of a human skull and an orang-utan jawbone 'reverberated not only through the halls of science but also through the halls of Parliament'. During this period of declining national prestige, the loss of such an apparently significant memory affected not only scholarly reputations but also national pride and the country's view of its place in the world. David Leon Higdon, *Shadows of the Past in Contemporary British Fiction* (London: Macmillan, 1984), p. 140. For a detailed and persuasive reading of Wilson's novel, including a discussion of 'the authenticating force of historical origins in a narrative of Englishness', see Connor, *English Novel*, pp. 49–55. In *Treasures of Time* Lively offers an alternative perspective on the relationship between historical finds and national identity. Tom Rider, a Ph.D. candidate engaged to the daughter of a famous archaeologist, considers new evidence that ancient British culture was more sophisticated than previously thought and finds it 'odd' that 'earlier archaeologists should have been so anxious to attribute everything to continental influence'. He thinks that to claim the nation's treasures as originating domestically 'would have fitted in with good old imperialist chauvinist days', but puts this disparity down to 'the conditioning of a classical education: anything that is culturally worth having comes from Greece or Rome'. Lively, *Treasures of Time* (London: Penguin, 2010), p. 92.

23 Lively, *Moon Tiger*, p. 22.

24 Lively, *Moon Tiger*, pp. 1–2.

25 Lively, *Moon Tiger*, pp. 65, 1.

26 Here the sense that Claudia is both narrator and author figure potentially breaks down. However, it remains possible that Claudia is imagining her future death rather than narrating it as it happens.

27 Lively, *Moon Tiger*, pp. 207–8.

28 Lively, *Moon Tiger*, p. 184.

29 Lively, *Moon Tiger*, p. 28.

30 Lively, *Moon Tiger*, p. 31.

31 Lively, *Moon Tiger*, p. 29.

32 Lively, *Moon Tiger*, p. 31.

33 Lively, *Moon Tiger*, p. 17.

34 Lively, *Moon Tiger*, p. 8.

35 Unknown, *The Anglo-Saxon Chronicle*, trans. by James Henry Ingram, in *Project Gutenberg*, www.gutenberg.org/files/657/657.txt (accessed 28 June 2010).

36 Lively, *Moon Tiger*, p. 144.

37 Lively, *Moon Tiger*, p. 154.

38 Lively, *Moon Tiger*, p. 80.

39 Lively, *Moon Tiger*, p. 75.

40 Lively, *Oleander, Jacaranda*, p. 19. Peter Mansfield, *The British in Egypt* (London: Weidenfeld and Nicolson, 1971), pp. xiii–xiv. Since Egypt's transition from a British protectorate to independence in 1922, Britain had retained control over the four key areas of defence, communications (meaning primarily the Suez Canal), the protection of foreign interests and minorities, and relations with the Sudan. Even after the 1936 Anglo-Egyptian Treaty, when some of these responsibilities were ceded to Egypt, significant numbers of British troops continued to occupy the country. For a concise survey of Egypt's modern history see Afaf Lutfi Al-Sayyid Marsot, *A History Of Egypt*, 2nd edn (Cambridge: Cambridge University Press, 2007).

41 Mansfield, *The British in Egypt,* p. xiv.

42 Although Claudia refers to 'the year of the canal' and a growing sense of outrage at the Eden government, it is the Hungarian revolution of the same year which claims her attention. Lively, *Moon Tiger*, pp. 171–2. Lively does, however, address Suez directly in her 'anti-memoir' *Making it Up* (London: Penguin, 2006; first published 2005), in which a series of stories trace the alternative paths her life could have taken: in the chapter 'Comet', she posits what might have happened had she followed up on a notion to return to Egypt and teach English. Her imaginary self dies when the aeroplane on which she was being evacuated crash lands.

43 Lively, *Oleander, Jacaranda*, p. 19.

44 Lively, *Moon Tiger*, p. 113.

45 Lively, *Moon Tiger*, pp. 72, 75.

46 Lively, *Moon Tiger*, pp. 88–9, 115–16.

47 Lively, *Moon Tiger*, p. 73. Artemis Cooper describes how 'Compared to London or Paris, Cairo had undergone little change since the war, and the Anglo-Egyptian upper crust carried on as they always had. The British still sipped their gin-slings on the terrace of Shepheard's Hotel ... [t]here was still polo and racing at the Gezira Club, dancing at the Auberge des Pyramides or Madame Badia's'. Artemis Cooper, *Cairo in the War, 1939–1945* (London: Hamish Hamilton, 1989), pp. 327–8.

48 Lively and Phillips, 'End of empire and English literature'.

49 Lively, *Oleander, Jacaranda*, p. 59.

50 Wm. Roger Louis, *The British Empire in the Middle East, 1945–1951* (Oxford: Clarendon Press, 1984), p. 747. Louis closes his narrative with this event and clearly identifies it as a watershed. See also Cooper, *Cairo in the War*, pp. 333–6.

51 Lively, *Moon Tiger*, p. 116.

8

'I am not the British Isles on two legs': travel fiction and travelling fiction from D.H. Lawrence to Tim Parks

Suzanne Hobson

Time and again, D.H. Lawrence made it clear that his argument was above all with English, the language in which his society's values were enshrined, to the extent, he claims, that he had to invent 'a foreign language' to write his first great novel, *The Rainbow*. (Tim Parks[1])

Tim Parks does not see his novels as belonging to the archive of Anglo-British fiction. As noted by an interviewer in 1999, Parks locates himself firmly in the European literary context: any national literature, he argues, can become parochial.[2] In this respect, Parks invites comparison with D.H. Lawrence, who having spent most of his adult life outside England writing fiction and essays which sought to expose English parochialism wherever he detected it, would no doubt have been surprised to know quite how central his novels would become to the Leavisite 'English tradition' after his death.[3] But central they became and have remained and this is not, this chapter argues, in spite of Lawrence's carefully crafted posture of foreignness or what Rick Rylance calls his 'oxymoronic Englishness'.[4] Rather, it is often because this posture reveals both to critics and novelists coming after Lawrence ways of articulating 'England and its ethnic forms' at their most natural (whether this means white working-class men, 'drawing-room' women or colonial pioneers) while also signalling their discomfort with the imperial forms of racial and sexual hierarchy which are conjured up by these means. Lawrence's foreignness thus serves as a distancing device, a way of inhabiting Englishness uneasily, with irony or more directly under protest: 'I am not the British Isles on two legs.'[5]

In the first part of this chapter, I explore how readings of Lawrence's foreignness have, since the 1950s, tracked and often focalised more general anxieties about the relationship between the English novel and empire. If Lawrence's difference from the 'English' was once perceived as one of class, then he is now more likely to be seen by critics and novelists such as Margaret Drabble, Helen Dunmore and Tim Parks as a traveller whose movements provide a critical lens through which to see both the home culture and the actions of that culture abroad.[6] In the subsequent sections I consider how, for Parks, Lawrence offers a model of ambivalent attachment to Englishness; a means of locating his novels within an 'English tradition' precisely at the point where the centre of this tradition shows itself divided, uncertain about what it means to write fiction in English after the end of empire and anxious to know how the novel can move beyond the various kinds of reductivism associated with parochialism and its close shadows, imperial nostalgia and writing back.

Lawrence as traveller

Since Raymond Williams it has been common to read Lawrence against a background of cultural crisis although, as Simon Gikandi points out, it would not have occurred to Williams to link this crisis to post-imperial decline.[7] In *Culture and Society*, Lawrence's novels provide a window on a crisis which reveals itself first in the industrial heartlands of England. They track the effects of the imposition of the cash nexus and the machine on collective and spontaneous modes of living. Re-reading Williams's book in the light of the recent emphasis on Lawrence's travels, it is striking how pointedly he resists the temptation to read Lawrence as a perennial outsider, a belated incarnation of romantic wanderlust. He insists instead that Lawrence is an 'exile', meaning someone who wishes the system to change so that he might return home.[8] What matters here is less Williams's definition of exile – which as Edward Said points out is problematic when used to refer to the various forms of expatriation 'chosen' by modernist writers – than his imagined repatriation of Lawrence: the manner in which Lawrence comes to stand for an indigenous working-class culture which is opposed to the kinds of romantic and post-romantic cultures for which aimless wandering (facilitated, though Williams does not say this, by colonial networks and infrastructures) was both a privilege and a rite of passage.[9]

Lawrence experiences a similar fate in novels from the 1950s and 1960s, which name him as a predecessor, both to establish their own cultural authority (their claim to speak beyond the provinces despite their provincial interests) and to signal that this authority does not, as is often presumed to be the case with Lawrence, originate with a connection to the metropolitan elite. Lawrence's trajectories are curiously circumscribed in these novels: usually they follow the movement from the North to the London art-world, from which the protagonists maintain a critical distance (John Braine, Stan Barstow);[10] or more unusually from the city to Northern seaside resorts and tourist-spots, such as Lincoln Cathedral where Edwin Fisher, the central character in Stanley Middleton's *Holiday*, imagines an argument with his wife that is lifted almost word for word from *The Rainbow*. Edwin's decision to stay in the Lawrentian Midlands for his holidays is explicitly contrasted with that of his friends and fellow professionals who take advantage of the burgeoning tourist industry to book foreign holidays to such places as 'Ibiza, Majorca, Costa Brava, Costa del Sol'.[11]

For this 1950s and 1960s generation, Lawrence offered a way out of an impasse: the means to distance their own novels from a version of 'Englishness' which already included within it the privileges of travel outside England and, more importantly, the right to choose when and where to (dis)own the identity of an English man or woman. These privileges are recognisably colonial in nature, although it seems unlikely (following Gikandi) that many of this generation would have seen them in these terms. More immediately, these novelists sought to distance their work from the Englishness they associated with British modernism and Bloomsbury in particular or, decoupling Englishness from national and ethnic identity, from the kind of American identity which in novels by Henry James is often synonymous with the gentleman expatriate. In this context, Lawrence's travel writings are often ignored or, when emphasised, tend to focus on his anxieties over his relationship to his metropolitan and cosmopolitan peers. To V.S. Naipaul, Lawrence belongs squarely with the elite group of white, male writers who made travel writing an occupation reserved for the colonial elite: 'But the writers I had had in mind – and there could have been no others – were metropolitan people, Huxley, Lawrence, Waugh. I was not like them. They wrote at a time of empire; whatever their character at home, they inevitably in their travels became semi-imperial, using the accidents of travel to define their metropolitan personalities against a foreign background.'[12] Anthony Burgess saw Lawrence's position vis-à-vis the likes of Waugh and Huxley differently. In his introduction to the 1972 Viking edition of Lawrence's Italian travel writings, he brought Lawrence's class back into play as his saving difference from Naipaul's 'metropolitan people': 'Lawrence was essentially an educated working-man, the product of a "phatically" loquacious Midland mining community, not a cold taciturn Southerner educated in an expensive, though austere, centre of learning, condescending, assured of certain certainties, including the British superiority to foreigners.'[13] Neither of these positions seems quite right as a final assessment of Lawrence's travel writings, not least because, as Howard Booth points out, he is anything but consistent in his attitudes both to his own metropolitan roots and to the 'foreigners' he meets.[14]

How, then, have Lawrence's foreign travels once again become a powerful part of his myth and an attraction for critics and novelists alike? And what might this reveal about the changing relationship between the English novel and the end of empire? While, as this collection attests, the postwar English novel often disavows empire by relocating debates over Englishness closer to home, the travel book has often struggled to free itself from what Debbie Lisle calls 'the embarrassment of its colonial past'.[15] Naipaul and Burgess point to two different versions of this embarrassment. More recently, critics have found a whole range of imperial tropes including the 'imperial-I', clubbability and cliché in books by the most recognisable of British travel writers such as Bruce Chatwin and Redmond O'Hanlon.[16] This does not mean, however, that the colonial embarrassments associated with the Anglo-British traveller can be confined to travel writing. Fiction and travel have always been intimately connected and, even in a present-day era which usually separates fiction from travel writing, there is frequently a passage between the two: novelists from Lawrence to Parks have often turned to travel writing, rightly perceiving it to be a more profitable undertaking than writing fiction. In addition to these specific connections, cultural historians and anthropologists have argued that travel in general should be moved to the centre of the cultural studies agenda. James Clifford's influential 'Travelling cultures', from which I borrow the title of my chapter, argues that 'travel' rather than dwelling ought to form the basis of cultural comparison and this because of, rather than in spite of, 'its historical taintedness; its associations with gendered, racial bodies, class privilege, specific means of conveyance, beaten paths, agents, frontiers, documents and the like'.[17] Clifford's work has refocused attention on travel while attempting to avoid the concept of exile and with it the metropolitan privileges which are associated with 'exiles' in modernist cultures.

It is in this context that critics have returned to Lawrence's travel books to find a writer whose emphasis on spontaneity, difference and the imperfect stands in sharp contrast to the imperial tendencies revealed in, variously, the authority of the Victorian travelogue, the 'romance of a lost unity' found in Eliot, and the quest for a rapidly disappearing 'England' revealed in backward-looking travel books from the 1930s.[18] The most recent Penguin edition of *D.H. Lawrence and Italy* (2007) is introduced by Parks, who as a travel writer, novelist and expatriate who has lived most of his adult life in Italy, seems ideally positioned to make a case for the continued relevance of Lawrence's travel books to the current generation. Lawrence's antagonistic relationship to the British empire is crucial in this respect for Parks grounds his argument in Lawrence's hostility to imperialism (particularly in 'Sketches of Etruscan Places') rather than in his class difference or his narrative style: 'In particular, [Lawrence] is eager to underline the deep alliance throughout history between the brutal will to power and puritanical morals, an alliance, as he sees it, still alive in 1927 both in imperial Britain and Fascist Italy.'[19] As glossed by Parks, Lawrence's account of empire seems ahead of its times, much closer to a postcolonial critique than the fashionable left-wing anti-imperialism that, for the likes of Graham Greene, was rooted in altogether English values such as fair play, tolerance and decency. Though Lawrence does not go quite so far as to argue that England is itself an effect of empire, he insists that it is a fiction, conceived after the fact to justify the same kind of expansionist and homogenising practices as were demonstrated by the Romans in their relationship with Etruria:

> In Etruria there is no starting point. Just as there is no starting-point for England, once we have the courage to look beyond Julius Caesar and 55 BC. ... What does the word England mean, even? What clue would it give to the rise of the English, should all our history be lost? (437)

Elsewhere Lawrence exposes the fallacy at the heart of imperial nostalgia (the erasure of the imperial hand in the destruction of an 'innocent' culture which the former subsequently mourns as a lost golden age): if the Italian workers are now politicised and materialistic then that is 'our own English fault'; 'we have set forth, politically, on such a high and Galahad quest of holy liberty and have been caught so shamelessly filling our pockets' (176). Yet it would be misleading to suggest that Lawrence's travel books ever break out of the 'semi-imperial' mode of travelling or that they play down, rather than up, Clifford's 'associations with gendered, racial bodies, class privilege, specific means of conveyance, beaten paths, agents, frontiers, documents and the like'. Italian men turn red in the sun like Etruscan paintings and 'American Indians' (372); Lawrence and Frieda travel first class on the steamer though, to their annoyance, this means they have to share a berth with three others (301); the agent who demands to see Lawrence's passport is a 'fool' (349); and the main reason for their trip to Sardinia, as opposed to Naples and Rome, is to get off the beaten track or outside 'the net of this European civilisation' (143).

Rylance points out that there is something odd in the urge to understand Lawrence as either normative or deviant, to read his books as either central or eccentric to a dominant English culture. Few other writers, he points out, have received this kind of scrutiny. He adds that this urge is particularly curious at a time 'when British culture has become more open to multi- and cross-cultural perspectives and a bit more comfortable with its own ambiguities.'[20] There is undoubtedly something troubling about the level of investment in Lawrence as a possible salve to post-imperial consciences in their encounters with modernist cultures. But the relevance which Lawrence's 'foreignness' retains for recent novelists and travel writers is not necessarily an anomaly. British culture is not yet altogether comfortable with the ambiguities of Englishness, and if this is not so clearly manifest in the novel as in the travel book which finds it hard to disguise its debts to the colonial past, then this discomfort nonetheless emerges in other, less obvious ways: in Parks's reworking of Lawrence's utopian geographies, for example, or in his Lawrentian concern with the homogenising potential of English as a global language.

Parks and Lawrence in the Tyrol

Parks published ten novels prior to 2000, in which he divided his attention between England and Italy – before, in *Europa* (1997) and in *Destiny* (1999), turning to the question of Europe itself. He also wrote two travel books in this period based on his experience as 'an Englishman in Italy' (*Italian Neighbours* [1992] and *An Italian Education* [1996]); a collection of essays (*Adultery and Other Diversions* [1998]); and a book on translating modernist writers, first published in 1998 and republished in 2007.[21] In the mid-2000s, Parks's writing became more directly and indirectly concerned with Lawrence: he published an introduction to the new Penguin edition of Lawrence's travel writing (2007); a second collection of essays, *The Fighter* (2007), containing an essay on Lawrence; and a novel, *Cleaver* (2007), which, as I suggest below, reworks a number of key themes from Lawrence's travel books and fiction. After *Cleaver*, Parks wrote *Dreams of Rivers and Seas* (2009) in which he moves away from the more obvious Lawrentian themes of *Cleaver*, but in so doing takes Lawrence's exploration of travel and its relationship with national character into the postcolonial space inhabited by his protagonists, John James and his family, as they move between London and Delhi.

Like many of Parks's books, *Cleaver* focuses on the consciousness of a middle-aged man placed under particular stress by a family crisis and by the increasing difficulty of his ignoring the signs of his declining health and sexual virility. The internal monologue in this case belongs to a television journalist, Harold Cleaver, who has abandoned his family at the height of his success (following an interview with the American President) to live in isolation in the mountains of the South Tyrol. The purported reason for his flight is a book written by his son which, though marketed as fiction and nominated for the Booker, appears to his father to be a defamatory account of his son's childhood: 'Look, doesn't the Booker, Cleaver had shouted to his wife at breakfast that morning – he seemed to remember she was grinding coffee beans – have to be a novel, fiction?'[22] Following a pattern established by Parks's earlier books, the seeming triviality and ultimately personal nature of Cleaver's immediate concerns are offset by the loaded nature of the cultural and historical material they touch upon: the role of America's unilateral foreign policy; the unstoppable rise of tourism as the privileged mode of travel and preferred way to encounter otherness (as opposed, for Cleaver, to the otherness of the black boyfriend that his daughter brings home (229)); and finally, offering a means of approach to Lawrence, the place of Englishness and the English language in the new Europe.

Within Lawrence's Europe, or what Earl Ingersoll calls his 'psychic geography', Cleaver's destination – the South Tyrol – has particular personal and cultural significance.[23] The Tyrol was where Lawrence took Frieda soon after their elopement and where she betrayed him for the first time; it features in three of Lawrence's travel essays; and it's the destination chosen, for similar reasons to Cleaver, by Rupert Birkin when he makes his escape from England with Ursula at the end of *Women in Love*. More importantly, the Tyrol is the site of Gerald Crich's death and it operates in the novel as the white screen on to which Lawrence projected his nihilistic vision of the Northern races, and of the English in particular, as having reached the end of their active history. This is a landscape, in other words, which is saturated with Lawrentian portents regarding the fate of the national character; portents which in Cleaver survive, but only just – being part-erased or co-opted by the more prevalent (or noisier) cultural forces of the twenty-first century including tourism, European secularism and the spread of global media and communication networks.

The most significant of these portents is the crucifix. The Penguin edition of Lawrence's Italian essays begins with 'The crucifix across the mountains', drafted in 1912–13 and revised in the early years of the first world war. Here, Lawrence interpreted the many crucifixes which he encountered on the road from Munich to Verona as the physical traces of 'forgotten imperial processions' and of the 'imperial vanity' which still sticks to the German soul (5). Lawrence made a pointed distinction between the crucifixes in the valleys which were 'factory-made' and 'weak and sentimental', and those in the mountain passes which responded instead to the peasant's sense of his labouring body as both the source of his vitality while at the same moment functioning as a constant reminder of his weakness and mortality (5, 12). While the former were easily ignored, the latter registered as a shock, evoking in the contrast between the stubborn body of the Christ and the frozen eternity of the mountains something of the nature of life itself, as forged in the struggle between opposing forces. The meaning of these crucifixes was missed, however, by most visitors to the region: mountain guides and their entourages; distant descendants of the imperial processions who 'tramp slowly, heavily past, not observing the presence of the symbol, making no salute' (14). Cleaver too sees crucifixes throughout the South Tyrol: in the homes and lodgings of the people he meets, on a shrine high up in the mountains and, on one memorable occasion, being carried at the head of a funeral procession (9, 30, 53, 95, 106). Like Lawrence's mountain guides, he is simply at a loss to know what to make of these relics from a religious past and quickly dismisses the crucifixes as part of the clichéd package to be consumed by tourists as 'standard South Tyrolese bric-a-brac' (30). He imagines presenting this stuff to the audience of one of his TV documentaries: 'Observe, he would tell the audience, the unusually large, carved wooden crucifix hanging over the bench in the corner, the Christ's twisted limbs, the sombre resignation of the upturned eyes' (9). What is, in Lawrence, a sign of a forgotten imperial ambition which had been claimed by a people and a locale as an expression of their own particular circumstances becomes, in Parks, the kind of local flavour beloved of a tourist industry that encourages the forgetting of its own imperial ambitions in order to preserve the value of the cultural differences which are its most desirable product. The spectres of forgotten empires are overcome by the omnipresent spectre of tourism, which has no connection to the past except to the extent that it can be packaged and sold as a commodified instance of local character.

In this respect, the most significant crucifix in *Cleaver* is the one which is not there. Cleaver (almost) re-enacts the death of Gerald in *Women in Love*, venturing out into the snow on his own and gradually succumbing to cold and exhaustion. The passages describing his adventure are close enough to those in Lawrence to suggest a kind of homage. In both novels, the landscape is a formless, blank screen: 'astonishingly white and shapeless' in Parks and an 'illuminated darkness' in Lawrence. Both convey the uncanny sensation, emphasised through the shift from indirect reported speech to interior monologue, that one's own death is happening to someone who is not quite oneself:

> There was something standing out in the snow. He [Gerald] approached it with the dimmest curiosity.
>   It was a half-buried crucifix, a little Christ under a little sloping hood at the top of a pole. Somebody was going to murder him. He had a great dread of being murdered. But it was a dread that stood outside him like his own ghost. ...
>   Lord Jesus, was it then bound to be – Lord Jesus! He could feel the blow descending he knew he was murdered.[24]

> His leg sank in thigh deep. Jesus! Cleaver sat and tried to put the shoe on again. The strap had broken. ...
>   I can't get up. For Christ's sake. This is it, Cleaver decided then. It's happening. He didn't feel angry or desperate. Only yesterday you dreamed of it. Now it had come much sooner than he imagined.
> (248–50)

Conspicuously missing from Cleaver's near-death experience is the religious icon – 'the half-buried crucifix' – which turns Gerald's demise into an epitaph for his entire race: the Northern European Christians who worship the 'God which is Not-Me', first, in the form of an abstract Christ and then, and nowhere more so than in England, in the form of the machine.[25] Gerald, the ruthless industrialist, is the perfect expression of this race, and his death in the snow the inevitable outcome of its striving to reach total self-abnegation in the pursuit of an impersonal God. In the passage from Parks, Cleaver's curses – 'Jesus!', 'For Christ's sake' – serve as a verbal echo, a distant memory of Gerald's death and Lawrence's prophesies concerning the fate of the Christian races. So too does the first line of the next chapter, which cuts to Cleaver's recovery after being rescued by his hosts: 'Cleaver is in a state of beatitude' (251). But in Parks these ghosts of empire (or ghosts of ghosts given that Gerald is himself the last gasp of an almost extinct race) meet a less tragic end than in *Women in Love*. Far from the pathos and ambivalence of Gerald's death in the snow, Cleaver's near-death is immediately undercut with caustic irony and the bathos of his rescue. Cleaver is no more the epitome of Englishness than he is a martyr or a saint. In the sort of tabloidese into which he often slips to narrate and denigrate his own life, he is a man who has had a lucky escape. And maybe even this is to stretch the point as it quickly transpires that Cleaver was never as far from his nearest neighbours as he had imagined: indeed, it turns out that the remoteness of the spot was artfully fabricated to attract walkers: 'People liked that there was … keine Elecktrizitat. It was an adventure' (271).

Gabriella Nouzeilles argues that mountaineering is one of the 'last resorts' of alternative travel, a final refuge for the kind of imperial nostalgia which breeds an expectation that travel will be difficult, demanding a heroic effort from the traveller and offering in return an encounter with the 'real'.[26] She touches on one of the most enduring myths of the end of empire: the idea that the world is shrinking and that the traveller has arrived too late on the scene to discover anything new. (In fact, this particular ending was already evident in the beginnings of empire. Clifford calls the uncanny experience of meeting Westernised natives in far-flung corners of the world the 'Squanto' effect, after the English-speaking Indian who greeted the pilgrims in Plymouth in 1620.)[27] This myth does not, however, endure unchanged and in this instance the distance of almost a hundred years between Lawrence and Parks is critical. When Lawrence talked of getting outside 'the net of the old European civilisation' in *Sea and Sardinia*, he divided the world along familiar colonial lines: at the centre was an acquisitive (if aged) European civilisation beginning in Greece and spreading outwards across Italy and the western part of the Eurasian peninsula; beyond lay the primitive, the untarnished and – before the Squanto effect, in the form of Italian soldiers and Communists, disabused him – the realm of the entirely other (143). In the mountaineering guides discussed by Nouzeilles, as well as in *Cleaver*, the point is also to get beyond the net of civilisation. But the meaning of 'civilisation' is much less strong than in Lawrence; in Parks it becomes a cliché, an off-hand way of referring to the deterritorialised 'net' of electricity and mobile phone networks, the internet and GPS. To Cleaver, for example, it is a relief to think that he would be able to pick up his mobile phone messages 'while he was down in civilisation' (47).

This is one of many occasions both in *Cleaver* and *Dreams of Rivers and Seas*, where travellers seem implausibly fascinated by mobile phone networks. Despite loudly advertising his wish for isolation, Cleaver is soon observed in the act of waving his mobile phone in the air in the hope of picking up a signal: 'the busy gadget sending its feelers into the busy air for some welcoming network to lock into' (21). In *Dreams of Rivers and Seas*, John James has barely arrived in India before he is texting his girlfriend and commenting, in no less extravagant and clichéd terms than Cleaver, that it 'was fantastic that you could send text messages back and forth between India and Maida Vale … and yet you couldn't find your mother round the corner'.[28] Parks thus re-stages the imperial shock of getting off the beaten track and being greeted with 'the coke can carrying local' as the faux shock of discovering that even 'above the noise level' (33, 99, 167) it is impossible to disengage entirely from modern communication.[29] The variation on the cliché 'getting off the beaten track' suggests that, as in the ideal scientific experiment, it is only after eliminating all the background noise that you can be sure your experience is empirically valid or, indeed, 'real'.

Travelling fiction

The shift in emphasis from the net of European civilisation to a global media and communication network has moved debates about the English novel from the flat plane of the map, with its two-way traffic between centre and periphery, into a deeper and more fluid space crossed and re-crossed by the many channels through which the English language circulates around the world. This new space is no less haunted by the spectres of empire than that of old, but for Parks as well as for advocates of new theories of cosmopolitanism it also offers fresh opportunities for staging the encounter between the novel in English and other languages and cultures. Lawrence's writing retains its significance in these new debates, in part because, as Parks points out, he was a translator as well as a novelist. Yet there is no equivalent in Lawrence to the kind of anxiety which inhabits many contemporary novelists – one might think of J.M. Coetzee, Amitav Ghosh and Parks himself – consequent upon the attempt to narrate in their fiction a non-English speaking world to a predominantly English-speaking market. Indeed, Lawrence was remarkable among contemporaries for the rapidity and impunity with which he approached the task of translating unfamiliar territories and peoples into English. Rebecca West remembers arriving in Italy to discover him already at his typewriter:

> This was faintly embarrassing, because on the doorstep Douglas had described how on arriving in a town Lawrence used to go straight from the railway station to his hotel and immediately sit down and hammer out articles about the place, vehemently and exhaustively describing the temperament of the people.[30]

As a travel writer Parks is more cautious. The author's note to *An Italian Education* explains his decision to make extensive use of untranslated Italian phrases, partly because of his wish not to submit too readily to the demands of publishers that he present his readers with a familiar language.[31] Later, in

Cleaver, this caution is re-staged as a naïve resistance to any kind of translation, especially when this translation is a prelude to 'hammering out' an article or a documentary on a place. Even before arriving in the South Tyrol Cleaver announces that it is not his intention to write about the place: 'The culture such as it may turn out to be, Cleaver told himself firmly, of the South Tyrol need not be analysed, ironised, criticised or eulogised' (4). No Lawrence he, Cleaver will not try to capture the 'collective identity' of the locals; in fact he has chosen his destination because, not speaking German, the South Tyrolean identity will remain stubbornly untranslatable to him: 'There will be no more reading, he had decided. He just did not want to hear, even in a language he did not know, their shared life, their noisy collective identity' (6).

Rebecca Walkowitz argues that this sort of explicit comment on issues of language and translatability is the hallmark of a new kind of novel: the 'born-translated novel'. She coins this phrase with reference to Parks's work on translation to describe novels which are written to travel, and which in conception are designed to accommodate translatability. This is a concession to the conditions of a global marketplace, but according to Walkowitz this does not mean that the 'born-translated' novel sacrifices the possibility of a critique of its own commodified conditions. In fact, she suggests, comment on the 'political history of languages' better survives the process of translation in a 'born-translated' novel than in a novel which relies on a singular linguistic idiom. The contrast, implicit here but spelt out elsewhere in her essay, is to modernist literature which places a premium on such so that, in a phrase she borrows from Parks, the work becomes a 'thing made of language'. In born-translated novels, such as Coetzee's *Diary of a Bad Year*, this emphasis is turned on its head. The novel's quarrel with language is signalled at the level of typography – public essays and private diaries appear on facing pages as in a simultaneous translation – and of narrative – the novel traces the 'collaborative' process through which the essays themselves are composed. Besides Coetzee, Walkowitz also names Kazuo Ishiguro, W.G. Sebald, Caryl Phillips, Jamaica Kincaid and Tim Parks (as novelist rather than translator) as writers of 'born-translated' fiction.[32]

And yet in my view, despite his investment in these questions, Parks does not exactly fit the rubric of 'born-translated novelist'. His essay on translation begins with a similar question to that addressed by Walkowitz: how, and in what different forms, do the 'cosmopolitan styles' of modernism (part of what Walkowitz calls 'the project of imperialism'[33]) feed into new kinds of 'transnational' literatures concerned with global contexts of citizenship and decolonisation? But he is sceptical of the idea that novels can be 'accessible but not obsequious',[34] and suspects that there is a price to be paid for capitulation to the fundamentally conservative forces of the global marketplace. For a writer to rebel against his or her national identity – as Lawrence, Joyce and Beckett famously did – has rapidly become a rite of passage to international celebrity. Nothing is loved so much by other cultures as a 'rebel' from his own; a fact that novelists such as Doris Lessing – 'I look at England with an English eye and simultaneously a foreigner's eye too' – and Kazuo Ishiguro have not been slow to realise.[35] Parks quotes Ishiguro as the source of the idea, also explored by Walkowitz, that novels should be written with translation already in mind. Unlike Walkowitz, however, Parks does not equivocate over the question of whether this is better or worse for the novel; it is, he argues, 'depressing' to accept the inevitable losses of translation in advance, in the original. This demonstrates, he says, a 'dangerous willingness to split apart content and style'.[36]

This is not, or not just, a rearguard action on behalf of 'high modernist' linguistic experiment. It is also a defence of the prose found in Lawrence and, as I argue below, in Parks's own novels: a style which draws heavily on the resources of the vernacular, while also seeming simultaneously to denaturalise the vernacular from within. According to Parks, these features pose particular problems for translators of Lawrence's novels, as well as for the readers of these translations. Through the distorting lens of translation it proves all too easy to misrecognise Lawrence as a 'traditional novelist'. Parks recalls an experiment in which he provided his translation students (proficient speakers of English) with two versions of the same passage from *Women in Love*: the first was the original English version, and the second the Italian version back-translated into English. Eighteen out of twenty students in the class identified the Italian version as the original, citing 'extravagance of diction', the under-qualification of verbs and grammatical anomalies as their reason for selecting Lawrence's original version (wrongly) as 'foreign'.[37] For Parks, such 'foreignness' is precisely the point:

> a text which seeks to escape a classical 'housedness' in language is a text which unavoidably draws attention to and starts to be about language (and associated conventions) from which it is fleeing. It is this element of Lawrence's text which is lost, and for the most part inevitably, in an Italian that seems all too at home with itself and the conventional patterns of mind it enshrines.[38]

Lawrence's 'foreign language'

How to make English(ness) foreign to itself is, I want to argue, an important part of Lawrence's legacy for the English novel since 1945. Lawrentian styles including repetition leading to defamiliarisation, extravagant diction, rambling and elliptical syntax and, to borrow a phrase from Joseph Boone, 'a poetics of the perverse' have all been pressed into service to signal new and old forms of discomfort at being 'housed' within English.[39] In Parks's novels English(ness) invariably comes undone at the point at which liberal pieties crumble under pressure to reveal the residues of prejudice and violence beneath. At the level of the prose itself, this registers as a gradual deformation or crumpling of style: a phrase repeated until it takes on the violence and involuntariness of a tic, for example; or digressive paragraphs; or the interruption of lyrical or rhetorical prose with ugly, prejudicial language and cliché. In *Cleaver* this last technique is revealed in Cleaver's own account of meeting his daughter's boyfriend: 'To Cleaver's considerable surprise, Craig was black. He was tall, but stooped. The face was handsome, but lopsided. One ear stuck out. He was Negro' (229). Here the syntax gradually contracts until it solidifies into the prejudice which was thinly veiled beneath the first all-too-carefully worded statement of surprise.

It is in *Europa*, however, that Parks's English comes under the greatest strain. It does so because, as filtered through the consciousness of another middle-aged and world-weary Englishman abroad, the language of the novel rubs against the grain of what Parks sees as the 'conformity' of European optimism.[40] The source of this optimism is not named – it seems to Parks's protagonist too naïve to resemble a philosophy, much less a policy – but for purposes of illustration I refer to Zygmunt Bauman's *Europe: An unfinished adventure* which describes this mood. *Europa* is a first-person account of a journey to the European parliament to deliver a petition protesting the discriminatory treatment of foreign instructors in Italian universities. The viewpoint is that of an English teacher at the University of Milan, Jerry Marlow – a name, which in echoing Conrad, suggests there is something altogether darker at the heart of Europe than Bauman can allow. According to Bauman there remains at the core of the idea of Europe an ancient 'utopian spirit' which has been deepened rather than annulled by the atrocities of empire and by their associated sensibilities. As a result of post-imperial decline, Bauman argues, Germany, Britain and France have had to discover the possibility of 'modernisation without westernisation'. Further, they have had to learn that the value of Europe is not in the achieved state or union of states but in the search for a Europeanness which remains elusive, utopian and infinite: 'a forever not-yet-attained identity, vexingly elusive and always at odds with the realities of the day'.[41] In Parks's Europe, this kind of utopian language is broken down and, much as in Lawrence, the 'pieties' of democracy, progress and England are twisted beyond recognition. (In fact Parks suggests that Lawrence's 'willingness to offend' the supporters of democracy 'would not seem inappropriate to the present debate about the West's right to impose democracy on every corner of the world'.[42]) The coach on which Marlow and his colleagues travel across the continent becomes a symbol of Europe's blind faith in modernity. It is, remarks Marlow, investing the word with all the bitterness and disgust of a curse, and repeating it with the compulsiveness of a tic, an altogether *modern* coach: 'on the long back seat of this modern coach'; 'a modern coach to boot, with piped music and videos and synthetic smell'.[43] The object of their quest, Europe itself, is stripped of its 'utopian spirit' and mythic potency, becoming instead mere cliché, layered over an unprepossessing story of the indignities to which men will stoop when obsessed with 'a girl': 'a word like Europe has been diluted into thin air with all the times everybody says Europe this and Euro that, though once it was the name of a girl a god became a bull to rape and half the heroes hoped to find.'[44]

In a video on his website Parks describes Cleaver's flight to Italy (as well as his own) as a search for 'exoneration from being British' which succeeds only in locking his mind into a new language and, by these means, a new 'system'. In both *Cleaver* and *Europa*, a Lawrentian prose style and 'willingness to offend' offers a way of deforming these national systems from within, a means of showing the violence which lies behind their complacency – as well as the complacency which generates the sensibility that seeks to overcome this violence by invoking new 'transnational' languages and systems.[45]

In 1918 Lawrence had compelling reasons to turn his back on England: he had seen *The Rainbow* prosecuted for obscenity, experienced the ritual humiliation of the conscription board, and been expelled from Cornwall as a suspected spy. In *Zennor in Darkness*, Helen Dunmore provides a fictional account of these years. She sums up Lawrence's feelings towards the country of his birth in words which suggest his personal suffering as well as, with an allusion to *Heart of Darkness*, the collective suffering of peoples subject to England's rule: 'It is wonderful to have your back to the land, to the whole of England: to have your back to the darkness of it, its frenzy of bureaucratic bloodshed, its cries in the night. … He [Lawrence] refuses to let it contaminate his heart.'[46] This myth of a Lawrence uncontaminated by the worst of Englishness is, I have argued, a touchstone for the postwar novel in its continuing struggle with the 'embarrassments of the colonial past'. The problem of 'Englishness' after the end of empire has been a consistent, if not constant, factor in the various ways in which his foreignness has been conceived: a foreignness, for example, opposed to the metropolitan and cosmopolitan character of his Bloomsbury peers; one which refused the assurances of 'taciturn Southerners', educated to believe in 'British superiority to foreigners';[47] and one which was hostile to the 'drawing-room' version of female sexuality which, as John Marx suggests, was always an effect of empire.[48] In Parks, Lawrence's 'foreignness' is updated to signal a refusal both of uncritical parochialism and of newer forms of transnationalism which too easily believe they have escaped the 'conventional patterns of mind' preserved in language itself.

Notes

1 Tim Parks, 'Translating Individualism: literature and globalisation' in *Translating Style: A literary approach to translation, a translation approach to literature*, 2nd edn (Manchester: St Jerome, 2007), p. 241.

2 Tim Parks, quoted in Rudolf Freiburg and Jan Schnitker (eds), *'Do You Consider Yourself a Postmodern Author?'* (Munster: Lit Verlag, 1999), p. 169.

3 F.R. Leavis, *D.H. Lawrence: Novelist* (Harmondsworth: Penguin, 1981; first published 1955), p. 1.

4 Rick Rylance, '"I must go away": the reception of Lawrence's Englishness in an international perspective' in Christa Jansohn and Dieter Mehl (eds), *The Reception of D.H. Lawrence in Europe* (London: Continuum, 2007), p. 14.

5 D.H. Lawrence, *Sea and Sardinia* in Simonetta de Filippis, Paul Eggert and Mara Kalnins (eds), *D.H. Lawrence in Italy* (London: Penguin, 2007). Further references to this collection are given in parenthesis after quotations in the text.

6 See Amit Chaudhuri, *D.H. Lawrence and 'Difference'* (Oxford: Clarendon Press, 2003); Peter Childs, *Modernism and the Post-Colonial* (London: Continuum, 2007); John Marx, *The Modernist Novel and the Decline of Empire* (Cambridge: Cambridge University Press, 2005); and Eunyoung Oh, *D.H. Lawrence's Border Crossing: Colonialism in his travel writings and 'leadership novels'* (New York: Routledge, 2007). For novels featuring Lawrentian travels see Margaret Drabble, *The Peppered Moth* (London: Viking, 2001); Helen Dunmore, *Zennor in Darkness* (London: Penguin, 2007; first published 1993); and Tim Parks, *Cleaver* (London: Vintage, 2007).

7 Simon Gikandi, *Maps of Englishness: Writing identity in the culture of colonialism* (New York: Columbia University Press, 1996), p. x.

8 Raymond Williams, *Culture and Society, 1780–1950* (Harmondsworth: Penguin, 1961; first published 1958), pp. 210–11.

9 Edward W. Said, *Reflections on Exile and Other Literary and Cultural Essays* (London: Granta, 2001), p. 181.

10 'There were welcome signs that the novel and the drama were moving out of London and the Home Counties, and of course regional novels had been published before the war. But he hadn't the flaming genius of a Lawrence', Stan Barstow, *Ask Me Tomorrow* (Harmondsworth: Penguin, 1968; first published 1962), p. 196.

11 Stanley Middleton, *Holiday* (London: Arrow, 2008; first published 1974), pp. 163–73, 89.

12 V.S. Naipaul, *Literary Occasions: Essays* (London: Picador, 2005), p. 16.

13 Anthony Burgess, 'Introduction' to *D.H. Lawrence and Italy* (Harmondsworth: Penguin, 1985; first published 1972), p. xii.

14 Howard J. Booth, 'Lawrence in doubt: a theory of the "Other" and its collapse' in Howard J. Booth and Nigel Rigby (eds), *Modernism and Empire* (Manchester: Manchester University Press, 2000), p. 208.

15 Debbie Lisle, *The Global Politics of Contemporary Travel Writing* (Cambridge: Cambridge University Press, 2006), p. 3.

16 See for example Lisle, *Global Politics of Contemporary Travel Writing*, p. 7; and Patrick Holland and Graham Huggan, 'Varieties of nostalgia in contemporary travel writing' in Glenn Hooper and Tim Youngs (eds), *Perspectives on Travel Writing* (Aldershot: Ashgate, 2004), pp. 143–4.

17 James Clifford, 'Travelling cultures' in his *Routes: Travel and translation in the late twentieth century* (Cambridge MA: Harvard University Press, 1997), p. 39.

18 Oh, *Lawrence's Border Crossing*, p. 26; Chaudhuri, *Lawrence and 'Difference'*, p. 133; and Childs, *Modernism and the Post-Colonial*, p. 126. See also Stefania Michelucci, 'The fortunes of D.H. Lawrence in Italy' in Jansohn and Mehl, *The Reception of D.H. Lawrence*, p. 83.

19 Parks, 'Introduction' in *D.H. Lawrence and Italy* (2007), p. xxi.

20 Rylance, '"I must go away"', p. 22.

21 See Gillian Fenwick, *Understanding Tim Parks* (Columbia: University of South Carolina Press, 2002).

22 Parks, *Cleaver*, p. 51. Further references to this novel are given in parentheses after quotations in the text.

23 Earl Ingersoll, 'Lawrence in the Tyrol', *Forum for Modern Language Studies* 26 (1990), p. 5.

24 D.H. Lawrence, *Women in Love*, eds David Farmer, Lyndeth Vasey and John Worthen (London: Penguin, 2000), pp. 473–4.

25 Lawrence, 'The lemon gardens' in *Lawrence and Italy*, p. 34.

26 Gabriella Nouzeilles, 'Touching the real: alternative travel and landscapes of fear' in John Zilcosky (ed.), *Writing Travel: The poetics and politics of the modern journey* (Toronto: University of Toronto Press, 2008), pp. 199, 195–6.

27 Clifford, 'Travelling cultures', p. 19.

28 Tim Parks, *Dreams of Rivers and Seas* (London: Vintage, 2009), p. 6.

29 Nouzeilles, 'Touching the real', p. 197.

30 Rebecca West, 'Elegy', in *Rebecca West: A celebration* (London: Penguin, 1978), p. 388.

31 Tim Parks, *An Italian Education* (1996; repr. London: Vintage, 2000), p. vi.

32 Rebecca L. Walkowitz, 'Comparison literature' *New Literary History* 40 (2009), pp. 569–70.

33 Rebecca L. Walkowitz, *Cosmopolitan Style: Modernism beyond the nation* (New York: Columbia University Press, 2006), p. 19.

34 Walkowitz, 'Comparison literature', p. 571.

35 Parks, 'Translating individualism', p. 244.

36 Parks, 'Translating individualism', p. 245.

37 Parks, *Translating Style*, pp. 57, 10–11.

38 Parks, *Translating Style*, p. 56.

39 Joseph Allen Boone, *Libidinal Currents: Sexuality and the shaping of modernism* (Chicago: University of Chicago Press, 1998), p. 7.

40 Freiburg and Schnitker, 'Do You Consider Yourself a Postmodern Author?', p. 162.

41 Zygmunt Bauman, *Europe: An unfinished adventure* (Cambridge: Polity, 2004), pp. 37, 18, 37.

42 Tim Parks, 'The fighter [D.H. Lawrence]' in his *The Fighter: Literary essays* (London: Harvill Secker, 2007), p. 11.

43 Tim Parks, *Europa* (London: Vintage, 1999), p. 2.

44 Parks, *Europa*, pp. 28–9.

45 See 'About *Cleaver*' at http://tim-parks.com/videos/ (accessed 30 July 2010).

46 Dunmore, *Zennor in Darkness*, pp. 65–6.

47 Burgess, 'Introduction', p. xii.

48 Marx, *Modernist Novel and the Decline of Empire*, p. 123.

9

Queer histories and postcolonial intimacies in Alan Hollinghurst's *The Line of Beauty*

Sarah Brophy

Funny how mere living in a house like this could have the look of a burglary. (Alan Hollinghurst, *The Line of Beauty*, 2004)

Heritage, home and spatial infiltration

Alan Hollinghurst's *The Line of Beauty* (2004) de-familiarises a decade which, from the rise of neo-liberalism to the politicisation of gay identity in the context of AIDS, 'seems to have determined so many things about the way we live now'.[1] That the novel's retrospective account of the 1980s focuses on the sumptuous homes of the ruling elite tellingly associates it with the heritage industry, itself a product of the 1980s. Yet while English heritage texts since the 1980s have generated a mood of melancholic guilt and nostalgia which works to revive identifications with older traditions of white Englishness,[2] at the same time many seemingly conservative English heritage texts readily yield to queer interpretations.[3] Since the 1980s queer writers and directors, such as Jeanette Winterson, Jackie Kay, Derek Jarman and Isaac Julien, have been reworking 'heritage' topics and forms in ways that harness them to social critique. In *The Line of Beauty* Hollinghurst's protagonist, Nick Guest, faces the realisation that at the end of his four years in London, and after many compromises, he cannot sustain his erstwhile intimate relationship with the Tory establishment -- a political formation which, it is ultimately revealed, can only locate him and his sexuality as a monstrous affront to upper-class white propriety. With the emergence of HIV/AIDS Nick's previous, tacit social acceptance is quickly and violently turned around by his Conservative friends and acquaintances, including the

Fedden family with whom he has been living in London; they pathologise Nick and his lovers, who are primarily men of colour, charging him with treachery. I see Hollinghurst's novel as a critical meditation on the sexual and racial inclusions and exclusions of English society in the wake of empire. By drawing attention to the tenuousness of belonging for 'outsiders', *The Line of Beauty* questions the political costs for queers of investing in a nostalgic England defined by heritage, family, wealth and power, while at the same time taking queer desires for social belonging seriously as they have been lived.

I open with the term de-familiarise in order to anchor my engagement with *The Line of Beauty* in a theoretical conception of heritage and home-space. For Andrew Higson, 1980s heritage culture, with its focus on 'visual splendour', evacuates history of class struggle and negates the possibility of critical distance; the combination of the 'intimate' and the national 'epic' in sumptuous cinematic form can, he argues, only ever be ideologically mystifying.[4] However, as Gayatri Gopinath points out, because 'past national space' is contingent on 'heteronormative evocations of home, family, and community', narrating the past from a queer diasporic perspective can shift how we understand foundational categories, not only of kinship, but also of civic belonging. In other words, queer domesticities and intimacies can play the familial/familiarising logic of heritage against itself.[5] Nostalgia in *The Line of Beauty* is alternately 'vicious', on the one hand, suggesting an immersion in sensual delight against one's better instincts, and 'acute', on the other, implying painful self-scrutiny.[6] In 1987 Hollinghurst wrote a review of the Merchant Ivory production of E.M. Forster's *Maurice*, protesting that 'the society that Forster is criticizing becomes almost involuntarily an object of veneration'.[7] In *The Line of Beauty*, Hollinghurst takes the problem of admiration as an instantiating theme, describing Nick Guest to one reviewer as 'someone who is not just looking on in horror, but is actually susceptible to the glamour of it all'.[8] By investigating Nick's tendencies towards 'veneration' and 'susceptibility to glamour', the novel puts pressure on the troublingly 'suppressive' nostalgia of England after empire.[9]

I can illustrate the potential of a focus on home-space by analysing a scene which tethers the novel firmly to the tradition, in Victorian and modern fiction, of depicting grand houses as domestic symbols of imperially derived wealth, power and stability. Just before the Tory sex scandal breaks, a decisive moment in the narrative, Nick Guest returns home to visit his parents in Barwickshire, where he has a vivid dream of a house with two stairways:

what a difference there was between them: the narrow back stairs,
dangerously unrailed, under the bleak gleam of a skylight, each step
worn down to a steep hollow, turned tightly in a deep grey shaft;
whereas the great main sweep, a miracle of cantilevers, dividing and
joining again, was hung with the portraits of prince-bishops, and had
ears of corn in its wrought-iron banisters that trembled to the tread.
... How quickly, without noticing, one ran from one to the other,
after the proud White Rabbit, a well-known Old Harrovian porn
star with a sphincter that winked as bells rang, crowds murmured
and pigeons flopped about the dormer window while Nick woke and
turned in his own little room again, in the comfortable anti-climax
of home.[10]

The White Rabbit, figure of drugs and desire, beckons Nick towards
novel experiences of pleasure and danger. The sequence continues with a
daydream in which Nick becomes conscious of 'vicious nostalgia' for his
friend Toby Fedden, for their Oxford days and for Toby's lavish twenty-first
birthday party at his uncle Lord Kessler's Victorian estate, Hawkeswood.[11]
Nick is fitfully conscious of the outsider status he shares with Portuguese
waiter Tristão, who waits tables at several of the grand Tory gatherings,
as Nick himself has done in the recent past.[12] Together with the dream's
visual rendering of the servants' staircase as a 'deep grey shaft', the audible
difference in Tristão's voice (he pronounces house as 'arse') identifies that
the house itself is something to be penetrated, and that that he, Nick, is
figuratively sodomising Kessler (the bachelor uncle), Gerald Fedden (the
Ur-masculine yuppie MP) and the rest.[13] The dream encodes Nick's fear
of the association between anal penetration, and literal and social forms of
death, an association which was discursively redeployed in the 1980s, to gay
men's and others' great cost, in the context of AIDS.[14] Illicit and boundary-
crossing, the memory of courting sexual possibilities at the party under the
noses of an esteemed Tory family is a pleasurable one. It is riskily reactivated
throughout the novel by Nick and Wani Ouradi, heir to his Lebanese father's
supermarket fortunes and devotee of decadence, who surreptitiously snort
coke and fuck as Conservative Party members and their investor friends
gather nearby in more public rooms.

Nick's dream invites readers to reflect on the instability of boundaries
between the two spheres of the English grand house, its legitimate public
face and its recesses. His giddy discovery of anal sex is accompanied by
an unconscious anxiety that his sodomitic desires – and the racial and
class crossings which they propel – are antithetical to the material and

social structures of the upper-middle-class London society which he wishes to make his new home. Far from abandoning the idea of home, argues Anne-Marie Fortier, coming-out narratives 'repeatedly reproce[ss]' the idea of home 'through multiple returns to the past – physical or mnemonic'.[15] Like Gopinath, Fortier highlights the dynamic, transformative qualities of 'homing desires' and the attachments they produce.[16] If we consider Nick Guest as *migrating* from Barwick via Oxford to London, then occupying a room 'up in the roof, still clearly the children's zone' at the Feddens's Kensington Park Gardens town house, he 'reprocesses' both the concept of home and through it his relation to the forms of Englishness promoted by Thatcherism. 'Passed on as a friend' by Toby, Nick is both harmless and serviceable in Gerald and Rachel Feddens's eyes: due to his 'gravity, a certain shy polish', he plays the (old imperial) role of manservant, care-giver, literary intellectual, a 'perfect little courtier', useful for 'making up numbers' – a hybrid, feminised role which is eventually revealed as a symbolic representation of the ambiguous, vulnerable status of gay men in the Thatcher era.[17]

The Thatcherites sought to return Britain to a pre-sexual revolution, pre-immigration era by challenging the citizenship claims of both queers and racial minorities. Section 28, which curtailed local government funding for sex education by prohibiting the 'promotion' of homosexuality, is referenced towards the end of *The Line of Beauty* in Gerald Fedden's 1987 re-election speech, which Nick's mother, Mrs Guest, praises for holding the Conservative line against 'these, you know, lesbian workshops'.[18] As Anna Marie Smith demonstrates, Tory discourse re-activated imperialist fears of miscegenation and degeneracy: 'The Section 28 supporters explicitly linked the promotion of homosexuality with the promotion of multiculturalism. They drew extensively upon already normalised racist metaphors around disease, foreign invasions, unassimilable "other" cultures, dangerous criminals, subversive intellectuals, excessive permissiveness and so on.'[19] Against such imagined contamination, the property-owning English family, a figure of imperilled national and imperial cohesion, must, for conservatives, be defended, even avenged. While he belatedly recognises how, as a gay man, he is at risk of being othered and criminalised, protesting to Gerald that he's 'not some alien invader',[20] Nick never embraces a politicised queer identity, in contrast to the more radicalised perspectives of his first lover, black city-council worker, Leo Charles, and of Leo's mentor, Pete Mawson.[21] Rather, Nick's worries are inchoate, displaced and confusingly bound up with his sexual desires as, for example, when he suddenly fears that passers-by might see Leo holding Nick against a wall as a 'mugger' rather than a 'lover'.[22] In this sense, the novel can be read as a critique of gay men's – especially white gay men's – complicity with the Thatcherites, a complicity, the novel suggests, driven by a desire for access to the glamour of wealth. While it anticipates Nick's violent expulsion from the Feddens's home and social circle, the dream of the servants' staircase as an anal passageway provides a preliminary incitement to reflect on how precarious projects of social inclusion and accommodation can be.

Queer cosmopolitanism in and beyond the 1980s

Alan Sinfield analyses 'homosexual disturbance' in the twentieth-century English novel by noting structural parallels between homosexuality and femininity and by highlighting the implications of gay men's boundary-crossing: 'the homosexual, leisure-class, literary intellectual was ... in a strikingly contradictory position. He was *inviting in* the working class that was believed to be about to overwhelm civilised standards. He was a Trojan horse within the citadel of cultural power, smuggling in the class enemy.'[23] At the end of *The Line of Beauty*, Gerald Fedden's accusation is that Nick has played 'the old homo trick' of attaching himself to the family and then betraying its trust: 'all we asked for was loyalty.'[24] Gerald associates Nick's sexual orientation with his failure as caregiver – specifically, his failure to inform them that their daughter, Catherine, had tried to harm herself during their holiday in France. Gerald's anger at Nick is connected to his anxieties about the fate of the next generation of Feddens, Toby and Catherine, and about the future of the institutions of social power. As Lee Edelman has shown, reproductive futurism dreams of securing the replication of its own image in the continuation of a heterosexual family line.[25] Even as Nick nurtures the memory of his first night with his first lover, Leo Charles, he fears being left behind by 'the great heterosexual express' which the rest of 'this efficiently reproductive species' seems ready to board.[26] When Nick visits Rachel in the bedroom which she shares with Gerald, he sees himself as 'as an intruder in the temple of marital love; his own love fantasies had taken envious possession of it, like squatters, in the married couple's absence.'[27] Here, late in his time with the Feddens and just before Gerald commands him to leave, Nick self-critically recasts his 'friend of the family' status as that of a 'squatter' who threatens, by his illegitimate presence and desires, the private space and idea of reproductive marital couple-hood so venerated in the Conservative imagination.

While Sinfield and Edelman emphasise the threatening qualities attached to the figure of the treacherous queer, in *The Line of Beauty* the rhetoric of baroque lines, and their complication of smooth, regular, polished perceptions, opens up an alternative interpretation. The 'Ogee' references the double curves of English baroque architecture:

> English and exotic, like so many things he loved. The Ogee curve was pure expression, decorative not structural; a structure could be made from it, but it supported nothing more than a boss or the cross that topped an onion dome. ... the snakelike flicker of an instinct, of two compulsions held in one unfolding movement.[28]

Defining cosmopolitanism as social practices which 'work in encounters with other human beings across gaps of space, time, and experience',[29] my reading of *The Line of Beauty* emphasises a queer cosmopolitanism which can imbue the figure of the queer-as-Trojan-horse with more enduring and transformative social effects than an emphasis on infiltration, annihilation, or expulsion would allow. I want to think in terms of queer cosmopolitical agency which, though by definition elusive, claims critical force for *The Line of Beauty*'s unstable 'double curves', for its simultaneously sensuous and ironic renderings of bodies and home-spaces. Within this conceptual frame, I suggest that Hollinghurst's novel retroactively intervenes in the debates about heritage to conjure – more forcefully than Merchant-Ivory's adaptations could imagine – a sense not only of pleasurable attraction and attachment, but also of loss, uncertainty, shame and of erotic memories of male same-sex relationships which treacherously exceed the imperially derived hierarchies of race and class.[30] In turn, such deviations from the straight world precipitate for Nick Guest unsettling analyses of his own political evasion and complicity.

In her important critique of queer complicities with neo-imperial and neo-national projects, Jasbir Puar is (shrewdly) inclined to be sceptical of the 'individualism' and 'liberal humanism' implied by 'elite cosmopolitan' formations of queerness.[31] But I am intrigued by Rebecca Walkowitz's repositioning of cosmopolitanism 'not simply as a model of community but as a model of perversity, in the sense of obstinacy, indirection, immorality and attitude'.[32] By putting Walkowitz's emphasis on the aesthetic legacies of (1890s) decadent style for cosmopolitanism into dialogue with Sara Ahmed's queer phenomenological work on lineages and trajectories, it is possible to rethink how we might employ the idea of cosmopolitanism: 'queer desire "acts" by bringing other objects closer, those that would not be allowed "near" by straight ways of orientating the body'.[33] Through the parsing of attachments, or the 'microintimacies of domesticity', *The Line of*

Beauty points toward the possibility of new forms of thinking and feeling: a nascent, politically ambiguous, sometimes scandalous, but nonetheless perceptible queer cosmopolitanism.[34] Such queer cosmopolitical lessons are mobilised powerfully, though learned incompletely and belatedly, raising questions about the seductive hold that the Fedden family – and the Tory wealth, property, entitlement and influence they embody – has on Nick. As a figure for redoubled representational and reading practices, the Ogee can take us through the novel looking not only for transgressive desire but for the layered, receding ironies which expose the conditions and limits of the social acceptance for which Nick yearns. Departing from criticism's common reading of the novel, in which Jamesian ironic style is interpreted as collusion, on the one hand, and self-indulgent mourning, on the other,[35] I suggest that *The Line of Beauty* pursues irony in order to reframe the 'different things [Nick] wanted, beautiful jarring futures for him', including the seductive draw of belonging to the English elite whose luxurious homes and lavish parties constitute the dominant vision of 'heritage'.[36]

Recesses and peripheries

In this section I focus on the domestic spaces – entrances, kitchens, formal front rooms, dance floors, gardens and passageways – which at various moments are occupied by Nick and his lovers. As the novel traces the 'microintimacies of domesticity' it becomes increasingly apparent that Nick is not a force of disruption. Unwilling to risk an openly feminised position (like that of self-destructive rebel, daughter Catherine) he becomes a guardian of the very family unit against which he also strains. In other words, he performs a classically liberal feminine role, one which (temporarily) secures his own social foothold by supporting the patriarch's power and authority, even when it is against his own self-interest and ethical principles to do so.

In contrast to the perceived cohesive 'fondness and efficiency' which stabilise Gerald and Rachel Fedden's household, Nick's relationships with his lovers, Leo and Wani, are characterised by a sense of being 'homeless'.[37] These affairs are conducted in momentarily claimed spaces, through oblique glances and gestures, and – literally – in the peripheries and recesses of the Feddens's properties. With the otherwise putatively liberal Rachel Fedden's expressed belief that gay sex is 'vulgar and unsafe' echoing in his thoughts, Nick brings home 'the risk of it', 'the scandalous idea', when he and Leo conclude their blind date by paying a visit to the key-holders' garden (which like Hawkeswood, is never open to the public).[38] Symbolised by the fucking pair's proximity to the compost heap, the erotic fecundity of Nick's new life in the city is suddenly brought inside the gates, and sex is made essential to the very idea of the garden as an urban retreat. The post-coital reverie is interrupted, however, by a 'legitimate occupant', Tory stalwart and key-holder Geoffrey Titchfield, who conspicuously averts his gaze from Leo, whose black body he sees as automatically out of place, suspecting a criminal threat. Counterpointing the mounting tally of AIDS deaths amongst the men Nick knows, the novel recreates tense and yet pastoral scenes of sex in public and semi-public spaces: on Hampstead Heath, for example, or in the pool house of the Feddens's Dordogne summer home. Reminiscent of the riotous all male bathing scene in *A Room with a View*, these scenes can be read as heterotopic, in the Foucauldian sense: as everyday sites which become generative for the utopian, non-normative pleasures and intimacies they bring into being.[39] The 'acute nostalgia' which Nick feels for sex in the private garden with Leo suggests that, like the other *al fresco* episodes, it is, for Nick, a site of pleasure and reciprocal recognition. Leo, however, ruefully dwells on the arrival of Geoffrey Titchfield, teasing Nick – who placates Geoffrey by informing him that he is a friend of the Feddens and a key-holder – for engaging in 'two sorts of arse-licking in ten minutes'.[40] Nick, it seems, is enamoured of the garden and of those who mediate access to it, and is as set on pleasing *them* as he is his new lover.

Leo Charles is significant not just as Nick's first fuck and, later, as the first death he must grieve, but for his caustic humour, which is tied to a political analysis that confounds Nick's bourgeois fantasies of joining the elite. Casually but consistently, Leo uses sarcasm to tutor Nick in matters sexual, racial, aesthetic and political; but against Nick's allegiance to the Feddens he is engaged in a losing battle. Leo questions the superficiality of Nick's aestheticism:

> Nick hesitated. 'There is a sort of aesthetic poverty about conservatism, though, isn't there.'
> 'Yeah?'
> 'That blue's an impossible colour.'
> Leo nodded thoughtfully. 'I wouldn't say that was their main problem,' he said.[41]

Leo's sarcasm cuts through the over-subtle ironies of Nick's aesthetic judgment and points towards the larger problem of Thatcherism's will to annihilate not only difference but, as Denis Flannery aptly points out, 'to extinguish forms of collective life' which exceed the model of the conventional heterosexual family.[42] Leo's critical observation creates the context for Nick's later, more sceptical, reading of the Feddens's preparations for a visit by 'the Lady' – by Margaret Thatcher herself – on the occasion of the couple's twenty-fifth wedding anniversary, when Gerald decides to repaint their front door Tory blue in her honour.[43] Yet Nick himself has persistently personified this very air of 'gravity' and 'polish'.

One of the most troubling features of Nick's narration is the chronic fragmentation of his subjectivity – and of his allegiances. On meeting Toby and Toby's girlfriend Sophie, Leo remarks on the fact that he was 'not invited' to join the family for lunch, and 'Nick raced away from the mere idea of it, as a nexus of every snobbery and worry, a scene of tortured intercessions between different departments of his own life: Leo – Gerald – Toby – Sophie – Lady Partridge …'.[44] As the punctuation suggests, the line of Nick's thoughts leads away from Leo as object of desire, and ultimately towards Gerald's staunchly Conservative mother as the person whose opprobrium he fears most.[45] Implicitly, Leo's perspective becomes the moral and political standard against which Nick's mental 'racing away' (not only his haste, but fleeing from race, erasing, whitening?) from the consequences of political insistency is measured.[46] Despite Leo and Pete's tutoring, however, it seems that Nick does not confront the implications of his erotic interest in, and intimate bonding with, men of colour; perhaps he is a mere 'chocoholic', as Pete tauntingly labels him, suggesting that Nick's taste for black men is an imperialist, consumerist indulgence.[47]

The limits of Nick's interest in, or capacity for, translating his attraction to Leo into a political solidarity become apparent when, towards the end of the relationship, Leo invites him home. Nick, proud of his centrally located *pied á terre*, thinks it obvious that Leo is submitting himself to a claustrophobic world signalled by his mother's clutter, bad art and lower-middle-class religiosity; he perceives Leo's bicycle as out of place in the 'heaped, stacked, jammed, crowded' kitchen and front room, reading it as a symbol of 'trapped velocity'.[48] The 'tiny flat in unknown Willesden' triggers a memory of superior class positioning: 'school afternoons of community service, going into the homes of the old and disabled, each charitable visit a lesson in life and also – to Nick at least – in the subtle snobbery of aesthetics'.[49] From Leo's perspective, at least, it is bizarre that the one point of interest which emerges to bridge the gap between his mother and Nick is 'Mrs. T.'[50] In the absence of any other common ground, the figure of Thatcher, anti-gay and anti-immigrant, provides the *lingua franca* for this meeting of gay and migrant.[51] Only retrospectively, when he finds himself telling Leo's sister how 'wonderful' her mother is, does

Nick begin to question these interactions. After all, like Leo's mother, who denies her son's death is AIDS-related, Nick too turns away in the street from an evidently ill Leo.[52]

If Nick is paralleled with the conservative politics and class aspirations of the West Indian matron, he is also, importantly, aligned with another conservatively inclined matriarch and upholder of English proprieties, Rachel Fedden. Originally from a wealthy Jewish banking family, her friends are mostly left-wing, from her art and theatre days at Oxford, which make her, as much as Nick, a potential Trojan horse. However, when Gerald's reflexive racism becomes shockingly plain Rachel demurs and it falls to their son, Toby, to point out that Gerald's racism belies the Feddens's own mixedness: 'You'll be calling me a bloody Jew-boy next.'[53] Just as important, while Rachel skirts the question of her own brother's sexuality, Lord Kessler inspires in Catherine the knowing question 'What do you think, he's not gay, is he?', and in Nick a 'subtle bachelor sympathy'[54] – while to other gay men at the party he is 'wicked old Lionel Kessler' who ought to be praised for hiring gorgeous boys as waiters.[55] Rife with internal tensions, the Fedden family, Rachel elegantly in the lead, tactically marginalises, euphemises and forgets what is most troubling.[56]

Like Rachel, who retreats to shed tears over the AIDS-related death of her friend Pat Graydon, Nick's responses to overt racism and homophobia are muted. When Rachel covers up Pat's queerness by assigning his illness a foreign origin ('some extraordinary bug he picked up in the Far East last year') Nick feels 'a kind of relief that this sinister fiction was being maintained'. Reluctant to assume 'the AIDS question' as 'somehow his responsibility, as the only recognised gay man present' his 'cheerful genteelisms' about safer sex are an ineffectual counter to Sir Maurice Tipper's view that 'they had it coming to them'.[57] 'The upper-class economies of [Rachel's] talk, her way of saying nothing except by hinted shades of agreement and disagreement' is a style which Nick 'longed to master',[58] and his vagueness creates an entrée for Wani to play directly into the Tippers's hands by boldly affirming the most conservative view of heterosexual destiny: 'I'm probably just old-fashioned on these things, but actually I was brought up to believe in no sex before marriage.'[59] Moreover, the subterfuge concerning Pat's death recalls the earlier surge of fear and collusion in the household when Catherine's friend, fifty-ish West Indian taxi driver Brentwood, is rendered suspect at the door of the Fedden home when he escorts a distraught Catherine home. Rachel's role is to remove her daughter as quickly as possible while Nick, after an initial angry outburst which serves only to bring a 'sly smile' to the face of the arch conservative dinner-guest Barry Groom, is to show 'the completely and critically different' Brentford the door.[60] Nick is adept at analysing Rachel's evasions precisely because they mirror his own.

Wani Ouradi's luxurious Clerkenwell house crystallises the contradictions of Nick's conservative feminine role. For Wani, whose Tory-aligned Lebanese parents have hired a woman, Martine, to appear in public as their son's fiancée, Nick performs the roles of housekeeper; procurer of boys, porn and drugs; business partner; and travelling companion. Comparing the two households, and his place in them, in self-mocking terms, Nick analyses the attitude of 'old wistful keenness' as a 'fantasy of prosperity' and prosperity as entwined with the enjoyment of 'love'.[61] The comparison points toward an insidious pattern; the intimacies which Nick desires are everywhere prone to sudden attenuation. Wani prefers 'danger' and 'everything that's the opposite of what it seems', and when Rachel confronts Nick about Catherine's attempted self-harm, her 'dryness', 'hard gasp', 'sharp resentful sigh' and repeated emphasis on Nick's abnegation of 'responsibility' deflect the possibility that the crisis might yield 'a new intimacy'.[62] The habitual diminishment of affect means that, while Wani and Rachel are potential allies for Nick, they never become actual ones. Throughout the novel it is Rachel's 'sudden harsh formulation' that gay sex is 'vulgar and unsafe', internalised by Nick, which forcibly keeps him in line, as he sustains, through strategic omissions, his place within the Feddens's closely guarded private circle.[63] To name 'wistful keenness' as a longstanding orientation constitutes, then, for Nick a movement towards considering his own implication in 'suppressive nostalgia'.

'Dancing with Maggie': on turning back and away

The HIV/AIDS epidemic profoundly shapes the novel's third and concluding section, 'The end of the street', set in 1987, in which Nick witnesses Wani's decline and receives word of Leo's death, and in which Thatcher and the fictional Gerald Fedden are both re-elected. Nick's cohabitation with the Feddens is summarily ended by Gerald when his own, and Nick's, sexual secrets are exposed. In campaign-trail hotels and at a borrowed 'fuck-flat' Gerald has been carrying on an affair with his office assistant.[64] Gerald and Nick are paralleled in their crossing of normative familial boundaries in their choice of sexual partners and in their seeking out of hidden, recessed spaces in which to conduct their affairs; but Gerald, like the paparazzi who descend on Kensington Park Gardens, has no compunction in scapegoating Nick. For Gerald, the press's feasting on Nick's relationship with Wani conveniently shifts the tabloids' focus away from his own indiscretion, and he makes the most of this displacement by refusing any comparison between the two situations. His rage on seeing Nick grips Gerald passionately, 'like a physical seizure'; Barry Groom's insults vividly illustrate his contempt for gay men occupying feminine, receptive positions: 'stupid little pansy', 'little cunt', 'little cocksucker'.[65] Nick has to face the fact that the Conservatives' visceral homophobia – as, in other instances, their racism – protects their positions of privilege even (or especially) when hypocrisy is evident.

In the context of such hate, the earlier scene of a coked-up Nick grooving with Mrs Thatcher to the Rolling Stones's 'Get off of my cloud' at the Feddens's anniversary party becomes not only aesthetically but ethically and politically grotesque.[66] Nick's re-evaluation of this episode is spurred by the visit which Leo's sister, Rosemary, and her partner, Gemma, pay to the Clerkenwell flat to inform Nick of Leo's HIV/AIDS-related death and to urge him to get tested. Their reading of Nick's domestic surroundings reveals the distance between their politics and his complicity:

'There's a picture of him dancing with Maggie!'
It was one of the photos from the Silver Wedding, Nick red-faced and staring, the Prime Minister with a look of caution he hadn't been aware of at the time. He wasn't sure Gemma would get the special self-irony of the lavatory gallery. It was something he'd learnt from his public-school friends.[67]

The Line of Beauty offers 'dancing with Maggie' as a metaphor for gay men's complicity with conservatism and the Conservatives in the 1980s, for the desire to be included in the party even if not belonging to or voting for the Party.[68] By hanging the anniversary photograph in the toilet, a space both private and not, and assigning it the status of a joke, Nick mimics Gerald, for whom being rendered in the form of a *Spitting Image* puppet would be the sign that he had arrived. A cartoon-like persona is associated with Thatcher herself, whose persona, in Jacqueline Rose's terms, thrived on 'the ambiguity of femininity appealed to and denied, masculinity parodied and inflated'. As Rose elaborates this point, it 'is the worst of a phallic economy countered, and thereby rendered permissible, by being presented as masquerade'.[69] The 'special self-irony' which propels such self-imagining is re-framed here as a 'learnt', class-specific mode. Challenged by Rosemary and Gemma, Nick realises he has been playing the comic villain's merry-making minion. Simultaneously, HIV/AIDS has transformed the faces and bodies of Leo and Wani, making them almost – but not quite – beyond recognition.[70] What becomes newly apparent, then, through the receding ironic frames attached to the photograph, is that during his four years with the Feddens, Nick has not, in fact, interrupted the dance but has been swinging along all the while.

Echoing the prophetic Hawkeswood dream which linked anality to social anxieties, Rosemary and Gemma's visit makes Nick feel 'a momentary vertigo'.[71] Subsequently, his view of the news headlines ('Peer's Playboy Son Has AIDS', with the subtitle 'Gay Sex Link to Minister's House') gives him a 'strange subliminal sensation that the banister wasn't there and that the hall floor had hurtled up to meet him', not least because he has a fresh explanation for Rachel's 'indignation': a complicity with homophobia which belies her liberalism.[72] In these circumstances of loss and scapegoating, Nick's emotional disorientation, like that of many gay men of his generation, is intense.

Given Thatcher's intractability (exemplified in her infamous phrase 'the lady's not for turning'), the concluding image of Nick hesitating and then turning away from the Kensington house significantly re-imagines his relation not only to the Feddens and to Thatcher, but to the opulent, nostalgic version of English 'heritage' from which he is being ejected.[73] As he hovers on the doorstep and then slips the last of his keys (the one for the garden) in the letterbox of the glossy blue door, Nick finds that:

> The emotion was startling. It was a sort of terror, made up of emotions from every stage of his short life, weaning, homesickness, envy, and self-pity; but he felt that the self-pity belonged to a larger pity. It was a love of the world that was shockingly unconditional. He stared back at the house, and then turned and drifted on.[74]

While Nick and Catherine had fantasised about Thatcher 'doing the twist, or pissed' and receiving a kind of aesthetic come-uppance in the process, at the end of the novel it is Nick who finds himself twisting and turning, this time alone.[75] Nostalgia for the pleasures of which he once partook in the Fedden home overlaps and competes with the pressures of necessity. As Ahmed writes, in finding some way not to heed the 'violent' straightening pressures entailed in received 'social forms', which rely on manipulating the desire to belong, 'we would not aim to overcome the disorientation of the queer moment, but instead inhabit the intensity of its moment'.[76] Nick's dwelling in the ambivalence of his departure counters the uncritical turning back associated with a 'vicious' and 'suppressive' nostalgia. To experience nostalgia and longing as 'startling' is to understand it as 'acute' or, in other words, as piercing, and surely here Nick, as he touches for the last time the object associated with his first weeks in London, is remembering the pleasure he took in having access to this space while seducing and being seduced by Leo.

Nick's falling out with the Feddens demands to be read as more than a cruelly enforced expulsion, for it inaugurates the possibility that Nick might now relinquish his naive desire to immerse himself in the splendours, material and imagined, of English heritage. Importantly, when Nick is reduced to 'cheap sarcasm' by Gerald's rage, he is not only being rendered marginal and robbed of agency. He may also be on the verge of learning Leo's lesson that some forms of self-serving irony cannot, and should not, be afforded by gay men in times of political danger. Nick's future, like his past, is inevitably shaped by his cross-racial and cross-class identifications with the men he has loved. What he struggles to comprehend is that erotic ties with men of colour are perceived as profoundly threatening to the resurgent homogenising visions of Englishness promoted in both politics (Thatcherism) and in culture (the heritage industry of the 1980s). As second-generation Black Britons, Leo and Wani can be read as figures for the shifting post-imperial re-constitution of Englishness, and Nick's contradictory, exciting alignment with them can be read as an implicitly critical comment on the narrowness of characteristic familial norms of whiteness and heterosexuality reproduced within heritage forms. Put another way, the men's erotic bonding represents the nascent, but politically thwarted, potential for a multi-racial, sexually diverse future for Englishness. By tracking Nick's delusions and their undoing, then, Hollinghurst not only confronts us with the pain attendant on recognising one's own outsider status, but also makes a significant contribution to theorising queer cosmopolitism: losing one's illusions about gaining a comfortable place amongst the ascendant class may be a necessary condition for translating erotic ties into more concerted, sustained forms of political allegiance. Shifting to an intrusive authorial narrative voice, The Line of Beauty offers the observation that Nick 'was young, without much training in stoicism',[77] reminding us to read it as a coming-out narrative which critically 'reprocesses' the ideas of (national) home and 'homing desires'.[78] In tune with current work on orientations, migration and home at the intersection of queer and postcolonial theory, Hollinghurst's novel anticipates queer claims on social and national belonging which will be something different from 'wistfully keen' and which will go beyond simplistic myths of pluralistic accommodation to recognise the necessity for scepticism, for alliances which necessarily transgress everyday boundaries, and for endurance. In time, if we take pains to grapple with complicities of all sorts, The Line of Beauty suggests, then cross-racial and cross-class queer intimacies, impure and vulnerable as they are, may perform their work of critique and social re-formation.

Notes

I am indebted to Sarah Trimble, Jessie Travis and Melissa Carroll for discussing *The Line of Beauty* with me in ways that I have found tremendously illuminating. Sincere thanks, too, to Michael Ross, Rachael Gilmour and Bill Schwarz, whose collaborative ethos, encouragement and insightful criticisms have helped me hone my argument. This research was supported by the Social Sciences and Humanities Research Council of Canada.

1   Stephen Moss, 'I don't make moral judgments. Interview with Alan Hollinghurst', *Guardian*, 21 October 2004, p. 8.

2   Paul Gilroy, *Postcolonial Melancholia* (New York: Columbia University Press, 2005), p. 99.

3   See Clair Monk, 'Sexuality and the heritage' *Sight and Sound*, October 1995, pp. 32–4, and Julianne Pidduck, *Space, Place and the Past: Contemporary costume drama* (London: BFI, 2005).

4   Andrew Higson, *English Heritage, English Cinema: Costume drama since 1980* (Oxford: Oxford University Press, 2003), p. 95; in chs 2, 5 and 6, Higson modifies his position on heritage forms to emphasise the ambivalence of reception. For a nuanced reading, see Raphael Samuel, *Theatres of Memory*, vol. 1 (London: Verso, 1996).

5   Gayatri Gopinath, *Impossible Desires* (Durham: Duke University Press, 2005), p. 97.

6   Alan Hollinghurst, *The Line of Beauty* (London: Bloomsbury, 2004), pp. 231, 305.

7   Alan Hollinghurst, 'Suppressive nostalgia' *Times Literary Supplement*, 6 November 1987, p. 1225.

8   Tim Adams, 'A classic of our times. Interview with Alan Hollinghurst', *Observer*, 11 April 2004, p. 15.

9   Hollinghurst, 'Suppressive nostalgia', p. 1225.

10 Hollinghurst, *Line of Beauty*, p. 231.

11 Hollinghurst, *Line of Beauty*, p. 231.

12 Hollinghurst, *Line of Beauty*, pp. 75, 55.

13 Hollinghurst, *Line of Beauty*, pp. 75, 339.

14 See Leo Bersani, 'Is the rectum a grave?' in Douglas Crimp (ed.), *AIDS: Cultural analysis/cultural activism* (Cambridge, MA: MIT Press, 1987), pp. 197–222.

15 Anne-Marie Fortier, 'Making home: queer migrations and motions of attachment' in Sara Ahmed, Claudia Castañeda, Anne-Marie Fortier and Mimi Sheller, *Uprootings/Regroundings* (Oxford: Berg, 2003), pp. 119, 123.

16 'Homing desires' is Avtar Brah's coinage in her *Cartographies of Diaspora* (London: Routledge, 1996), p. 180, and is reworked for queer theory by Fortier in 'Making home', p. 115.

17 Hollinghurst, *Line of Beauty*, pp. 4, 107. This chapter focuses on *The Line of*

Beauty in order to explore its critique of imperial legacies and Conservatism in the 1980s. For an illuminating analysis of *The Swimming Pool Library* (1988), see David Alderson, 'Desire as nostalgia: the novels of Alan Hollinghurst'. David Alderson and Linda R. Anderson (eds), *Territories of Desire in Queer Culture* (Manchester: Manchester University Press, 2000), pp. 29–48.

18 Hollinghurst, *Line of Beauty*, p. 360.

19 Anna Maria Smith, *New Right Discourse on Race and Sexuality: Britain, 1968–1990* (Cambridge: Cambridge University Press, 1994), p. 22. See also Stuart Hall *et al.*, *Policing the Crisis: Mugging, the state, and law and order* (London: Macmillan, 1978).

20 Hollinghurst, *Line of Beauty*, p. 419.

21 Hollinghurst, *Line of Beauty*, p. 104. The novel is haunted by the impact of Thatcher's social and economic policies on those outside the Conservative power bloc: Polly Tompkins, who later wins a Tory seat, comments in 1983 on the post-election 'mood in Whitehall – the economy's in ruins, no one's got a job, and they just don't care, it's bliss', p. 57.

22 Hollinghurst, *Line of Beauty*, p. 149.

23 Alan Sinfield, *Literature, Politics and Culture in Post-war Britain* (London: Continuum, 2004), pp. 75, 80.

24 Hollinghurst, *Line of Beauty*, p. 419.

25 Lee Edelman, *No Future* (Durham: Duke University Press, 2004), p. 21.

26 Hollinghurst, *Line of Beauty*, pp. 58–9.

27 Hollinghurst, *Line of Beauty*, p. 405.

28 Hollinghurst, *Line of Beauty*, p. 176.

29 Kwame Anthony Appiah, 'Rooted cosmopolitanism' in his *The Ethics of Identity* (Princeton: Princeton University Press, 2005), p. 258. See also Bruce Robbins, 'Introduction part I: actually existing cosmopolitanism' in Pheng Cheah and Bruce Robbins (eds), *Cosmopolitics* (Minneapolis: University of Minnesota Press, 1998), which makes the important point that: 'instead of an ideal of detachment, actually existing cosmopolitanism is a reality of (re) attachment, multiple attachment, or attachment at a distance', p. 3.

30 When Wani's companion, Martine, disparages the Merchant-Ivory adaptation of *A Room with a View*, Nick replies that 'everyone is in evening dress all the time these days aren't they'. Hollinghurst, *Line of Beauty*, p. 187.

31 Jasbir K. Puar, *Terrorist Assemblages* (Durham: Duke University Press, 2007), p. 22.

32 Rebecca Walkowitz, *Cosmopolitan Style* (New York: Columbia University Press, 2006), p. 13.

33 Sara Ahmed, *Queer Phenomenology* (Durham: Duke University Press, 2006), p. 92.

34 I draw here on Walkowitz's discussion of Kazuo Ishiguro's *The Remains of the Day* (1989), p. 31. Like Ishiguro's butler, Stevens, Nick achieves a limited belonging within a privileged, conservative household. Enamoured of the landed family on whose coat-tails he rides and whose son attracts

his erotic attention, Nick is also a reworking of Charles Ryder, of Evelyn Waugh's *Brideshead Revisited* (1945). Whereas Brideshead offers what Peter J. Kalliney, in *Cities of Affluence and Anger* (Charlottesville: University of Virginia Press, 2007), p. 67, calls 'a kind of satiric sympathy for the Flytes', a 'self-destructive and misunderstood minority', *The Line of Beauty* reveals the Feddens to be merciless protectors of their own self-interest.

35 I will not be replicating the close attention which has already been paid to Jamesian intertextuality and influence by Andrew Eastham, 'Inoperative ironies: Jamesian aestheticism and post-modern culture in Alan Hollinghurst's *The Line of Beauty*', *Textual Practice* 20: 3 (2006), pp. 509–27; by Denis Flannery, 'The powers of apostrophe and the boundaries of mourning: Henry James, Alan Hollinghurst, Toby Litt', *The Henry James Review* 26: 3 (2005), pp. 293–305; and by Daniel Hannah, 'The private life, the public stage: Henry James in recent fiction', *Journal of Modern Literature* 30: 3, pp. 70–94.

36 Hollinghurst, *Line of Beauty*, p. 42. Lord Kessler refers to Jamesian 'style as an obstacle', and Nick counters that 'style hides things and reveals things at the same time'. This moment opens up the possibility of a meaningful and politicised understanding of style while also suggesting Nick over-values it as oppositional: 'he grinned with pleasure and defiance, it was a kind of coming out', p. 50.

37 Hollinghurst, *Line of Beauty*, p. 42.

38 Hollinghurst, *Line of Beauty*, pp. 33, 323.

39 Pidduck argues that envisioning such 'spaces outside' was, in the context of Section 28, a particularly important artistic strategy for 'open[ing] up discursive and real "places" for the exploration of non-normative gender and sexual identities', *Space, Place and the Past*, pp. 143–5.

40 Hollinghurst, *Line of Beauty*, p. 38.

41 Hollinghurst, *Line of Beauty*, p. 93.

42 Flannery, 'The powers of apostrophe', p. 302.

43 Hollinghurst, *Line of Beauty*, p. 321.

44 Hollinghurst, *Line of Beauty*, p. 103.

45 Lady Partridge pronounces the idea of analysing 'racism' 'a lot of rot', though she persistently raises the topic of 'muggers' herself, p. 71 and p. 327. When Nick introduces her to Leo, she 'drift[s]' past him and is 'edgy for reassurance' from Rachel and Gerald, Hollinghurst, *Line of Beauty*, p. 92.

46 While Flannery, 'The powers of apostrophe', p. 302, suggests that 'both Nick and Hollinghurst's novel troublingly owe their futurity and their impact to the sacrifice of a black man', this reading does not give adequate weight to the book's critique of political complicity. Instead, I argue that the novel is critical of Nick's failure to address his obligation to Leo.

47 Hollinghurst, *Line of Beauty*, pp. 97, 167.

48 In recognising the 'evidence of little necessary systems' Nick may be read as drawing on his own lower-middle-class background to read the Charles family home in more sympathetic terms, Hollinghurst, *Line of Beauty*, p. 135.

For a history of British–West Indian domestic spaces, see Michael McMillan, *The Front Room: Migrant aesthetics in the home* (London: Black Dog, 2009).

49 Hollinghurst, *Line of Beauty*, p. 135.

50 Hollinghurst, *Line of Beauty*, p. 136.

51 Nick cites two Jamesian sentences which highlight his, and James's, concern with self-delusion, on the one hand, and 'homing desires', on the other. From 'The outcry' he quotes, 'The worse they are the more they see beauty in each other', and from 'The high bid', 'a man says to a butler in a country house, "I mean, to whom do you beautifully belong"', Hollinghurst, *Line of Beauty*, pp. 182–3.

52 Hollinghurst, *Line of Beauty*, p. 355.

53 Hollinghurst, *Line of Beauty*, p. 311.

54 Hollinghurst, *Line of Beauty*, pp. 52, 316.

55 Hollinghurst, *Line of Beauty*, p. 56.

56 Panikos Panayi, *An Immigration History of Britain* (London: Longman, 2010), maps the nineteenth- and twentieth-century history of anti-semitism in Britain: 'While positive attitudes towards Jews certainly existed, especially if they faced persecution at the hands of intolerant continental regimes, it always competed with a powerful strain of anti-semitism, which manifested itself especially in social prejudice', p. 278. It is noteworthy, however, that the Aliens Act of 1905, which provided 'the template for the history of British immigration control', explicitly targeted 'the immigration of poor Eastern European Jews into the East End of London', p. 62.

57 Hollinghurst, *Line of Beauty*, pp. 72, 290, 292.

58 Hollinghurst, *Line of Beauty*, p. 44.

59 Hollinghurst, *Line of Beauty*, p. 297.

60 Hollinghurst, *Line of Beauty*, p. 131.

61 Hollinghurst, *Line of Beauty*, p. 175.

62 Hollinghurst, *Line of Beauty*, pp. 307, 407.

63 Hollinghurst, *Line of Beauty*, pp. 23, 31, 38.

64 Hollinghurst, *Line of Beauty*, p. 399.

65 Hollinghurst, *Line of Beauty*, p. 413.

66 Jacqueline Rose, 'Margaret Thatcher and Ruth Ellis', *New Formations* 6, 1988, describes as 'grotesque' Thatcher's 'support for capital punishment' and the way she 'stood for … the desirability of war', p. 9.

67 Hollinghurst, *Line of Beauty*, pp. 354–5.

68 Hollinghurst, *Line of Beauty*, p. 355.

69 Rose, 'Margaret Thatcher and Ruth Ellis', pp. 19–20.

70 Hollinghurst, *Line of Beauty*, pp. 357, 374.

71 Hollinghurst, *Line of Beauty*, p. 347

72 Hollinghurst, *Line of Beauty*, p. 409.

73 Margaret Thatcher, Speech to Conservative Party Conference, 'The lady's not for turning', Thatcher Mss digital collection, 10 October 1980, p. 11.

74 Hollinghurst, *Line of Beauty*, p. 438.

75 Hollinghurst, *Line of Beauty*, p. 54.
76 Ahmed, *Queer Phenomenology*, p. 107. My reading of Nick's ambiguous 'drifting' is also informed by Heather Love's argument in *Feeling Backward* (Cambridge, MA: Harvard University Press, 2007) for the importance of dwelling with 'instances of ruined or failed sociality', p. 22.
77 Hollinghurst, *Line of Beauty*, p. 437.
78 Fortier, 'Making home', pp. 115, 123.

10

The return of the native: Pat Barker, David Peace and the regional novel after empire

James Procter

Killing in one context gets you a medal ... in another you spend years behind bars ... but maybe they're carried out in a similar state. (Pat Barker, *Guardian*, 16 August 2003)

Wogs Out, Leeds, NF, Leeds, Kill a Paki, Leeds. (David Peace, *Nineteen Eighty Three*, 2002)

The regional novel ... is from the beginning characteristically written by natives (Raymond Williams, *Writing in Society*, 1983)

Bounded, insular, self-consciously apart, the regional English novel would appear remote from the concerns of this volume. It is perhaps no wonder then that debates on empire and its aftermath have tended to flicker between metropolitan centre and postcolonial periphery while paying scant attention to the internal margins of provincial Englishness. Nevertheless, there is compelling evidence to suggest that the regional novel has played, and continues to play, a significant imaginative role during the period of empire's passing. In his comprehensive study of the British regional novel, K.D.M. Snell tracks book production between 1880 and 1990, observing that 'the genre as a whole has expanded since the Second World War, and noticeably during the 1970s and the 1980s'.[1] Snell goes on to speculate that these peaks in production coincide with periods of social and economic crisis, 'when older interior ways of life' are threatened and 'when changes in familiar and psychological "landscapes"' take place.[2] This is an intriguing observation within the context of a collection of essays looking at how the English novel responded to the disappearance of empire during the decades of decolonisation.

This chapter considers a series of novels that were either written during what Snell identifies as the boom decades of the 1970s and 1980s, or otherwise return to that period within works of historical fiction. My primary focus will be on the first novels of two authors closely associated with the north of England: David Peace's *Nineteen Seventy Four* (1999) and Pat Barker's *Union Street* (1982). However, I will also refer at points to the wider series of regional novels associated with these authors: Peace's 'Red Riding Quartet', which comprises, in addition to *Nineteen Seventy Four*, *Nineteen Seventy Seven* (2000), *Nineteen Eighty* (2001) and *Nineteen Eighty Three* (2002), and Barker's *Blow Your House Down* (1984) which, with *Union Street* and *The Century's Daughter* (1986), has been understood (problematically I would suggest) as marking a 'regional' phase in her career, which ended with the *Regeneration* trilogy (1991–95).[3]

Both Peace and Barker have used the historical events of the Yorkshire Ripper case as a fictional resource and point of departure in their early writing, subsuming their stories within fairytale frameworks which invoke the cautionary narratives of 'The Three Little Pigs' (*Blow Your House Down*) and 'Little Red Riding Hood' (the 'Red Riding Quartet'). These allusions to oral folk tales say something about Barker and Peace's shared interest in the vernaculars of working-class communities. More precisely, they point to the authors' joint preoccupation with predatory male violence against children and women. While their titles suggest the eternal and inevitable return of the archetypal 'wolf', both invite us to think locally and historically rather than universally about the conditions which produce serial acts of violence. At the same time seriality, doubling, mirroring and repetition all serve as devices in their work to multiply, magnify, extend as well as to question the origins of violence. Violence is not immanent for them, an evil or exceptional eruption from within; rather it connects with elsewhere and is intimately attached to empire. It is no coincidence then that images of rape and buggery, the 'master tropes of colonial discourse', appear as the most prevalent mode of violence.[4]

What follows is an attempt to understand the recurring but textually unelaborated, or 'unpacked', relations between empire, violence, race and region within these novels. Available readings of Barker's and Peace's work properly focus on issues of class, locality and gender, but this has involved a forgetting of the way their texts are also haunted by empire. While my attempt to recover empire in what follows risks attenuating questions of class and gender, it should be clear that the three cannot be detached. Just as rape is connected to both sexual and imperial politics in these novels, so too their concern with land occupation and property ownership has clear class and colonial connotations.

Empire appears on one level inconsequential to their fictional worlds. If a visceral, violent racism reverberates through their imagined communities then this is a fact which simply goes without saying; it is never explained, illuminated or resolved. In their north of England narratives, a spade is a spade, and race and empire are surface events rather than moments of profound revelation or epiphany. However, it is not that empire is merely outside, or even peripheral to, the insular landscapes of Peace and Barker's self-consciously non-metropolitan, white working-class fictions. If the West Indian character of Bertha in Barker's *Union Street* presents, in a text replete with doubles and mirrors, obvious parallels with Charlotte Brontë's *Jane Eyre*, Peace's is essentially a *tribal* locale described towards the end of the Quartet as 'heart of a darkness, belly of a nightmare' (*Nineteen Eighty Three*, 393). What critics have pinpointed in regional terms as Peace's 'Northern noir' comes to reside elsewhere in this context, in colonial stereotype: this is a world where the newly established Metropolitan police force has 'too many chiefs' (*Nineteen Seventy Seven*, 6), where the 'natives' are described as 'getting restless' (*Nineteen Seventy Four*, 175), which resounds with the echo of 'jungle drums' (*Nineteen Seventy Four*, 141–2), and where references to Mau Mau appear as a naturalised part of the local landscape (*Nineteen Seventy Seven*, 15).

Like Conrad's Kurtz, the communities of both Barker and Peace find themselves 'going native' when confronted by a series of local traumas and deep historical crises. The becoming-feral of Kelly Brown in *Union Street*, like the increasingly predatory, animal and savage acts of the police, press and paedophiles in Peace's 'Quartet', is not straightforwardly a 'becoming-local', or a regression into a set of regional stereotypes akin to the British television comedy, *The League of Gentlemen*. Going native in these novels demands to be understood in the more profound – imperial – sense of the term.[5]

Structured around three-year intervals, Peace's 'Quartet' encompasses the period from 1974 to 1983, with parts of the novels turning back to the late 1960s. Barker's *Union Street* is set in 1973 – and the interregnum between the miners' strikes of 1972–74 – while gaining much of its political urgency from the fact it was published in 1983, on the verge of the climactic 1984–85 strike. Like Peace's 'Quartet', Barker's *Blow Your House Down* fictionalises the Yorkshire Ripper killings, which took place during the years 1975 to 1981. While their carefully confined chronological focus fits well with the equally constricted regional visions of Peace's West Yorkshire and Barker's North East, both are also working knowingly across a wider watershed in national (and international) history. Among other things, the move from 1974 to 1984 marks the historical transition from consensus politics to a more militant Conservatism, from the collective vision of the welfare state and union activity to the privatised and individualist enterprise culture of Thatcherism, from the regulated to the free market economy, from the industrial to the post-industrial world.

This historical 'progression' appears in the fiction of Barker and Peace as essentially regressive, a move backwards which finds its counterpoint in the process of 'going native'. In *Union Street*, the elderly Mrs Bell notes that 'There wasn't much she'd learned in the Depression that still made sense in the seventies' (242). 'And yet,' she thinks, 'She was poorer now than she'd been then. And worse housed' (242). Regression is part of the very form of *Union Street* and of the 'Quartet', with the former presenting a sequence of seven women's lives, each older than the one before, and the latter organised around a serial structure which involves repetition and the compulsive return of the repressed.

These are regional narratives which testify to the social and economic wreckage brought about by the unleashing of a militant market politics. In 1974, the year of Peace's debut novel, the Chapeltown district of Leeds (a key venue in the 'Quartet') had an unemployment rate four times higher than the national average. The killers' lair is a disused mine, and the mills are described as 'silent' (28). The violent misogyny of the men in Barker's fiction has its foundations in the dereliction, redundancy and impotence of its industrial landscapes, which have no place, no use-value, in the new post-industrial society which is emerging elsewhere in England. In a different context, Peace has described Yorkshire as historically 'the place of the defeated, subjugated, and ultimately neglected people of England'.[6] He goes on to refer to the county as 'occupied land', akin to Northern Ireland. The extent to which both authors mobilise images of the Troubles is striking, and it is significant that the most tragic victims of Barker and Peace's novels – Kelly Brown and Michael Myshkin – are to be witnessed performing versions of the 'dirty protests' conducted by jailed Catholics in the Northern Ireland of the 1970s.

Yet it is precisely the point where such postcolonial parallels emerge that the relations between empire and region become most strained. Far from inviting a nostalgic vision of subaltern working-class communities, it is through images of empire, race and racism that these novelists trouble a romantic sense of community. Typically, the characters of these fictions are aggressively racist when confronted with what Salman Rushdie once called 'the new empire within'.[7] Empire appears in these novels as something which characters constantly misrecognise, seeing and living only the disconnections.

A closer look at Kelly Brown in Barker's *Union Street* illuminates these complexities. The novel is set in 1973 when fuel is scarce due to the miners' strike and to the oil crisis. In the opening chapter the eleven-year-old Kelly screws up a newspaper in order to make a fire: 'She picked up the first piece of newspaper. The face of a young soldier killed in Belfast disappeared beneath her scrumpling fingers' (4). The casual violence of the face of the dead soldier (not the page of the paper), collapsing beneath Kelly's clenching fingers, reverberates throughout a chapter in which hands and fingers are connected with displaced male sexual desire, and ultimately with Kelly's own violent rape. Earlier in the day, in what appears to be a prior encounter with her attacker, a stranger takes an unripe conker from her: 'She watched his long fingers with their curved nails probe the green skin, searching for the place where it would most easily open and admit them' (14). The latent violence of these connected episodes makes sense as a device to foreshadow the actual, and unflinchingly graphic, rape of Kelly later that day. What is less easy to explain is the way the novel parallels the (post)colonial violence of occupied Ireland with the sexual and class-based violence in the otherwise isolated world of *Union Street*.

Shortly after she has been raped, alone at night, Kelly seeks to block out the world by switching on the television:

> She watched anything rather than switch it off. Tonight, there was a programme about Northern Ireland. She settled down, expecting to be bored. But then there was this young man, this soldier, and he was lying in a sort of cot, a bed with sides on it, and he was shouting out, great bellows of rage, as he looked out through the bars at the ward where nobody came. What caught her attention was: they'd shaved all his hair off. You could see the scars where they'd dug the bullets out. His head like a turnip. That was what they'd done to him. They'd turned him into a turnip, a violent turnip, when they shot the bullets into his brain.
> The camera switched to gangs of youths throwing stones. But his eyes went on watching her. (48)

As with the newspaper story, the news of Northern Ireland fails to catch Kelly's eye. Yet if she is indifferent to the Troubles and to their political implications, she is at the same time transfixed by the image of the traumatised and wounded soldier, mesmerised by his mental state and bodily monstrosity. To be sure, this is an ambiguous image for Kelly to settle on: on the one hand the soldier, like Kelly, is young, presumably working-class, a wounded and scarred victim of penetrative violence. At the same time, he is an embodiment of the same aggressive masculinity (in its institutionalised, state-sanctioned form) which is inflicted upon Kelly and many other women in the novel. Moreover, the soldier is an extension of the politics of occupation and indirect rule imposed from Westminster, and a haunting reminder of the nation's internal colonial history. Caged, helpless and child-like in his barred 'cot', the soldier is by turns implicitly predatory ('his eyes kept on watching her') and dangerous. At the same time Kelly cannot take her eyes off him, and as she abstracts and strips the soldier of his political significance, closing her mind to the larger context of the coverage (the youths throwing stones), she connects with him completely, and only, as a victim of the violence of others.

Her deterioration in what follows involves a process of her 'going native' which closely parallels the physical and emotional state of the soldier. She too becomes a predator, holding the eyes of others as she haunts the streets after dark (48). At one point she breaks into a Victorian property in the wealthiest part of town, 'raping' its opulent interior with her fingers which have now become claws, 'clawing at the satin skin of the bed dragging her nails across the dressing table hard enough to leave scratches, claw marks, in the polished wood' (52–3). Kelly catches her image in the mirror, 'as wild and unkempt as an ape, as savage as a wolf' (54), before roughly shearing her hair with scissors, as if to mirror the turnip head of the shaven soldier. Condensed in her subliminal sexual assault on the property is a form of class rebellion which, via this other victim of violence in Northern Ireland, becomes tinged with the colonial politics of occupation. Before she is raped, the narrator (whose consciousness at this point is close to Kelly's) lingers over the middle-class diction and register of the rapist, particularly the way he pronounces 'steelworks': 'in that light, precise, slightly sibilant voice, it sounded as remote as the Pyramids' (24). Class is articulated through the image of the exotic, rendering the familiar locale in foreign terms.

Disgusted with her timidity after fleeing the house, Kelly later goes on to break into her school. As with the 'intimate' rooms of the house, she now seeks to make her headmaster's office 'vulnerable, to expose itself' (55). After smashing, vandalising and stabbing the furniture, she shits on the floor before smearing her 'hot, animal stink' across the room with her fingers (55). Although it is never explicitly stated, this act of rebellion mirrors the so-called 'dirty protests' conducted by IRA paramilitary prisoners who rebelled against their criminalisation during the late 1970s. Previously classified as political prisoners, not criminals, they protested by smashing cell furniture, refusing to wash and smearing excrement on walls. By leaving these connections open but unspoken Barker refuses to give Kelly a causal, conscious set of political motives, while at the same time suggesting the workings of a political unconscious.

The echoes between the politics of postcolonial struggle in Northern Ireland and Kelly's rape are tangible in the text, setting up a subtle mirroring of imperial and domestic violence in a novel full of reflections, doubles and ghosts.[8] There is something self-consciously Lacanian about Barker's mirrors, where recognition is a form of misrecognition which is repeatedly associated with splitting, fragmentation and the disintegration of identity rather than with the unity that both mirrors – and the novel's title – seem to promise. Yet union and unity remain a symbolic possibility at the close of the narrative, as Kelly's young hand joins with the elderly Alice Bell's, and so too the structural reflections, echoes and repetitions across the text invite the reader to explore the underlying connections both along and beyond the atomised, divided lives of the street. Through their insistent coupling, the traumatic violence of the Troubles and Kelly's rape become more than exceptional, isolated or random acts. They are presented as a function of a systematic (if, in Barker's fiction, unmappable) regional, national and nationalist aggression.

The resonances of haunting, doubling and mirroring are perhaps most pronounced in the story of Joanne Wilson, which follows directly after Kelly's. Jo works in a cake-making factory on a production line with three other women, one of whom, Big Bertha, is West Indian. The name is suggestive of Jane Eyre's dark double in Brontë's classic novel. But where Brontë's Bertha is given a biography, which allows us to explain her presence – albeit through a contrapuntal reading at the margins of the text – Barker's Bertha simply appears, is inexplicable to the other characters and unexplained by the text.[9] This aporia or blank in the narrative is suggestive of the limits of regional and working-class community, as imagined in Barker's text:

> The trouble had started when Bertha first came to work at the factory. Nobody liked it. She was the first coloured worker there. But Elaine had gone on louder and longer than most: there was 'nigger stink' in the cloakroom; why was she being allowed to use the same toilets when everybody knew what mucky buggers they were; and anyway if she had to be there at all, why sponges? There was chocolate cake upstairs; why not there? (81)

Free indirect discourse is deployed by Barker in order to merge Elaine's voice with that of the narrator. As a result there is no outside text or voice which can adequately explain, justify or judge the 'extreme' racism of the women, and which as a result appears as a normative, commonsense discourse. Thus a co-worker can illuminate the motivation of Elaine's racism – "'It's their Barbara. Her [Elaine's] eldest sister. She had three to a nigger'" – while still reproducing it herself (82). If the other factory women distance themselves from Elaine's extremism and silently respect Bertha's stoicism in the face of this ongoing barrage of insults, it is made clear they broadly share Elaine's ideological viewpoint, as does the narrator. When Bertha finally and ferociously reacts, beating Elaine until she bleeds, the women feel no sympathy for Elaine. At the same time, Bertha's innate difference from them is confirmed:

> Bertha's use of her fists, the silent ferocity of her attack, was something quite foreign to their experience. And they hated it. More even than the colour of her skin, it confirmed that she was an outsider amongst them. (84)

Ironically, and far from being foreign to their experience, violence (including the use of fists and of 'silent ferocity') is a mundane, matter-of-fact dimension of these women's lives (see, for example, p. 184 and the story of Iris King). Their emphatic rejection and racialised compartmentalisation of violence allows them to externalise and render safe a difference which is internal to them. The othering of Bertha among the women appears at least partly founded on the manner in which she reminds them of themselves, holding up a mirror to their own lives.

If *Union Street* exposes the regional poverty bequeathed by a post-industrial economy, it is by no means nostalgic for older ideas of industrial community. The novel suggests there is a more precise, local and class-based dimension to their treatment of Bertha which is closely connected to their conditions of labour. The aggressive division of time and space in the cake factory, which operates on a Fordist logic, is closely linked to the compartmentalisation of the women into isolated units of production. It is within this setting that the women become internally divided, alienated from one another, unable to connect or empathise as automatons within a segmented workplace. Even during the strictly timed breaks the women 'sat in much the same order they worked on the conveyor belt. … If any of them had been asked what they thought of this arrangement, the answer would probably have been "Terrible". Yet they continued to abide by it. It was easy; required no thought' (90). The noise of the machinery prevents conversation so that 'in this roaring cavern of sound each woman *was* alone' (85).

Following her attack on Elaine, Bertha extracts further revenge on the assembly line, breaking the enforced rhythms of the conveyer belt. 'This altered movement, repeated, as it would have to be, hundreds of times, would amount by the end of the morning to agonising pain' (88).

The assembly line produces not just confectionery but modes of alienated, automated subjectivity and serial violence, including racist violence.

Barker pursues her critique of reification further in *Blow Your House Down*, a novel set in an unnamed northern city where the women must choose between a life of prostitution or working in a chicken factory. Both options involve objectification, alienation and serial killing: when Brenda moves from prostitution to the conveyor belt in many respects she has stayed in the same place. Significantly, it is during her time at the factory that the reader realises Brenda is failing to see that her children are being abused by their carer, while at the same time she articulates her own sense of disconnection from those around her – from the lives of the Pakistani women (who never go out, leaving 'nobody in this street she could ask to sit with the children') and West Indian women ('"Mucky sods"'; 'tits like footballs, floor crawling with bairns') (38–9).

The inability of Barker's white working-class women to connect with other kinds of women, particularly Caribbean and Asian women, is in part a consequence of the atomised conditions of the street and workplace. It also underwrites their disconnection from wider national and international politics. In *Union Street*, following her day's work at the factory, Joanne Wilson is described watching television alone, in a scene which echoes the one with Kelly Brown earlier:

> She [Joanne] sat in the darkness and watched gangs of youths throwing stones on the streets of Belfast. Then turned the volume up for a story about petrol price increases. She wasn't interested, but Joss would be. His car was his god. (102)

Joanne, who may or may not be watching the same news item as Kelly earlier, certainly shares her lack of interest. Like Kelly's purely personal identification with the soldier in Northern Ireland, Joanne only thinks of politics at the level of the individual rather than the communal – the conditions for Thatcherism would already appear to be in place.

The novels of both Barker and Peace seem enclosed, sealed off from national and international changes which were constituitive of Britain's renegotiation of its imperial, or post-imperial, status. While their texts are littered with newspaper headlines, radio announcements and television items (both local and global) which provide a tantalising glimpse of these wider historical transformations, the characters themselves are conspicuously indifferent to them. In *Union Street*, newspapers typically constitute waste materials, a mundane feature of the decaying industrial landscape ('a sour, brick-strewn waste land, covered with dog shit, newspaper and beer cans'), or are otherwise used and recycled for something other than 'news' (22). More specifically newspapers serve a primary and pragmatic need: fuel for the fire (4); wrappings for chips (48); insulation from the cold (60); or otherwise operate as points of distraction rather than reflection and engagement, always about to be discarded. In Peace's 'Quartet', meanwhile, characters are repeatedly figured turning off or tuning out their radios to silence the news.

The isolated newspaper headlines which are seamlessly woven into the realist plotlines of Barker's *Union Street*, are elevated to become part of the fragmented or divisive texture of Peace's fictional world, whether in a proto-modernist newsreel format, or in the use of journalists and media men at the level of content and character. As part of the very form of Peace's novels, at points newspapers themselves become a vehicle of symbolic violence. Peace doesn't stitch together journalistic and fictional segments but tends to leave them as open wounds for the reader to traverse and confront. The segmented structures he deploys present readers with a scarred and wounded surface driven by the staccato rhythms of a speech cast in the imperatives of impoverishment and social disconnection.

Where this scarring is pronounced is at the boundary between the regional and the national/international. Press stories associated with the serial killings are described in emphatic terms as 'National. Not Local' (*Nineteen Seventy Four*, 27), or as 'Not going … National' (*Nineteen Eighty Three*, 39); the *Yorkshire Post*, *Radio Leeds*, *Calendar* and *Look North* cover the 'local hells' of Leeds and West Yorkshire, while *News at Ten* and the national media cover the election campaign of 1983, the moon landing of 1969 and the disappearance of Lord Lucan in 1974. The sense of informational excess which the 'Quartet' generates is on one level a simulation of the Yorkshire Ripper investigation where, in a period before computers, the accumulation of information far outstripped the capacity to process it. Disconnection is part of the 'crime' of the 'Quartet', which dwells on what the author has termed 'Yorkshire apartness' – a tribal condition he describes as part of the collective identity of the region. In the novels this syndrome is reproduced in the mismatch between national and local news, and it's apparent too in the mores of the newly formed West Yorkshire police, delighting in its status as a law unto itself. 'THIS IS THE NORTH. WE DO WHAT WE WANT' (265).

The reader of these novels is charged with the attempt to establish connections across the dismembered and striated surface of a serial narrative. If this emphasis on making connections is a generic convention of crime fiction, where certain clues need to be solved for the plot to be resolved, Peace takes this beyond the more limited sense of the crime itself to embrace the relations between regional, national *and* imperial history. 'Everything's connected' is a line which resonates across the books, and it is the inability, or the refusal, of the police to make connections – to take seriously the serial, repetitive nature of the crimes before them – which remains the most sustained injustice of the narrative (233). The reader is invited to understand the crimes of the 'Quartet' as more than the interior pathology of an individual or isolated consciousness. If hatred, greed, fear and loathing are the prevailing emotions that create the climate for killing and violence in Peace's Yorkshire, these are not abstract terms, but are closely linked to the rise of the New Right. New Right discourse, which spans the post-1968 politics of both Powellism and Thatcherism, and precisely parallels the period of serial killing in Peace's 'Quartet', handled empire in a new and distinct way. As Anna Marie Smith (1994) has argued, Enoch Powell, for example, worked through the trauma of decolonisation by presenting empire as something external, almost accidental, to the nation.[10] The consequences of this were complex. The structural forgetting of the dependency of the nation on its peripheries has meant that the internal black immigrant can be constructed as entirely external to, or foreign to, Englishness. This is the spatial (inside/outside) logic on which the exclusionary racial discourses of the New Right were established. In *Nineteen Seventy Four* there exists a revealing link between Detective Superintendent George Oldman's denial of the connection between the recent spate of killings in West Yorkshire and *the novel's* construction of racism and empire through the logic of what Peace calls 'apartness'.[11]

Nineteen Seventy Four tells of a Gypsy community targeted by the police after the killing of a Morley schoolgirl, Claire Kempley. Following a tip-off, local reporter Eddie Dunford finds himself witness to an infernal scene at the Hunslett and Beeston exit of the M1, where the Gypsy camp is razed to the ground under the cover of night. Looking down from the motorway embankment, Eddie watches with impotent rage as the caravans burn while police vans circle to stop the men, women and children trapped inside from escaping. Beyond this moving barricade of vehicles an outer ring of police encircle the ring of fire, beating their shields before slowly moving in. Officers shoot the Gypsies' dogs, destroy any remaining possessions, strip the women and children of their clothes, beat the men.

The Gypsies are more than racialised scapegoats for the murder of Claire Kempley: they also occupy the land on which Donald Foster and his men (including architect John Dawson, and the gaffer George Marsh) plan to build the biggest shopping centre in Yorkshire. It is an entrepreneurial vision from which senior police officers (the 'fat cats' (172)) stand directly to profit. The name of the proposed commercial development is the Swan Shopping Centre. Swans are the trademark of the serial killers who attach wings to the backs of their victims. Eddie Dunford and others drink in The Swan. Swan's wings are the inspiration for the roof of John Dawson's home. Eddie's journalist colleague, Barry Gannon, states that 'All great buildings are crimes'. (*Nineteen Seventy Four*, 82). The construction company linked with Dawson, Marsh and Foster is in turn caught up in the serial killings. Everything is connected.

As he watches the Gypsy camp burn, Eddie Dunford describes what he sees in the condensed phrase, 'Cowboys and fucking Indians, 1974' (*Nineteen Seventy Four*, 45). And then later, referring to the police beating their shields, '*Zulu*, Yorkshire style' (*Nineteen Seventy Four*, 46). Dunford's exotic and oxymoronic analogies appear entirely foreign to the reporter's native Yorkshire. Yet his appropriation of what were, in 1974, popular colonial stereotypes seems appropriate: the police themselves are to be witnessed 'going native', dancing around the fire and beating their shields – while elsewhere in the 'Quartet' the serial killers scalp their victims.

Dunford's reference points also reveal something of his own psychological limits. If the crime against the gypsies reduces him to tears, he still talks without hesitation of gypos, wogs, puffters and Pakis. He can fight heroically to resolve the police cover-up of child sex abuse, but anally rapes the mother of one their victims. Nobody is above, or outside, the logic and contradictions of the ugliness of everyday political realities. Everybody is compromised. It is not just the powerful, the police and the media, who produce a rhetoric of hatred. It is also the dispossessed, the anonymous and voiceless who express their feelings in graffiti on the borderlines of the city: 'Mandy Sucks Paki Cocks' (61); 'Yorkshire Whites' (61); 'FUCK THE IRA' (150). This is what the narrator of *Nineteen Eighty Three* calls 'the graffiti that hates everything, everywhere, and everyone but especially the IRA, Man United and the Pakis ...' (26).

In such sentiments we encounter a process of abjection not dissimilar to that found in Barker's novels. These anonymous slogans of hatred, rejection and expulsion work through the trauma of immigration by turning the inside out. At the same time Peace himself exposes the extent to which violence – directed at women, children and immigrants – should be understood as a mode of colonial violence which is *internal* to the history of Yorkshire and of the nation, which was of old 'exported' rather than being a phenomenon which has only recently been 'imported' into the nation.

Thus, Barry Gannon, the journalist who precedes Eddie Dunford in investigating Foster, Marsh and the others, indicates that his life is in danger because he has come close to uncovering the killers. Moments before he dies in suspicious circumstances, he confides to Eddie that he believes he will be killed by a 'Death Squad':

> You think that shit is just for the Yellow Man or the Indian? There are Death Squads in every city, in every country ... They train them in Northern Ireland. Give them a taste, then bring them back home hungry ... You really think it's gangs of Paddies in donkey jackets lugging round big bags of fucking fertilizer, blowing up all these pubs? (60)

Later in the novel, Barry Gannon's story is reiterated in a very different context when Eddie meets the shady underworld figure of Derek Box at an Indian restaurant, the Karachi Club on Bradford Road. Derek Box is Foster's partner-in-crime who offers a revealing insight into the formative experiences of a violent killer. Box met Foster when on 'Her Majesty's business', doing his National Service in the Kenyan Highlands:

> protecting fat cunts like I am now, fighting the fucking Mau Maus. ... They'd come down from the hills like a tribe of bloody red Indians, raping the women, cutting the cocks off the men, stringing them upon fence posts. ... We weren't angels, Mr Dunford. I was with Don Foster when we ambushed a fucking War Party. We shot them in the knees with .303s so we could have some fun. ... Foster took his time. He taped the screams, the dogs barking, claimed it helped him sleep. (*Nineteen Seventy Four*, 211)

Foster's pathological desires were forged in a colonial context, during the Kenyan struggles for independence in the 1950s. As the opening epigraph from Barker suggests, two otherwise very different modes of serial killing – one for queen and country, another for sexual gratification – are more intimately connected than we might care to think. Within Box's deranged yet incisive imagination the brutal treatment of the Mau Mau maps precisely onto the current situation in Leeds in 1974. As he concludes the revelation above: 'It was war, Mr Dunford. Just like now' (211). Several pages earlier, at the Karachi Club, Box elaborates in more detail on the nature of this war:

The government and the unions, the Left and the Right, the rich and the poor. Then you got your Paddys, your wogs, your niggers, the puffs and the perverts, even the bloody women; they're all out for what they can get. Soon there'll be nowt left for the working white man. (*Nineteen Seventy Four*, 186)

Box's easy move from politics, to class, to gender, to sex, to race wars is suggestive of a wider sense of a disorderly England as parasitic host to a series of invaders, 'out for what they can get' (186). What Box identifies (and himself endorses) is the value of aggressive entrepreneurial individualism. As he concludes: 'To the victor, the spoils' (186). Yet he is more eloquent on the politics of hatred (xenophobia, homophobia, misogyny) than about the wider practices of politics, understood more generally, and this is the rule rather than the exception in Peace's Yorkshire. The unrelenting bleakness of these narratives derives, as it does in Barker's *Union Street*, from the inseparability of the locals' recognition from their misrecognition. Yorkshire (like Union Street) *is* an occupied landscape, but it is not the wogs, niggers, Pakis, puffters, Paddies and gypos who have 'taken over', or illegitimately claimed the place for themselves. On the contrary, it is the police, the press and the politicians, those whom Barry Gannon calls, in an overarching allusion of the 'Quartet', Big Brother – who have colonised this corner of England.

Notes

1   K.D.M. Snell, *The Regional Novel in Britain and Ireland, 1800–1990* (Cambridge: Cambridge University Press, 1998), p. 27.

2   Snell, *The Regional Novel in Britain*, pp. 27–8.

3   David Peace: *Nineteen Seventy Four*, *Nineteen Seventy Seven*, *Nineteen Eighty* and *Nineteen Eighty Three* (London: Serpent's Tail, 2000; 2000; 2001; and 2002). Pat Barker, *Union Street* (London: Virago, 2004) and *Blow Your House Down* (London: Virago, 1986). When Justine Picardie spoke of Barker emerging 'from a kind of chrysalis' (cited in Elaine Showalter, 'Inner visions', *Guardian*, 23 August 2003) with the *Regeneration* trilogy, she arguably had in mind the 'ghetto' of 'regional' as much as of 'women's writing'. As the biographies of both Barker (born in Thornaby-on-Tees, Teesside; educated at the LSE) and Peace (born in Osset, West Yorkshire; currently living in Japan) attest, the term 'regional' can impose dubious and potentially patronising limits on the non-metropolitan imagination. This chapter will reveal that the regions with which these authors deal are not as self-contained or set apart as they first appear. Nevertheless, the term is worth retaining because it identifies much of what is distinctive about these two authors' work in terms of its

peripheral engagements with empire. In an interview in 'Immigrant fictions', a tellingly titled special issue of *Contemporary Literature* (47: 4, 2006), Peace notes his main motivation in writing the 'Quartet' was to ask 'why these crimes happened in this place at this time to these people. And by extension, to what extent are/were the people of Yorkshire, and the North in general, culpable in these crimes? What role, for example, did the language or the landscape of Yorkshire in the 1970s play in these crimes, similarly, the political and economic policies of the time?', Matthew Hart, 'An interview with David Peace', p. 561.

4   See Nancy Paxton, *Writing Under the Raj: Gender, race, and rape in the British colonial imagination, 1830–1947* (New Brunswick: Rutgers University Press, 1999).

5   As Sinead Caslin defines it, 'The term "going native" is employed to refer to the trepidation felt by the European colonizers in Africa that they may become desecrated by being assimilated into the culture and customs of the indigenous peoples. In today's liberal and anti-racist society, "going native" is understandably considered a derogatory and offensive term.' Going native within these novels has both global-imperial implications (for example, the connections between serving in Africa and serial killing in Peace), while also signalling an unreconstructed, provincial racism: 'Going native' in 'The imperial archive', www.qub.ac.uk/schools/SchoolofEnglish/imperial/key-concepts/Going-native.htm (accessed 15 August 2010).

6   Hart, 'Interview', pp. 562–3.

7   See Salman Rushdie, *Imaginary Homelands: Essays and criticism, 1981–1991* (London: Granta, 1991), pp. 129–38.

8   From the Hall of Mirrors and the Ghost Train at the fair, to the fish and chip shop in whose greasy reflective tiles she is brought into a discomforting unity with the rapist, she ends up mirroring his actions.

9   We might speculate, given her age and circumstances, that Bertha belongs to the first wave of West Indian immigration during the 1940s and 1950s which was invited to fill the menial jobs left vacant after the second world war.

10 Anna Marie Smith, *New Right Discourse on Race and Sexuality: Britain, 1968–1998* (Cambridge: Cambridge University Press, 1994).

11 Hart, 'Interview', p. 562.

11

Saturday's Enlightenment

David Alderson

The principal focus of this essay is on Ian McEwan's novel, *Saturday*. The motivation for writing it, however, is to engage with larger debates on the British left – including the liberal left to which McEwan in some sense belongs – about the US- and British-led invasion of Iraq in 2003 and more generally about the continuing imperatives of empire. Set on 15 February, the day of the anti-invasion protests – though published in 2005, and written therefore in the knowledge of all that had transpired – *Saturday* explores the ambivalent, though mostly pro-invasion, attitudes of the central character, Henry Perowne.[1] It does not reflect, but rather may be read in the light of, a certain disorientation on the left in relation to contemporary imperialism, and a tendency for prominent members of it, socialists as well as liberals, to side with the US in contexts where it has militarily attacked obviously authoritarian regimes, even though those regimes – Taliban Afghanistan, Saddam's Iraq – have owed their existence to US support in the past. It has been extraordinary and frustrating to witness a figure like Christopher Hitchens, author of a brilliant book confirming the criminality of Henry Kissinger,[2] declare that the US really was now in the business of promoting freedom, and this at a time when old hands in forging US foreign policy – Bolton, Cheney, Perle, Rumsfeld, Wolfowitz – were prominent in the Bush administration. But Hitchens was not alone in unrepentantly claiming that *he* is the one who has stuck to his Enlightenment principles: the Marxist academic, Norman Geras, and the journalists, David Aaronovitch and Nick Cohen, have consistently attacked the anti-war left for its supposed betrayal of rationalist principle. The short-lived Euston Manifesto launched in 2006 included among its signatories some who opposed the invasion of Iraq, but its defence of universal human rights and democracy was directed principally against those who were perceived to have allied themselves with reactionary – and especially reactionary Islamic – forces.[3]

Saturday, though, seeks to avoid definitive political commitments, substituting a family crisis and its reconciliation for the consideration of global questions. My view is that this substitution is actually a means of pursuing those questions in different ways through its deployment of ideological tropes which have been integral to the overlapping histories of imperialism and the Enlightenment, whose relationship will be the central theoretical preoccupation of this chapter. I am concerned therefore with the complex ways in which the legacies of British colonialism have served to legitimate a quite different form of imperialism, that of the US. This requires some explanation in relation to the work of a writer who has at times been critical of both British imperialist nostalgia and US hegemony, and in order to understand how this has come about it is necessary first to consider McEwan's responses in a variety of works to shifting postwar and post-cold war geopolitical relations.

Gender, family, politics

No moment was more important symbolically in generating a sense of imperial decline in Britain than the Suez crisis of 1956, during which Britain and France were humiliated into retreat by their ostensible ally, the US. The son of a British army officer, McEwan was living in Libya at the time, and records that Suez generated so much popular anger there that British families had to be rounded up into armed camps for their own protection:

> My mother happened to be in England at the time, and for some weeks I lived in a tent with other children not so very far from a machine-gun nest. My father was a remote, organizing figure with a service revolver strapped around his waist. Suddenly everyday routines belonged to a distant past and I understood for the first time that political events were real and affected people's lives – they were not just stories in the papers that grown-ups read.[4]

In casting himself in the role of that recurrent figure in his work, the vulnerable child, McEwan here strikingly recounts a moment of revelation and maturation in which politics were made 'real' to him through gendered social and familial roles, as well as through related forms of emotional, spatial and temporal alienation. That first sentence encourages us to view the machine-gun *nest* as an ironic, military and masculine, substitute for the protection of his absent mother. But if we are expected to recognise certain phallic qualities in the various guns which populate this scene, we must surely note the contrast between those directed at the Libyans and the tidily British, holstered and attenuated weapon strapped to McEwan's father's waist. This was, after all, a retreat of sorts, and is here symbolic of the larger retreat from colonialism which would help to condition British masculine sensibilities more generally in the postwar period. The reality of politics is associated principally with the loss of the feminine and the disruption of an idealised familial balance, for which a 'distant' masculinity offers few attractive possibilities by way of compensatory identification. Writing fiction, for McEwan, will self-consciously become a means of maintaining a fidelity to the maternal.

There is a further separation which needs to be registered, though, between the moment being described and the time of McEwan's writing about it, since this memory is presented in the introduction to his screenplay for *The Ploughman's Lunch* (1982). This focuses on a Tory historian, James Penfield, who is writing a revisionist account of Suez at the time of Britain's attempts to reassert some degree of military independence on the international stage during the Falklands/Malvinas war. McEwan's account of his personal experience in 1956 are therefore also mediated by his relations to Thatcherism and to its attempts both to restore Britain to the 'glorious' imperial past from which it had been severed, and to effect a break with the postwar consensus.

The Ploughman's Lunch, though, reminds us of the continuing subordinate status of Britain through the relationship which was rarely so 'special' as when Thatcher was in power. Penfield is, above all, a careerist and opportunist, and the history he writes is carefully tailored to appeal to patriotic sensibilities without offending the main market for the book, US undergraduates (47). Hence the precision of the symbolism of Suez: Britain's decline was bound up with the rise of US power, just as the protectionism integral to colonialism was incompatible with US imperialism's imposition of 'free' markets. Elsewhere in his work, McEwan repeatedly draws our attention to the *ressentiment* integral to US–British relations as they are mediated by masculinity, and in *Saturday* it conditions the competitive relations between Henry and his brash US colleague and squash partner, Jay Strauss. In one of those asides through which the novel questions Henry's confidence in his own objectivity, we learn that 'Whenever he talks to Jay, Henry finds himself tending towards the anti-war camp'.[5]

Strategically central to the achievement of global US hegemony was the containment and ultimate defeat of the Soviet Union, and the cold war has also been a recurrent preoccupation for McEwan. The renewed zeal with which it was prosecuted by the US and Britain in the 1980s provides the context for his libretto for the anti-nuclear oratorio, *Or Shall We Die?* (1982). Reagan invested unprecedented amounts in nuclear weaponry, and in trying to match him the Soviet Union ruined its economy, a factor crucial in precipitating its collapse. McEwan's words, though, cast a plague on both houses – 'Here one nation stands jailer to its people's minds, / here the other ransacks the globe, a freedom / sustained by greed' – and the work is determinedly non-partisan, liberal humanist in orientation (22). It expresses the hope that the proliferation of nuclear weapons might be reversed through an evolutionary development of human consciousness away from the Newtonian rationalism which had dominated the twentieth century, determining that sense of ourselves as standing 'separate from our world – and from ourselves and from each other – describing, measuring, shaping it like gods' (12). The Einsteinian revolution, by contrast, held the potential to teach us that subjective perceptions are bound up with the process of observing. McEwan notes that the struggle between objectivity and perspectivalism – and, by extension, between reason and feeling – has traditionally been seen as one between masculine and feminine qualities, and the oratorio consequently concludes that, if the human race is to survive, there must be 'womanly times' (23).

The defining characteristic of womanliness in the oratorio is nurture, though McEwan makes it clear that he does not regard this as a trait exclusive to women. Indeed, the genesis of the oratorio lay in 'private fears', including ones which strikingly prefigure those passages in *Saturday* in which Henry fears for his family's safety: 'Love of children generates a fierce ambition for the world to continue and be safe, and makes one painfully vulnerable to fantasies of loss. Like others, I experience the jolt of panic that wakes you before dawn, the daydreams of the mad rush of people and cars out of the city before it is destroyed, of losing a child in the confusion' (5). Fathers, too, can be womanly, and all of this helps to explain the absolute centrality of, and value placed on, the family in his novels. For McEwan the family functions as the source of an ethical investment in the other and as a commitment to a principle of futurity. However it is also inevitably the source of his conservatism, given the gendered and sexual norms which govern the family, as well as the conditions and limits it imposes on any extension of sympathy beyond the self, since the family has symbolically served to police all kinds of distinctions, extending outwards from public and private to those which define the communal or national, and even the human.[6]

Of course, families are not consistently idealised in McEwan's fiction, but that is because they are prone to perversities generated by the social and familial dominance of masculinity.[7] Before discussing *Saturday*, I want to consider two novels in which the relations between abstraction and concretion, gender and the body, are especially revealing: *The Comfort of Strangers* and *The Innocent*. In the first, Venice functions both as a concrete labyrinth in which the central characters get lost and a symbolic site of psychic exploration. Within it, the characters of the novella more or less embody, more or less transgress, conventional correspondences between men and masculinity, and women and femininity. Robert asserts ideologically and physically the principle of necessary male dominance, not only over other women, but also over the feminised Colin. Mary's feminism challenges, and yet reproduces in certain respects, masculine impulses: she admires, if only as 'a tactic', the radicalism of Italian feminists who propose castration for rapists.[8] This serves to draw our attention to the crucial issue within feminism about the precise relations between body and culture: Mary and the Italian feminists here suggest the problem and the solution might be biological. Robert, by contrast, grounds his patriarchalism in culture: "It is the world that shapes people's minds. It is men who have made the world. So women's minds are shaped by men. Now the women lie to themselves and there is confusion and unhappiness everywhere'" (55). Colin's androgyny, residing in the beauty and vulnerability which make him the object of both Robert and Caroline's sadistic desires, is substantially biological and bound up with sexual desire. He explains to Mary during their renewed bout of lovemaking after visiting Robert and Caroline how 'he felt an aching emptiness, close to desire, between his scrotum and his anus; he thought this might be an approximation of womanly desire' (61). This establishes a contrast to Mary's masculine forcefulness: when she massages his shoulder, briefly causing Colin pain, it reminds us of Robert's earlier erotic gesture of intimacy with him (70).

It is a further measure of the abstraction of this narrative that it does not confirm male homosexual desires, still less identities, even while it relies heavily on homosocial ones. Colin's unrealisable longing to be filled is located, impossibly, somewhere *between* scrotum and anus, and Robert's suggestive massaging of Colin's shoulder is followed by a punch to the stomach which foreshadows Colin's murder. Even when Robert takes Colin for his last visit to Robert's bar 'along streets relatively free of tourist and souvenir shops, a quarter from which women too seemed to have been excluded', the emphasis is on a foreign authenticity and homosociality, not on a relative subcultural autonomy. McEwan may be exploiting our sense of the relative weakness of gay identification in Italy, and the alleged casualness there of same-sex encounters, but this nonetheless conduces to the tale's juxtapositions and complications of (patriarchal) tradition with (feminist) modernity. After all, Robert and Colin do not finally have sex. Rather, in a kind of heterosexual snuff scene, the androgynous Colin is sacrificed to the lovemaking of Robert and Caroline, with Mary as viewer (further suggesting that her brand of castrating feminism is vaguely complicit with Robert and Caroline's impulses). Masculinity, in this novella, figures as an atavistic force: elemental, in some sense subconscious, it is the spectre which haunts the modern, more feminised, world.

Children are absent from all of this; they present no restraining influence, no demands to be nurtured. Mary's are being looked after by their 'womanly', biological father from her broken down marriage – he lives in a rural, vegetarian commune – while there is 'something wrong' with Robert's sperm, and Caroline's account of this fact leads into her description of the origins of their sado-masochism, as if the fact of Robert's impotence is sufficient to explain its evolution (86). By contrast, we are given no corresponding explanation for Caroline's submissiveness; it is as if there is no need for one, though there are obvious enough parallels to be drawn between nurture and masochism suggesting that the satisfaction she experiences results from her thwarted desire for children. Underpinning McEwan's exploration of perversion, as we might expect, are ultimately normative and heteronormative accounts of desire and the family.

The Innocent, by contrast, is more typical of McEwan's later, more historically specific work. Set in postwar Germany, it concerns the joint CIA–MI6 project, Operation Gold, to construct a spy tunnel across Berlin's West–East divisions. But this collaboration in fact turns out to be the means through which British–US tensions are explored, not least through the relationship between the central English character, Leonard, and his immediate boss from the CIA, Glass. The novel recognises that the British constitute the subordinate partner in the exercise, and the love affair between Leonard and his first girlfriend, the German, Maria, is set in the context of increasing US cultural influence, as suggested by the rock and roll played on the radio. Indeed, the affair itself is in part governed by the homosocial rivalry between Leonard and Glass over Maria, with Glass ultimately, and symbolically, victorious, though only as a result of a misperception on Leonard's part determined by the larger rivalry between them. Leonard resolves to correct things much later, on receiving a letter from Maria after the death of Glass in 1987, only two years before the fall of the Berlin Wall. One interpretation of this ending is that Leonard and Maria's reconciliation has been made possible by (an anticipated) political reconciliation – the fading of European tensions and the end of the cold war – but the other is that it is symbolic, indeed celebratory, of that reconciliation. In the first, love is that which struggles, and initially fails, to transcend politics; in the second, relationships generally are allegorical of politics. The earlier parts of the novel tend to confirm the former interpretation. Glass's death, by contrast, is key in suggesting the latter: it can only symbolise, given that it was not determined by, any weakening of the political hold of the US over Europe. The significance of this is that love, having been presented as that which may be defeated by history, finally comes to idealise history's supposed dissolution. McEwan's grasp and critique of the systemic nature of capitalism has weakened.

At one point, Leonard endangers his early relationship with Maria when he begins to act out rape fantasies which are bound up with relations between their respective nationalities. These fantasies also entail an acceptance, on Leonard's part, of 'the obvious truth that what happened in his head could not be sensed by Maria'.[9] It is only when he grasps that her protests are genuine, rather than complicit with the fantasy, that some balance is restored to his perspective. Maria is reminded of other instances of masculine aggression: the rape she once witnessed committed by a victorious Soviet soldier, and the violence of her estranged husband, Otto, whom she will later kill while, in feminine fashion, protecting Leonard in a way she never protected herself. But, for all the novel's recognition of the pervasiveness of rape and the way in which it brutally mediates through sexual difference other forms of power, it should be stressed that Leonard's sudden departure from, and equally sudden return to, innocence is never truly explained. Thus while apparently determined by specific social relations, masculinity also seems somehow instinctual – just as it is in the dehistoricised context of *The Comfort of Strangers* – a threat to the love which is also contradictorily bound up with, yet 'above', history.

McEwan's preoccupation with gender, then, emerges out of an idealisation of the balanced family, since it is the family which symbolically reconciles our gendered outlooks on the world (objectivity and subjectivity) and our dispositions towards it (aggression and nurture). The ideological consequences of this are multiple. They are bound up, first, with his persistent reifications of masculinity and femininity; and, second, with the ways in which gender is deployed in the novels as the basis for interpreting social and political relations more generally. In *Saturday*, ambivalence represents the best approximation to balance achievable. But this fetishisation of indecision is also the product of an inability to see the world as radically contradictory. Indeed, the novel's resolution achieves the symbolic expulsion of all that would be required to grasp it as such.

Enlightenment and its discontents

The fortuitous death of Glass in *The Innocent* suggests that McEwan had anticipated that the end of the cold war would bring about a reduction in US global influence. In fact, it paved the way for dreams of a New American Century. Central to this project was a now unrivalled military capability which underwrote a more flexible, because confident, imperialist strategy, characterised by an increasing disdain for the UN and even for NATO, and by a pursuit of *ad hoc* alliances in a commitment to 'war *without end*, either in purpose or time' because pre-emptive.[10] 9/11 provided spectacular justification for this, most obviously through its deployment as the pretext for the US-led invasion of Iraq. Blair's Atlanticism had already cast Britain in 'a hyper-subalternist role without historical precedent',[11] a role to which he zealously held fast despite widespread European dissent.

McEwan claimed not to be an enthusiast for the invasion, though he was certainly resigned to it: 'the hawks have my head,' he wrote, 'the doves my heart. At a push, I count myself – just – in the camp of the latter. And yet my ambivalence remains. I defend it by reference to the fact that nothing any of us say will make a difference: ambivalence is no less effective than passionate conviction.'[12] The distinction this statement sets up between head and heart maps on to the divided logics which determine the characterisation in *Saturday*: Henry, who prides himself on his rationalism, mostly thinks the invasion would be a good thing; his daughter, Daisy, a poet and sceptic towards her father's scientific certitude, is the most outspoken in her opposition. A sequence of familiar overlapping oppositions therefore overlays the pro- and anti-war positions: objective/subjective, science/culture, masculine/feminine. In privileging Henry's perspective, the novel's use of indirect free discourse does enable subtle ironisations of it, but for the most part *Saturday* surely impresses on its presumed liberal audience – probably anti-war, cultured and sceptical of the claims of genetics to explain human behaviour – the value and integrity of Henry's rather different values.

Henry's attitudes towards the war are bound up with his perspective on London itself. His anxious day begins prematurely when he witnesses a burning plane on its descent towards Heathrow in the early hours of the morning. He believes he is witnessing a terrorist attack, and this prompts his protective reflections on what it is that he values about the city, not merely as the place where he and his family live, but as the symbol of progress. At one point, he perceives that 'Life in it has steadily improved over the centuries for most people, despite the junkies and beggars now. ... At every level, material, medical, intellectual, sensual, for most people it has improved.' But this, he recalls, is not the view of Daisy's college lecturers who 'like to dramatise modern life as a sequence of calamities. It's their style, their way of being clever. It wouldn't be cool or professional to count the eradication of smallpox as part of the modern condition. Or the recent spread of democracies.' Henry even celebrates the 'consumerist and technological civilisation' he heard one of them traduce in a lecture (77). The implication is that their view is anti-Enlightenment, possibly postmodern. It is true that we shift from such unmediated thoughts to an appreciation of the subjective processes which in part determine them – Henry's antagonists are 'spectral entities ... figures of his own invention whom he can defeat' (78) – but the narrative on which his vision depends is not radically questioned by the text. The reference to 'the recent spread of democracies', for instance, is a fascinating piece of rhetoric. It alludes to the fall of the various authoritarian regimes of Eastern Europe, while glossing over the nature of the brutally neoliberal and inegalitarian societies which have replaced them. But it also anticipates the particular 'spread of democracy' with which the novel is explicitly concerned, and thereby connects the triumphalist rhetoric of a resolved cold war with the idealist register of the war on terror. Its grammatical construction manages to avoid specifying the active or passive voice, and there is consequently an ambiguity about whether democracies augment more or less spontaneously and beneficently, or whether they are imposed by other nation-states. This helps to mask disturbing implications underpinning Henry's thought, as the city here is both a normative abstraction, symbol of progress in general, and the specific embodiment of that abstraction, London, the centre from which historically much of the self-conscious and self-congratulatory business of spreading progress has taken place. Progress is, or should be, universal – the world is, or should be, rather like London – and, if it is not, there may at times be reasons for making it so.

It is a distinguishing feature of Henry's particular kind of scientific sensibility that he cannot tolerate uncertainty, the counterfactual, fiction, and is even impatient with thought experiments such as Schrödinger's. One of the most obvious ways in which this intolerance is ironised is that it is itself fictional, an imagined reality, though this is no simple matter, since the novel is technically characterised by a painstaking realism[13] and relates to the events of a specific, historic day; it carefully rehearses many of the debates about the impending invasion; it relies for much of its description on McEwan's observations of the work of a real surgeon; and famously it uses McEwan's own home as the model for Henry's. Fact and fiction are therefore intimate with each other in ways which complement the purpose of the book in destabilising the various divisions it treats.

This is because the novel is in part concerned with the limits of perspectivalism, and Henry's distrust of narratives establishes a further contrast to Daisy. Her belief that 'people can't "live" without stories' (68) is allied to what Henry regards as her relativism, evident, for instance, in her – Foucauldian, we are to presume? – belief that madness is a kind of social construct serving power (92). Hers is a relativism, then, of a certain section of the left, instilled in her, as we have seen, by her university lecturers. When she recites Larkin's poem, 'Water', Henry's response is to invoke the awe-inducing potential of evolution as an alternative, and superior, basis for religion. '"Now that's genuine old-time religion, when you say it happens to be demonstrably true",' she responds (56). Scientific convictions are for her equivalent to superstition: their foundationalism unites them. Daisy's perspective is implicitly postmodern.

Nonetheless, the various positions juxtaposed and embodied in Henry and Daisy do not obviously represent any right/left political division – each is surprised by the position the other takes up in their argument about the war – and their different perspectives are suggestive of those splits on the left I identified at the start of the chapter. In these, too, questions of fidelity to Enlightenment principles and accusations of relativism have been important, and this is the context I want now to discuss. In doing so, my focus on Fred Halliday – as a representative of the pro-war, supposedly pro-Enlightenment camp – takes its cue from Henry's own citation of his claim that 9/11 had precipitated 'a global crisis which, if we are lucky, will take a hundred years to resolve'.[14] I do not wish to suggest a detailed indebtedness to Halliday on McEwan's part, not least because Henry questions this assertion at various points. Rather, I intend to explore their common indebtedness to Enlightenment traditions which have a complex relation to contemporary political questions. In the process, I want to question the novel's suggestion that resistance to those traditions must direct us towards relativism or postmodernism.

Marxism, imperialism, temporality

Halliday's own account of his trajectory is revealing. Formerly an editor of *New Left Review*, he left that journal in 1983 after falling out with other editors, Tariq Ali in particular, over the specific commitment to national self-determination which defined the journal's anti-imperialism. In explaining this moment, Halliday invokes a striking narrative: 'About 20 years ago I said to Tariq that God, Allah, called the two of us to His presence and said to us, "One of you is to go to the left, and one of you is to go to the right." The problem is, He didn't tell us which was which, and maybe He didn't know himself.'[15] That sense of Halliday and Ali divided and disoriented through a shared origin which is incapable of correcting them goes to the heart of the problem that confronts us here.

One very powerful influence on Halliday's thinking was Bill Warren's book, *Imperialism: Pioneer of capitalism*, in which Warren argued positively the case often made negatively against Marxism within postcolonial theory: that Marx had supported imperialism as a progressive force globally. Both Warren and postcolonial theorists have claimed warrant for their cases in Marx's comments on India in a series of articles he wrote for *The New York Daily Tribune* in 1853. In these, Marx describes British rule as having been 'the unconscious tool of history' because it revolutionised the traditional village system of production that had 'restrained the human mind within the smallest possible compass'.[16] This authentic emphasis in Marx, Warren claims, was supplanted in Marxism by subsequent, and erroneous, theories of underdevelopment and neo-colonialism influenced Lenin. The result was an inversion of Marx's insight: 'It is now not the character of capitalism that determines the progressiveness (or otherwise) of imperialism, but the character of imperialism that determines the reactionary character of capitalism.'[17] Warren died before he could advance the political conclusions he wished to draw from his analysis, but his arguments go to the heart of genuinely difficult issues in Marxist thought which have been addressed only inadequately by postcolonial theory.

Inadequately, for a specific reason: postcolonial theory tends to evade engagement with Marx's principal claim to radicalism, his materialist inversion of dialectical thought. Rather, insofar as it is a branch of poststructuralism, it treats Marxism merely as discourse, effectively bracketing off its claims to be describing a systemic reality. In a specific critique of Marxism, for instance, Robert Young once wrote that 'in recent years theorists have turned their attention back to the question of the historicity of historical understanding, to its status as interpretation, representation or narrative, and, more radically, to the problem of temporality as such', and there has been little sign of this abating.[18] Central to the dialectical features of Marx's work, though, and determining his view of the situation in India, is the claim that capitalism is progressive in the very precise sense that it expands the productive capacity of human societies and thereby generates qualitatively and quantitatively new kinds of freedom, while *at the very same time* introducing new forms of exploitation. The dynamic, expansive system of capitalism which revolutionises traditional societies is destructive and always spread by force through forms of 'primitive accumulation' which expropriate common land and resources. Aijaz Ahmad's account of Marx's writings on India, moreover, provides us with a corrective, implicitly, to Warren's complacency about them.[19] It also explicitly corrects Edward Said's reductivism in assimilating them to that more general Orientalist outlook which he claims produces discursively the reality it claims to be describing.[20] While Ahmad acknowledges Marx's positivism, his Eurocentric rhetoric, and his failure thereby to live up to his own materialist methods of analysis, he points out that Marx both emphasised the violence of the colonial project, and supported indigenous anti-colonial movements which now had the opportunity to seize possession of the technological developments colonialism had introduced by force. Ahmad also contrasts Marx's progressivist view with the indigenous romanticism of a figure like Gandhi, who celebrated Indian primitivism and poverty in a tradition of nationalism which has still not disappeared. The point at issue is whether anti-imperialism should embrace a repudiation of 'development' as 'Western' because it is governed by the Enlightenment's supposedly imperialist prescriptions. As Young has written more recently, 'Marx forces contemporary readers to face up to the question of how much critiques of colonialism are driven by a form of longing for a pre-industrial way of life altogether.'[21]

The relevance of this to Halliday's position, and to McEwan's novel, resides precisely in the conviction of both that Western imperialism may still be acting as 'the unconscious tool of history' by bringing democracy to Iraq. This is effectively the view articulated by Perowne's Iraqi friend, Miri Taleb: '"It's only terror that holds the nation together. ... Now the Americans are coming, perhaps for bad reasons. But Saddam and the Ba'athists will go"' (64).[22] Thus the invasion will bring progress even if, and perhaps because, it is determined by the priorities of US capital. One feature of the pro-war faction, indeed, has been to defend the US against what they claim is a crude 'anti-Americanism' pervasive on the left. This is Halliday: 'For all its faults, the USA is, to date, the most prosperous country in human history, the one to which many people, possibly half of the world, would like to emigrate and work, whose vitality in a range of fields, from music to medicine, outstrips all others. It must be doing something right.'[23] Similarly, the Euston manifesto is full of praise for this 'great country and nation' in spite of its 'failings'.[24] What is striking about such defences, because surely obvious to socialist sensibilities, is their failure to recognise that what the US does 'right' is precisely bound up with all that it does wrong, both through the systemic, and largely racialised, immiseration it produces at home, and in the imperial power it exercises abroad. Henry's undialectical perspective on London compares with Halliday's on the US, but their correspondences go further than this.

Halliday has written that twentieth-century anti-imperialist forces had traditionally combined socialist and Marxist with nationalist impulses in a belief that capitalism could not fulfil the promise it generated, but that increasingly after the 1970s, 'ambivalence towards modernity that was always latent within nationalism came to the fore in movements of religious fundamentalism, a politics of national identity, valorisations of nature and other, irrational, forms', while 'an increasing part of the remaining traditional anti-imperialist movement came to be dominated by forms of authoritarian politics that represented the worst of the traditional left'.[25] Contemporary anti-imperialism has inherited this twin legacy, in his view, and this accounts for its reactionary qualities. Hence his comments on the protests against the Ministerial Conference of the World Trade Organisation in 1999: given that

> critique has to be linked both to the potential for improving on what already exists and on the identification of the forces capable of realising such a critique … [o]ne shudders to think what the more hard-headed of the socialist traditions of the twentieth century would have thought if they had seen that the last great global mass event of the twentieth century would be the motley agglomeration on the streets of Seattle.[26]

Provocative as they are, these comments demand to be taken seriously. One means of engaging critically with them is provided by David Harvey's crucial discussion of what he calls the New Imperialism of the Bush regime. Crucial, because it poses serious challenges, both to Halliday's position and to those various constituencies on the left which oppose it.

Harvey's case is that the 'primitive accumulation' which Marx saw as the fundamental motor that got capitalism going was not simply a feature of capitalism's origins; rather, it has persistently attended capitalism's development, providing one means by which problem of capital overaccumulation can be solved, not least through the specific 'spatio-temporal fix' of imperialism. Thus Harvey prefers the term 'accumulation by dispossession' to 'primitive accumulation', and distinguishes this from the 'accumulation through expansion' which we have tended to regard as definitively capitalist.[27] The peculiarly rapacious quality of what we have become used to calling neoliberalism has, since its inception, been determined by its pursuit of accumulation by dispossession, according to Harvey, and it remained a fundamental determinant of the New Imperialism of the Bush administration, along with specifically neoconservative aims of maintaining US global supremacy through force if need be and restoring order at home.

Let us now turn to Harvey's views on resistance and the contrast they establish to Halliday:

> the struggles within the field of expanded reproduction (that the traditional left [including Halliday's 'hard-headed' socialists] placed so much emphasis upon) have to be seen in a dialectical relation with the struggles against accumulation by dispossession that the social movements coalescing within the anti- and alternative globalization movements [Halliday's 'motley agglomeration'] are primarily focusing upon.[28]

Harvey's dialectical grasp here refuses simply to privilege one tradition over the other, and retains a commitment to evaluating the social and political aims of anti-globalisation movements in relation to the continuing need for forms of development – for safe and adequate water supplies, let us say, or effective anti-HIV education, as well as social and political equality and democracy.

Harvey's overall argument also suggests a need to revise our understanding of temporal processes. If primitive accumulation should be understood not as 'primitive' at all but as persistent, contemporary, then resistance to such forms of accumulation should not simply be dismissed as 'primitive' either, destined merely to become obsolete in some progressive unfolding of the dialectic of capitalist advance. After all, neoliberalism was advanced as a project of accumulation by dispossession in the West too – the 'rolling back' of the state, the selling off of nationalised industries, and so on. If Thatcher wanted us to believe that she was a traditionalist, however, it largely fell to Blair to try to convince us instead of the progressive nature of neoliberalism, euphemised and inevitabilised as 'modernisation'.

Art and utopia

It has been necessary to take this detour in order to recognise the significance of the analogy we might draw between Halliday's 'motley agglomeration' and the marchers who help to ruin Henry's day in McEwan's novel, since one of their most striking features is their archaism and primitivism. Unthreateningly at first, the scene of the gathering marchers 'has an air of innocence and English dottiness' (62). This turns sinister, though. During Henry's first confrontation with Baxter after colliding with his car, the demonstrators file past the scene, and 'the unrelenting throb of drums' (85), of their 'tribal drums' (87), becomes the accompaniment to it.

This brings us to the figure of Baxter himself, the gangster who will later invade Henry's home in revenge for his humiliation over the car incident. Numerous critics have noted that he represents the coalescence of threat in the novel and is not just some random thug.[29] My sense, though, is that Baxter's symbolic properties are capable of subsuming various possibilities in a way that can only be fully understood once we realise that the novel comprises something other than a contingent set of events loosely strung together. Rather, its structure is overdetermined by various narrative logics. First the striking (fictitious) coincidence of the burning plane's appearance in the sky on the day of the anti-war protest facilitates the connection in our mind between 9/11, Al Qaeda and Saddam Hussein repeatedly invoked, if increasingly subliminally – because evidently false – by the Bush and Blair administrations in the lead-up to the invasion. The connection is not made explicit, and Daisy will repudiate it in her argument with Henry, but the novel's ultimate reliance on this association is more revealing of the effectiveness of the US and British governments' insistence for all that.

This is complemented by a series of narrative shifts, and a symbolic logic of substitution and concretisation, through which the forces inimical to Enlightenment progress as perceived by Henry – terrorism, the marchers – come to be embodied in Baxter. 'Simian' in appearance and afflicted with Huntington's disease, he is a moral and physical degenerate of the sort which for long has haunted the racially inflected imperial imaginary. He appears here as the sign of a social system anxious about its own precariousness, as well as the vulnerability of the reason, virtue and order it sustains (88). The attack on reason and virtue is carefully registered as Baxter's revenge on Henry is exacted through the rape with which his daughter is threatened. When she undresses to reveal that she is pregnant, Baxter's elemental masculinity is directed malevolently against the condition which epitomises womanliness – against, that is, the very principles of sympathy and future hope.

Baxter is, of course, defeated and expelled, though in ways which preserve the civilisational superiority of the Perowne family over him. He is disarmed when Daisy recites 'Dover Beach' and is spontaneously transformed by his condition into an aesthete in a way that Max Nordau[30] would surely have understood. This confirms those qualities of unself-governability he shares with the fanatic, since 'he finds nothing extraordinary in the transformation of his role, from lord of terror to amazed admirer. Or excited child' (222). And it is perhaps this childishness which from their first encounter prompts in Henry a sympathy for Baxter, such that he will go on to save his life and resolve to drop criminal charges against him. The restoration of order entails a balance of force and compassion.

This is in keeping with the more general mood at the end of the novel. Henry's ambivalence remains. But now it is bound up with the equilibrium achieved in and through the family, and through the family's defeat of Baxter. When Henry first discovers that Daisy is pregnant, he thinks 'What perfect sense it makes; the variations of mood, her euphoria, that she should cry over a dedication' (218). At the end he considers that this fact endows her with a specific authority in relation to their differences over the invasion (277). The certainty that London will receive its terrorist bombs is therefore balanced by the certainty that Baghdad will shortly do so too, a rhetorical parallel which is both disproportionate – nothing the Islamists possess could match the forces about to be unleashed in Operation Shock and Awe – and renews the implication that there is a connection between Al Qaeda and Saddam Hussein's regime. They are linked in a more abstract way too by Henry's sense of the Islamists as 'utopianists, zealous men certain of the path to the ideal social order … totalitarians in different form', in a line stretching back through 'Hitler, Stalin, Mao' (276–7). And others, since we first encounter such sentiments while Henry is listening to his son's band:

> Out in the real world there exist detailed plans, visionary projects for peaceable realms, all conflicts resolved, happiness for everyone, for ever – mirages for which people are prepared to die and kill. Christ's kingdom on earth, the workers' paradise, the ideal Islamic state. But only in music, and only on rare occasions, does the curtain actually lift on this dream of community, and it's tantalisingly conjured, before fading away with the last notes. (172)

So, art and reality should ultimately thrive on their separation; to confuse them, as visionaries do, is dangerous. *Saturday* will assert only this much and leave its final ideological work to character, form and sensibility. The reality into which McEwan claims to have been pitched by Suez can only be redeemed momentarily by the art which aspires to humanise, not politicise, and in much the same way as the nurturing family, by making us understand the perspectives of others. Just as there is an ideal balance between art and reality, so there must be between the family and the society which both lies beyond and sustains it, such that the existing order of things is naturalised. In *Saturday* any such naturalisation must be grasped ironically. We smile in a superior kind of way at Henry in his car, thinking of 'An ancient evolutionary dilemma: the need to sleep, the fear of being eaten. Resolved at last, by central locking' (121). But then a real genetic loser invades his house and such thoughts no longer seem absurd.

And so, of course, this talk of 'utopianists' as always somewhere else precludes the possibility that they may actually, and right now, be in charge – indeed at the time of the invasion of Iraq, directing it. In 1944, the historian, Karl Polanyi, claimed as virtually inevitable the collapse of the nineteenth-century 'idea of a self-adjusting market [since it] implied a stark utopia. Such an institution could not exist for any length of time without annihilating the human and natural substance of society; it would have physically destroyed man and transformed his surroundings into a wilderness.'[31] Polanyi's case was directed against a then minority of economists, such as Friedrich Hayek, whose time would nonetheless come with the neoliberal revolution of the 1970s and 1980s, and with consequences this paper has been in part concerned to trace.

So what did the market utopians bring to Iraq? Those of us who marched against the invasion will not feel any sense of satisfaction that the subsequent history of the occupation proved us, terribly, right. Our conviction was that any further extension of US power could not be beneficent. Even so, few of us could have anticipated the scale of the disaster which was to result from the uncompromising pursuit of accumulation through dispossession: the massive rolling back of the state, in part justified as de-Ba'athification which, in conjunction with the unprecedented levels of unemployment it assisted in creating, threw people back on the resources of their communities, and facilitated sectarian bloodshed; the decimation of an infrastructure already fragile as a result of sanctions, and the corrupt failure of the privatised 'reconstruction' which nonetheless lined the pockets of US companies;[32] the everyday, random killing of ordinary Iraqis by trigger-happy or anxious, uncomprehending US and British troops and private security agents;[33] the murderous assaults on Fallujah and other towns and villages; the far from exceptional torture in Abu Ghraib; the lack of concern for the Iraqi dead evinced by the Allies' failure even to attempt to count them; and, more generally, the warrant granted by the illegality of the war on terror to other terrorist states, from Russia to Israel to Sri Lanka and beyond, to pursue their various military campaigns in defiance of basic principles of justice and human rights, or international law and opinion. Now Iraq's oil is being sold off in what the *New York Times* has called 'the biggest oil field auction in history'.[34] It took some time, as the oil companies used the 'security situation' to bargain for a better deal, but we are reassured that private management will bring new efficiencies (we know what that means) and new investment in order to modernise an industry 'battered by years of war and sanctions'.[35] The ironies multiply bewilderingly, but one stands out. If the US and Britain have, in a sense, acted as 'the unconscious tool of history' in Iraq they have done so by demonstrating that any progressive side to capitalism has long since played itself out. It is time – way past time – for other narratives of progress: not new forms of idealism, but other ways of making history.

Notes

1 I do not here follow the practice of the book in reserving for Henry the authority of the family name.

2 Christopher Hitchens, *The Trial of Henry Kissinger* (London: Verso, 2001).

3 www.eustonmanifesto.org/the-euston-manifesto/ (accessed 7 January 2010).

4 Ian McEwan, *A Move Abroad: Or shall we die?* and *The Ploughman's Lunch* (London: Picador, 1989), p. 27. Future references included in the text.

5 Ian McEwan, *Saturday* (London: Jonathan Cape, 2005), p. 100. Future references included the text.

6 Claire Colebrook, 'The Innocent as anti-oedipal critique of cultural pornography' in Sebastien Groes (ed.), *Ian McEwan* (London: Continuum, 2009), pp. 43–56, effectively makes an opposing case.

7 Kiernan Ryan stresses these dynamics in *Ian McEwan* (Plymouth: Northcote House, 1994).

8 Ian McEwan, *The Comfort of Strangers* (London: Jonathan Cape, 1981), p. 12. Future references included in the text.

9 Ian McEwan, *The Innocent* (London: Jonathan Cape, 1990), p. 78. Future references in the text.

10 Ellen Meiksins Wood, *Empire of Capital* (London: Verso, 2003), p. 149.

11 Tony Wood, 'Good riddance to New Labour', *New Left Review* 62 (2010), p. 9.

12 Ian McEwan, 'Ambivalence on the brink of war', www.opendemocracy.net/debates/article-2-114-882.jsp (accessed 12 January 2003).

13 The irony of Henry's fictitious mistrust of fiction informs Mark Currie's reflections in *About Time: Narrative, fiction and the philosophy of time* (Edinburgh:

Edinburgh University Press, 2007), pp. 124–32. Peggy A. Knapp considers the novel to be hyperrealist, characterised by 'over-specification': 'Ian McEwan's *Saturday* and the aesthetics of prose', *Novel* 41: 1 (2007), pp. 122–43.

14 Fred Halliday, 'September 11, 2001, and the Greater West Asian crisis' in his *Two Hours That Shook the World. September 11, 2001: Causes and consequences* (London: Saqi, 2002), p. 24.

15 Danny Postel, 'Who is responsible? An interview with Fred Halliday', *Salmagundi*, 150/1 (2006), p. 221.

16 Karl Marx, 'The British rule in India' in Marx, *Surveys from Exile* (Harmondsworth and London: Penguin and New Left Review, 1973), pp. 306–7.

17 Bill Warren, *Imperialism: Pioneer of capitalism*, ed. John Sender (London: Verso, 1980), p. 47.

18 Robert Young, *White Mythologies: Writing, history and the West* (London: Routledge, 1990), p. 22.

19 Aijaz Ahmad, 'Marx on India: a clarification' in *In Theory: Classes, nations, literatures* (London: Verso, 1992), pp. 221–42.

20 Edward Said, *Orientalism* (London: Routledge and Kegan Paul, 1978), pp. 153–6.

21 Robert J.C. Young, *Postcolonialism: An historical introduction* (Oxford: Blackwell, 2001), p. 109.

22 Note too Halliday in Postel, 'Who is responsible?': 'The key issue is not: Is the US intervening? Nor: What are the US's motives? The key issue is will that intervention plausibly help those people or not', p. 223.

23 Halliday, 'September 11', p. 49.

24 www.eustonmanifesto.org/the-euston-manifesto/ (accessed 7 January 2010).

25 Fred Halliday, 'The pertinence of imperialism' in Mark Rupert and Hazel Smith (eds), *Historical Materialism and Globalisation* (London: Routledge, 2002), p. 85.

26 Halliday, 'The pertinence of imperialism', p. 87.

27 I am summarising Harvey's general argument in *The New Imperialism* (Oxford: Oxford University Press, 2003), but on the terms 'spatio-temporal fix' and 'accumulation by dispossession', see pp. 43–4 and 139–40.

28 Harvey, *The New Imperialism*, p. 176.

29 See Rebecca Carpenter, '"We're not a friggin' girl band": September 11th, masculinity, and the British-American relationship in David Hare's *Stuff Happens* and Ian McEwan's *Saturday*' in Ann Keniston and Jeanne Quin (eds), *Literature After 9/11* (New York: Routledge, 2008), p. 151; Robert Eaglestone, '"The age of reason is over … an age of fury was dawning"', *Wasafari* 22: 2 (2007), pp. 19–22; Michael L. Ross, 'On a darkling planet: Ian McEwan, *Saturday*, and the condition of England', *Twentieth Century Literature* 54: 1 (2008), pp. 90–1; Elizabeth Kowaleski Wallace, 'Postcolonial melancholia in Ian McEwan's *Saturday*', *Studies in the Novel* 39: 4 (2007), p. 476.

30 Nordau, theorist of the nineteenth-century *fin-de-siecle* condition, believed

that aestheticism was one sign of physical degeneration. See his *Degeneration* (New York: Appleton, 1895).

31 Karl Polanyi, *The Great Transformation: The political and economic origins of our time* (Boston: Beacon Press, 2001), p. 3.

32 Naomi Klein's account of the neoliberalisation of Iraq is unrivalled: *The Shock Doctrine: The rise of disaster capitalism* (London: Allen Lane, 2007), pp. 325–82.

33 Accounts of such shootings permeate Patrick Cockburn's account of *The Occupation: War and resistance in Iraq*, 2nd edn (London: Verso, 2007).

34 'Iraq's oil industry poised to re-enter world stage' *New York Times*, 15 February 2010, www.nytimes.com/2010/02/15/business/energy-environment/15reniraq.html (accessed 7 January 2010).

35 'Shell Signs Iraq Oil Field Deal', *BBC News Online*, 11 December 2009, http://news.bbc.co.uk/1/hi/8407274.stm (accessed 7 January 2010).

Afterword:
The English novel and the world

Elleke Boehmer

Parochial, introverted, historically myopic – until very recently words like these have been used to describe the response that the English novel has made, or indeed only partially made, to the rest of the world – a world over whose waves England and English capital once confidently claimed to have command.

The essays collected in this book throw a rather different light on the matter, though it is the end-game of empire, the decline and fall, rather than empire as such, the grand theme of England's imperial power, that is of particular concern to the contributors. The question left begging, even following these many excellent exegeses of England's late and post-imperial condition as represented in post-1945 fiction, is whether the English novel, or Western narrative more broadly, has to date properly addressed, in a substantive way, rather than tangentially or obliquely, the fact of European empire, let alone its demise. To what extent and in what ways has the English novel satisfactorily contended with empire, whether its early dawn, its heyday or its passing? I will return later to this difficult question – a question that probes the interrelationship of the novel, a genre conventionally relating to nations, with the broad scope of world literature and world history.

For several decades, since at least the emergence of postcolonial discourse theory and the rise of the postcolonial or migrant novel in English, the critical consensus has been that the English novel, defined in terms of ethics and consciousness, as Bill Schwarz describes, has primarily involved itself in the immediate and the domestic. Small enclosed tales have mapped onto a small self-involved island. English novelists have allegedly favoured heaths over harbours, crises of character over world conflicts, storms in teacups over military and political tempests out on the open seas. Steven Connor's telescopic *The English Novel in History, 1950–1995* (1996) with its suggestive argument as to how the novel structurally encapsulates a nation's story, expanded from Benedict Anderson, put its thesis to work in respect of the English novel in part by enlisting writers like Hanif Kureishi and Salman Rushdie as English writers, thereby subsuming their fictions of race and immigration to the island story.[1] Yet what this move entailed, curiously, was that the end of empire, or empire as such, was eclipsed as a topic, even though it was linked to race. The assumption seemed to be that it could be taken for granted as a historical given, or was no longer worth addressing in so many words.

As is clear from the essays collected between these covers, while empire surely throws up issues and concerns as central to the English novel as to English politics and social life, these have not generally manifested at the heart of the literature. True, the repercussions of the imperial experience have been expressed through a variety of formal and thematic complexes, many of them linked to matters of race and migration, yet these, too, have not received significant literary or critical attention. Indeed, on the basis of the readings given here of William Golding, the Mills & Boon romance, and William Boyd, amongst other topics, the English novel postwar emerges from between sharply distinct poles of contradiction: it speaks now of imperial denial, now of a concomitant yearning for empire; it seesaws between a mawkish late colonial humour and a belated grief at colonial retreat. Trauma – a troubling memory trace, a stylistic tic, a nameless distress – runs like a crooked seam through all the writing discussed. Following Paul Gilroy's 2004 thesis of postcolonial melancholia in contemporary Britain, the nation's and hence the novel's symptoms appear to be unmistakeable.[2] The predominant mode through which the post-1945 English novel has registered the British imperial experience as well as the retreat from world dominance more specifically, is melancholic.

Faced with the loss of empire's moral legitimacy after 1945, the English novel (let stand English society) shows clear signs of having avoided, repressed or erased the full implications of what that loss entailed at a variety of different levels, emotional, psychological, social, cultural and ethical. It has not allowed itself properly to mourn the diminishment of global power, nor fully to process the trauma represented by a centuries-long history of colonial violence, nor yet to understand what is involved when 'a new national identity' is to be rebuilt 'from the debris of ... broken narcissism'. In this precarious situation, as Gilroy writes, incoming strangers, as might be depicted in the novel, are forced like scapegoats not only to '*represent* the vanished empire' but also to carry the burden of the complicated feelings that this vanishing occasions: pain, shame and grief.[3] There is a provocative analogy to be developed here with post-apartheid writing in South Africa, where the charge is that even following the partial successes of the Truth and Reconciliation Committee (TRC) in the mid-1990s, with its gathering together of victims' testimonies and perpetrators' confessions, literary narrative is yet in the process of coming to terms with apartheid's passing, and with the position of the stranger in society. Not only the trauma of that experience of state-sanctioned racial segregation, but also the moral responsibilities, uncanny intimacies and bitter-sweet complicities it represented for all parties, which register in some texts as a non-specific Naipaul-reminiscent 'disturbance', have yet to be fully worked through.[4]

In criticism of the novel in English to date, the seeming occlusion of empire from discussion of the ethnically defined 'Anglo-British' novel, as against the overriding preoccupation with empire and its cognate issues in postcolonial or international writing, has produced a discursive bifurcation, which Bill Schwarz in his opening essay at once perceptively outlines and rejects. On the one hand is the near overdetermination of the postcolonial novel in English by its historicity, or by the process of decolonisation of which it is held to be a definitive expression. On the other hand is the English novel 'at its most centred', that point where, according to the criticism, it is most insular, most monadic, most amnesiac, most shrinking, certainly with respect to English imperial history.

Against this false split, the contributors to *End of Empire and the English Novel* pitch, with some heuristic boldness, their variegated readings of the literary English novel, as well as of English romance, crime fiction, sci-fi and travel writing. As they contend, the British empire in these fictions can be seen to be not so much (or not only) out there, beyond the waves, as in here at the dead centre, captured in a range of morbid symptoms, or sensed as the unacknowledged grief outlined by Gilroy, as distress, unease, unsettlement, 'attesting to pasts that couldn't otherwise be spoken'.[5] The interpretative approaches developed by postcolonial critique are thus extended to work that falls outside 'the postcolonial field of vision' – legitimately and appropriately so. The centre is shown to be striated by its margins, just as the margins have always been by the centre. There is as much British world history to be discovered embedded in the relatively closed category of English narrative, as in postcolonial writing by authors like Kamila Shamsie, Bernardine Evaristo or David Dabydeen. To this extent at least, despite the contributors' overall loyalty to the narrow definition of the 'English novel', the collection participates in and upholds that 'convergence of the English novel ... with its multiple postcolonial, Anglophone manifestations' that criticism has increasingly come to register across the past fifty years.

Inchoately but persistently, it would seem, the memory of empire has impinged on the English novel in the second half of the twentieth century. Or has it? One of the tasks to be undertaken by an afterword is to address questions that a book has left pending, and this question of influence and effect, of the extent to which what was once called Greater Britain shaped the English novel at home, is one that this collection despite its many fresh critical perspectives cannot quite lay to rest. That this is so, however, relates not to the definitions of literature and history that have been brought to bear, as might be assumed, but rather to a larger issue concerning the English novel's relations to the world – that world once dominated by British power. This larger question can be simply expressed by drawing on terms already put in play. To what extent has the English novel, past or present, imaginatively confronted that world in which, in the nineteenth and early twentieth centuries, the English played so significant and repressive a role? Quite apart from the theme of empire endings, has the empire at any point in its history been registered, in a fundamental, thoroughgoing way, within the Anglo-British novel? Is there an English novel that provides a symbolic cartography, however incomplete, of the global webs and circuits of the burgeoning empire?

From the extensive evidence presented by novels written in English, produced by those with some form of colonial, colonised or decolonising background, when compared with fiction by writers belonging to England without other ties, it remains the case that from 1790 to the present day, the world-spanning dimensions and dynamism of the British empire have been more vividly registered and embodied within that first category of writing than within the second. The imaginative projection of the self upon the other that distinguished the Victorian domestic novel, as it did the adventure story, continued into early twentieth-century writing and its ongoing imaginative complicity with colonial and metropolitan perspectives, even despite the modernist interrogations of inherited knowledge of a Virginia Woolf or a W.B. Yeats. 'Self-criticism' in many cases produced no more than 'self-repetition'.[6] Aliens – whether colonial travellers, anthropological exhibits or foreign products – consistently feature in Anglo-British writing from across this long time-span as figures on the edge, whereas in work by writers with colonial co-ordinates like Joseph Conrad or Olive Schreiner, Olaudah Equiano or J.E. Casely Hayford, the alien or the 'out there' is drawn into the core structures of the narrative, into the integument of character and plot.

Something of the same applies even to contemporary English novels that look back to the height of formal imperialism, of which A.S. Byatt's 2009 *The Children's Book* set in the 1890s *fin de siècle* and the Edwardian era, is an interesting case in point.[7] A finely textured work concerned with *avant-garde* and fringe movements in the arts of the period, this family story is laden with details at once lucid and lucent of such characteristic events and developments as experimentation in puppetry, sculpture and nudism, the 1900 Grande Exposition Universelle de Paris, the first staging of *Peter Pan* in 1904, and, most importantly, the efflorescence of children's writing, here channelled through the character of Olive Wellwood, closely modelled on E. Nesbit. Empire, however, never more expansive and confident than at this time in British history, never more implicated in the warp and weft of English social life, figures very small in the novel – mainly, and sporadically, in the oddly and inaccurately termed 'Kaffir market' in which Geraint Fludd, of the younger generation of characters, makes money, presumably after the opening of the Johannesburg mining markets to British capital following the Anglo-Boer war. The rest of the wider British world however – India, wracked by famine in the 1890s; Australia, coalesced into a new continental nation in 1901; the Boxer Rebellion in China – none of it features, its presence is not even marginal. In *The Children's Book* the Greater British world barely exists.[8]

These observations should not be taken as suggesting that the place of empire in the metropolitan imagination whether past or present, is entirely suppressed. By any reckoning, Byatt's novel constitutes a fairly extreme example of imperial occlusion in fiction. Since at least as far back as Edward Said's *Culture and Imperialism* (1993), with its readings of slavery in Jane Austen and of the 'Mutiny' in Rudyard Kipling, it has been widely understood that in English writing imperial effects do not come unmediated.[9] The different shifting phases in English literary history are marked by at least this one constant: whatever the period concerned, empire consistently appears under the sign of trauma, that protective shield that the literary work, like the psyche, mounts in relation to violence, pain and loss. From the beginning of what C.A. Bayly and others have called the second British empire, the English novel experienced an allegedly expanded England as a series of inchoate psychological after-effects.[10] Throughout, the margins have manifested in translated and coded forms.

On this basis it might justly be submitted that special pleading for post-1945 writing in respect of empire is to a degree unwarranted. Empire is everywhere present in British fiction as something resembling that undiagnosed 'pain' of which Nina repeatedly complains in Evelyn Waugh's

Vile Bodies (1930). And if this is so, then it will also be the case that the 'end of empire' hermeneutic which is powerfully developed with this book need not be restricted only to the closing phases of British colonial history. If the wraith-like shapes of 'what the [imperial] twilight says' repeat like recurring dreams, or like Olive Wellwood's nightmarish stories, back through the past of British culture, then *End of Empire*'s critique of imperial forgetting, too, will in due course be productively extrapolated back into the English novel in history.[11]

Notes

1   Steven Connor, *The English Novel in History, 1950–1995* (London: Routledge, 1996); Benedict Anderson, *Imagined Communities*, 2nd edn (London: Verso, 1993).

2   Sigmund Freud, 'Mourning and melancholia', *Journal of Nervous and Mental Disease* 56/5 (November 1922), pp. 543–5; Paul Gilroy, *After Empire: Melancholia or convivial culture* (London: Routledge, 2004).

3   Gilroy, *After Empire*, pp. 109–10.

4   A thoroughgoing study of apartheid's complicities in the light of the TRC may be found in Mark Sanders, *Complicities: The intellectual and apartheid* (Durham: Duke University Press, 2002). Naipaul's 'disturbance' is taken from Bill Schwarz's discussion of imperial effects above.

5   Gilroy, *After Empire*, p. 20.

6   I make this case at some length in my *Colonial and Postcolonial Literature*, 2nd edn (Oxford: Oxford University Press, 2005), see in particular pp. 132–52.

7   A.S. Byatt, *The Children's Book* (London: Chatto and Windus, 2009); see, for example, p. 405.

8   In defence of *The Children's Book* it might be asked why empire should in any sense be the concern of a fictionalised history of the growth of British children's literature. A fair point – were it not for the fact that that efflorescence was shaped in virtually every respect by imperialism. Consider only the child character's Indian connections in Frances Hodgson Burnett, the Indian relations in *The Railway Children* or the colonial motifs in J.M. Barrie's *Peter Pan*.

9   Edward Said, *Culture and Imperialism* (London: Jonathan Cape, 1993).

10 C.A. Bayly, *The Birth of the Modern World, 1780–1914: Global connections and comparisons* (Oxford: Blackwell, 2004).

11 I refer to Derek Walcott's essay 'What the twilight says' in his *What the Twilight Says: Essays* (London: Faber, 1998).

Lightning Source UK Ltd.
Milton Keynes UK
UKOW06f1823180615

253742UK00007B/79/P